Bases for Effective Reading

Bases for Effective Reading

By Miles A. Tinker

Professor Emeritus
University of Minnesota

UNIVERSITY OF MINNESOTA PRESS • MINNEAPOLIS

© Copyright 1965 by the University of Minnesota. All rights reserved

Printed in the United States of America at
the Lund Press, Inc., Minneapolis

Library of Congress Catalog Card Number: 65-25098

Second printing 1966

Typography by Miles A. Tinker

PUBLISHED IN GREAT BRITAIN, INDIA, AND PAKISTAN BY THE OXFORD
UNIVERSITY PRESS, LONDON, BOMBAY, AND KARACHI, AND IN CANADA BY
THE COPP CLARK PUBLISHING CO. LIMITED, TORONTO

Preface

The aim in writing this book has been to present a clear, simple, and well-coordinated exposition of available information on the reading process which is so fundamental to most of our daily activities. Much of the research reported here was carried out by the author during his 32 years at the University of Minnesota. Materials from related research by others have been added to provide a comprehensive picture of the areas covered.

There are five parts to the book: Part One is concerned with the nature of reading, perception, and comprehension. In Part Two, five chapters deal with various aspects of eye movements in reading. The seven chapters in Part Three on scientific typography cover data on printing for easy and efficient reading. Materials on visual functioning and illumination for reading are summarized in the four chapters of Part Four. And the last three chapters, which constitute Part Five, deal with appraisal of reading proficiency.

It is hoped that the material in this book will promote among both teachers and research workers an adequate understanding of what is basic for effective reading.

The writer is deeply indebted to the late Dr. Donald G. Paterson for encouragement to work in the field of applied experimental psychology and for his contribution as co-author on many joint research studies. Particular thanks are given the Iowa State University Press for permission to paraphrase certain materials in *Legibility of Print*. Grateful acknowledgment is also given to the University of Minnesota Graduate School for the financial aid which made possible much of the research reported here.

The writer is especially indebted to the editorial and production staffs of the University of Minnesota Press for their cooperation and helpful suggestions during the writing of this book.

Miles A. Tinker

Santa Barbara, California
June 1965

Contents

Part One: About Reading, Perception, and Comprehension

1 *Introduction*

The importance of proficient reading in this day and age can hardly be overemphasized. Reading is undoubtedly indispensable for satisfactory adjustment to contemporary living conditions. There are few activities in business, recreation, school, homemaking, and other aspects of daily life that do not require some amount of reading to perform well. And as pointed out by Gray and Rogers (106), reading books, newspapers, magazines, and the like satisfy needs which other media of communication, like television and radio, are unable to meet. Indeed, the ideas of creative minds of human history, as well as the concepts and values of present-day civilization, can probably be comprehended best through the printed word.

As noted by Russell (228), people, whether children or adults, will read if they are thus helped to cope with their problems. One may read to learn how to assemble a bicycle, another to find out how to eliminate pests on rose bushes or fruit trees, and still another to satisfy a psychological need such as that for relaxation or for escape from a workaday world. Motivation derived from interests provides the drive for continuing to read. What one reads in his free time depends partly upon the amount of his leisure but even more upon his individual interests and personality characteristics.

Reading is a complex, developmental process. As the child moves through school, he acquires skill in word recognition, increases his vocabulary and his knowledge of concepts, and enlarges his ability to comprehend ideas. Gradually the materials read become more complicated in vocabulary and concepts and in intricacy of sentence structure and language. Even greater de-

3

mands are made upon his capacity to grasp meaning and appreciate style in writing. Finally, the proficient reader learns to do more than passively recognize and accept the meanings that printed symbols represent. He interprets, evaluates, and reflects upon those meanings. Reading used as a tool to acquire knowledge is relatively ineffective unless it is accompanied by thinking — unless, that is, the reader is critical and uses his accumulated experience and knowledge to understand what he encounters for the first time.

A desirable and important goal is to become a mature reader. Not everyone reaches this goal. The study of Gray and Rogers (106) revealed that the reading performance of our adult population ranges all the way from gross immaturity to a very high level of achievement but that the number of highly mature readers is small. Apparently level of education does not alone determine degree of maturity in reading, for some eighth-grade pupils are mature readers while many college graduates are not.

Reading maturity appears to be closely associated with general maturity. "Maturity in reading as one aspect of total development is distinguished by the attainment of those interests, attitudes, and skills which enable young people and adults to participate eagerly, independently, and effectively in all the reading activities essential to a full, rich and productive life. It is assumed that, in the satisfaction of interests and needs through reading, a mature reader will continue to grow in capacity to interpret broadly and deeply." (106, page 56.)

The developmental nature of progress in reading has been recognized by the National Committee on Reading of the National Society for the Study of Education (227). Six stages of development are listed: the prereading stage, birth to sometime in grade 1; the beginning reading stage, grade 1; the initial stage of independent reading, grade 2; the transition stage, grade 3 and early grade 4; the intermediate or low maturity stage, grades 4 to 6; advanced stages of reading, grade 7 and later.

Many school systems, considering these six stages to be only rough descriptions, organize their program in 10 or 12 steps: readiness level, pre-primer, primer, first-reader, second-reader, and so on to the eighth-reader level or above. Although a child may reach a specified level at a particular time, the alert teacher realizes that the so-called stages in reading ability are not mutually exclusive. The level to which a child has progressed is merely one stage in continuous growth as he acquires reading proficiency in the developmental sequence.

What Is Reading?

Many people have attempted to define reading. Pronunciation of words, contrary to the views of certain authors (78, 261), is not reading. Many seem to believe that reading is getting meaning from the printed page, but this is misleading. The printed page contains no meanings but only symbols which stand for meanings. Printed symbols as such merely stimulate one to recall some familiar concepts. That is, recognition of a word or group of words brings recall or arousal of previously encountered meanings. And any new meanings are derived from manipulation by the reader of recalled concepts, not from symbols as such. Concepts possessed by the reader are readily recalled. But when the concept is new, manipulation of related materials and meanings in the formation of the concept becomes a kind of problem-solving process with emphasis on the thinking side of reading. In the full sense, reading is creative. It involves all the complicated mental processes activated in the interpretation of concepts and meanings that are aroused by recognition of printed symbols. What any reader derives from a printed page, therefore, is not exactly what some other reader would get or even what the author had in mind, but to a certain degree at least a personal re-creation on the part of the reader. Sometimes this process becomes highly creative.

Tinker and McCullough (320) have summed up their definition of reading as follows: "Reading involves the recognition of printed or written symbols which serve as stimuli for the recall of meanings built up through past experience, and the construction of new meanings through manipulation of concepts already possessed by the reader. The resulting meanings are organized into thought processes according to the purposes adopted by the reader. Such an organization leads to modified thought and/or behavior, or else leads to new behavior which takes its place, either in personal or in social development." (Page 13.)

Fundamental Aspects of Reading

Any attempt to make a complete list of the aspects basic to an understanding of the reading process doubtless would be unrewarding since a consensus of the experts is most unlikely. However, it is probable that the following partial list would be accepted by practically everyone in the field of reading:

Perception of words is fundamental to all reading. In learning to read, words must be identified and recognized. But perception of a word occurs only when the recognized word is meaningful to the reader. For instance, one can learn to pronounce "aardvark" and to recognize it when met again but the word will mean little or nothing until the reader finds out that an aardvark is a large, nocturnal, burrowing mammal of Africa, living largely on termites or ants, and having a long slimy tongue capable of being extended to catch the insects. The development of visual perception of words is a continuing activity, extending throughout the school years and, for those who continue to read, throughout adult life. So word perception implies identification, recognition, and an understanding of the meaning of a word.

Concepts, vocabulary growth, and comprehension are intimately interrelated. Effective reading depends upon the acquisition of a meaningful vocabulary correctly connected with an adequate stock of concepts. Each word in such a vocabulary is a label for some concept. A concept is a generalization about related data. It is derived from percepts, images, and memory. Understanding and interpretation, i.e., comprehension, of printed material is possible only when vocabulary meanings are adequate and concepts are clear and precise.

Measurement of eye movements while reading has furnished much of our fundamental knowledge of the reading process. Although recording of eye movements is a research procedure, the results of oculomotor research find broad application in understanding and teaching reading.

6

Introduction

Legible printing is necessary for rapid and easy reading. Research has provided enough information for the editor, publisher, and printer to specify and use legible typographical arrangements in material for both children and adults.

Proper *illumination for reading* is also necessary for rapid and easy reading. This requires application of research findings on intensity, color, and distribution of light in relation to vision in reading.

Evaluation of growth in reading is required for appraisal of teaching effectiveness and of various aspects of reading performance. Testing methods have been developed which greatly facilitate this evaluation.

Plan of This Book

This book is written to bring to workers in the field the research findings and the conclusions of systematic studies dealing with the reading process. It is planned to provide readers with an understanding of a series of psychological factors which are fundamental to the development of proficient reading. Those who have become, or are in training to become, specialists in the teaching of reading will find here certain important facts and principles that are not treated fully in texts on the teaching of reading. How to achieve more effective reading in school or later will be better understood when the basic factors here described are seen in focus.

Chapters 2 and 3 are concerned with how adults and children perceive words. They explain why perception goes beyond mere word identification and recognition. Also the differences and similarities of word perception by children and adults are clarified. Word identification and recognition, use of verbal context to aid in understanding words, phrasing, vocabulary development, and study skills are all considered along with accuracy and speed of comprehension.

In Part Two, Chapters 5 through 9 deal with eye movements in reading: their nature and measurement; time relations; variation; adaptation in special reading situations; and role in improving reading.

Part Three, Chapters 10 through 16, is concerned with scientific typography: printing for easy and efficient reading. These chapters deal with the nature of legibility, and the roles played by typefaces, size of type, line width, leading (spacing), color and paper surface, and spatial arrangement of the printed page in printing for children and adults. Separate chapters discuss newspaper typography and special printing situations.

Chapters 17 through 20 (Part Four) take up the problems of specifying illumination for reading: color, intensity, and distribution of light for effective vision; illumination standards; and the hygienic reading situation.

Chapters 21 through 23 (Part Five) discuss evaluation of progress in reading: measurement, interpretation, and applications.

2 *Perception in Reading among Adults*

The general process of perception includes stimulation, preparation for a response, and the culmination in a response, the perception. The pattern in reading is along these lines. The graphic symbol is the stimulus, the meanings and interpretations (perception) are derived from the reader's past experiences, and the response relates meaning to the symbol. In this discussion some attention will be paid to the relation of perception in reading to general perception, i.e., perception in the nonreading situation, but there is no plan to explore the complexities of perception in general. As pointed out by Vernon (339), the perception and reading of words need to be dealt with apart from perception of other visual objects since they involve processes that are not essential to the latter.

Those persons who have achieved a fair degree of maturity in reading have also mastered procedures of perceiving words that are somewhat different from those employed by children. Therefore, word perception by adult readers will be dealt with first. This will be followed in Chapter 3 by an explanation of how children learn to perceive words and how they gradually acquire mature procedures in such perception.

Word Identification, Recognition, and Perception

First of all, it is desirable to differentiate between or define word identification, word recognition, and word perception. The initial inspection of a new word involves identification of its printed or written symbol in terms of its visual appearance and its sound. That is, its correct pronunciation is achieved either aloud or mentally as inner speech as the visual form is matched with its sound. The meaning that is present with identification may be slight or great, depending upon the experiences of the reader associated with the identified word and the amount of help available from the context in which the word occurs. Thus, identification of a printed word that is already in the reader's oral comprehension vocabulary, and that he uses in his speech but has not met in print before, will of course carry much meaning. But, if the new word is not in the reader's understanding and usage vocabulary, the meaning upon identification (matching the printed symbol with the correct sound of a word) is apt to be slight. Increased meaning comes with repeated contact with the word in various contexts.

Word identification and word recognition are interrelated. As pointed out by Tinker and McCullough (320), to recognize a word means to identify it as a word previously known, i.e., the visual form of the printed symbol leads to correct revival of the sound of the word, with association between the sound and the sound's meaning and the visual form. Immediate or relatively rapid recognition occurs only with words that are well known through frequent encounters in previous reading. But other words which a reader has met but which are less familiar are recognized less promptly, usually after a slight delay. With such words, a slightly more thorough visual inspection in which the reader is aided by one or more word recognition clues will ordinarily result in ready recognition.

Perception is involved both in identification and in recognition of words. Keep in mind that the more meaning that is present, the more adequate the perception. Vernon (339) states that there are two important factors which must be considered in studying the perception of words. Since all words are primarily speech units, the word as written and read derives directly from the word as spoken. And some traces of auditory and vocal processes always occur during reading. Secondly, perception of a word is not completed just by apprehension of its visual and its auditory form or structure. "Every word is a symbol, and awareness of its meaning requires at least some appreciation of the idea or experience it connotes. It follows that the complete perceptual act involved in reading a word is one of great complexity." (Page 17.) When a word is recognized, the meaning attached is apt to be broader and perception clearer and more complete than if the word is merely identified. Recognition implies familiarity which may have been enhanced by having met the word in several contexts. The perception of words, therefore, depends upon the meanings that are present in identification and recognition of the words. And since the meaning aroused by a printed or written symbol depends upon the reader's background of experience associated with the sound and spoken use of the word, perception is basically associated with experience. All this tends to emphasize the role of experience and verbal facility in reading. And we may repeat that the person who brings the most extensive experience to his reading gets the most from the printed page.

As pointed out by Vernon (338), the process of perception in normal reading is somewhat different from perception in general (of objects, geometric figures, pictures). As letters and words are learned, the sensations of meaningless groups of straight lines, angles, and curves are organized by the reader into definite groups and configurations, each of which is intimately related to some language form. Each configuration must acquire the meaning of a language form (a word) and then become organized with others into phrases and sentences through association of meaning. In reading, word recognition and assimilation are rapid. And the imagery, associated thought, interpretation, and evaluation which follow tend to be rich and varied since they are taken over together with acquired meanings derived from language configurations of word, phrase, and sentence. The adult (presumably mature) reader, according to Vernon (338), seems to pass directly from the visual perception to these meanings and processes of thought.

From the discussion above, it appears that perception in reading is dependent upon the meaning that occurs when visual impression is matched with the sound of a word in language usage. Also the meaning present in word identification and the early stages of recognition expands to ever greater richness as the

11

word is encountered again and again in new contexts. Probably few readers achieve mastery of the maximum meaning of many words. The mature reader, as defined in Chapter 1, will of course acquire greater fullness of word meanings than less mature readers.

How Adults Perceive Words

We now turn to a consideration of word perception by adults who have learned to read well. In this discussion, it is necessary to keep in mind that facile word perception is essential for effective reading. Without accurate word perception, the thinking side of reading and all that this implies (interpretation, evaluation, skill in comprehension) would be impossible.

In most of the investigations designed to discover how words are perceived, a short exposure device called a tachistoscope has been employed. This apparatus can be adjusted to give the subject or reader a single glimpse of a word, phrase, or sentence, a situation resembling what occurs in normal reading. In reading, the eyes make several stops, or fixation pauses, along a line with rapid saccadic moves between the pauses (see Chapter 5). The printed material is perceived only during the fixations of the eyes. On the average, these pauses are about 250 ms. (milliseconds) in duration in the ordinary reading of adults. Since a subject is limited to one fixation per trial by the timing of the tachistoscope, his perception is similar to what might occur during one fixation pause in reading.

To what degree does the area of clear vision during a fixation pause or a tachistoscope exposure determine accuracy and amount of perception in reading? At the normal reading distance, the fovea of the retina of the eye subtends an angle of about 70 minutes. In reading, therefore, only about 4 letter spaces of normal sized print fall in the fovea, the place of clearest vision. In the surrounding area, vision becomes gradually less distinct toward the periphery. Ruediger (225) has mapped out the field of distinct vision. He determined the distances from the fixation point (center) of fovea at which the letters u and n in 11 point type could be perceived correctly when viewed at 12 inches from the eyes. He found that this field has no distinct boundaries, but that clearness of form definition fades off gradually. Shape and extent of the field varied from one person to another. At one inch (12 to 15 letter spaces) from the fixation point, the accuracy of recognition was still fairly good. Images of words need not be at maximum clearness in all details to be perceived accurately. The unclear images of words to the right of the fixation point have important cue values. Hamilton (112), in studying the reading of continuous prose by means of successive short exposures, found at each fixation a small area of distinct vision along with marginal impressions of words and letters situated mainly to the right of the clearly defined fixated area. These impressions, which vary greatly in clearness, provide preliminary partial perception of successive words. In addition they orient the reader for the perception of successive words in the sentence or phrase as well as provide essential stimuli for successive fixations of the eyes. These vague word forms and letters or letter groups seen in peripheral vision to the right of the fixations also provide premonitions of coming meanings which are cleared up enough in successive fixations to yield correct word perception. That is, in reading all words need not be seen with maximum clearness (foveal vision) to be perceived.

The perceptual span in reading is the number of items, such as letters, digits, or words, that can be perceived and reproduced when the subject or reader has had a single glimpse at the material. Ordinarily, a tachistoscope or other short exposure technique has been employed to present words or other stimuli for an interval short enough (100 ms. or less) to assure the use of only one fixation by the subject at each trial. Much information about the perception of printed symbols including words has been obtained by use of this method. The terms "span of visual apprehension" and "perceptual span" are employed synonymously in the literature.

In this discussion we shall be concerned only with printed symbols occurring in reading situations. Cattell (47), Erdmann and Dodge (70), Tinker (268), Hoffmann (123), and others obtained perceptual spans for adults of 3 to 4 unrelated letters for the most part, but occasionally 5. When letters are grouped in the form of nonsense syllables (combination of letters which can be pronounced but which do not make a meaningful word, as "tuk" or "daux") the span for letters is increased to about 7 items. When groups of unrelated words are presented tachistoscopically, the number of letters apprehended is greater than for nonsense syllables although the number of words grasped is comparable to that of letters in nonsense series, i.e., 3 to 5 words or up to 19 letters. And when words are presented in phrases or sentences, the perceptual span is further increased by about one word over that for unrelated words. The sources above are sample citations. A survey of the literature indicates in a convincing manner that there is a natural tendency for a person to combine the different elements of a visual impression into higher perceptual units whenever grouping is possible. This occurs in perceiving letters organized in the form of nonsense syllables or words, and in the perception of words in phrases or sentences. These findings indicate that, in perceiving symbols presented momentarily as in a short exposure or a reading fixation pause, adults tend to organize the materials subjectively in accordance with the meaning. As the meaning becomes clearer, this organization achieves a greater perceptual span, i.e., there is an increase in the number of letters perceived when words are grasped as units.

We may then ask what roles are played by individual letters, small letter groups, and word form or shape in perception in the reading of adults. Does an adult with considerable skill in reading read by letters or by words? Actually, the answer is not simple or unequivocal. We shall find that both letters and word form provide important cues to perception in reading.

The fact that during a reading fixation pause a person may at times read in a sentence words containing 20 to 30 letters, with a typical average of 8 to 10, but can perceive only 3 to 4 unrelated letters suggests that in reading perception must take place by some means other than the recognition of letter after letter as was once supposed (131). The old and deeply rooted assumption was based in large part on the belief that the eyes passed from letter to letter along a line of print and that recognition

14

followed the successive fixations. Since research has shown how the eyes move in reading and that perception occurs only during the pauses, we know that it is impossible to read by letters. It is now obvious that, during each fixation, stimulations from several letters affect the reader simultaneously and that separate acts of recognition for each successive letter do not occur.

As early as 1885, Cattell (47) secured data which led him to conclude that proficient readers perceive printed material in units — whole words, sometimes even a phrase or sentence. He discovered that, when single words were briefly exposed, they were recognized as quickly as single letters. In fact, with accurate measurement of response time, it took longer to name single letters than to name whole words. And recognition without naming took only slightly longer for a word than for a single letter. He states that educated adults, therefore, perceive a word as a whole.

On the basis of their findings in numerous experiments, Erdmann and Dodge (70) strongly support the view that perception in reading is by word wholes. According to them, practiced readers recognize a word by the visual whole made up of the length of the word and its characteristic general shape. This conclusion was supported by the following findings. Subjects recognized words that were printed in type too small for individual letters to be identified; too far in peripheral vision for recognition of their component letters; and exposed beyond the distance at which the letters could be recognized. The authors state that it is not the constituent parts of any given form that make it recognizable, but the familiar total arrangement, the word form or shape. As emphasized by Huey (131), a familiar word form should be recognized and named just as a familiar house or wall. "The arrangement, the total form, is the main thing, whether in the recognition of letters, numbers, words, or objects of whatever sort" (page 75).

There has not been complete unanimity of opinion, however, on how words are perceived. Apparently, letters and small letter groups have cue values in word perception. Are such cues sufficient for the perception, the whole answer, or do they at times replace the cues from word form, or do the letters and small letter groups merely provide one or another aspect of word form? Evaluation of a number of experiments will help to answer these questions.

Goldscheider and Müller (100) point out that certain letters and letter complexes are more influential than others in determining the recognition of words. They call these "determining letters" as opposed to the "indifferent" ones. The first letter of a word belongs in the class of determining letters. Consonants, because of their characteristic form, are more often determining letters than vowels. However, vowels at times are determining letters, probably because they give a clue to the number of syllables in the word. Goldscheider and Müller found that the determining letters were more important in the recognition of words than other factors because they gave characteristic form to the word. This was particularly true of the more familiar words. They pointed out that one may, from time to time, read by letters, by groups of letters, by syllables, or by word wholes. The procedure in any particular instance is determined largely by the familiarity or difficulty of the word. If the reading is by word wholes, the characteristic form of the word is conditioned mainly by the determining letters present. Their conclusion was that the determining letters or letter complexes aroused the auditory image of the word and the word was then filled out through association. Erdmann and Dodge (70) do not deny that determining letters condition word form, which they consider to be the essential thing in word perception, and that words are read as units.

In a report based upon a tachistoscopic study, Zeitler (356) agrees with Goldscheider and Müller that the real stimulus in word perception consists largely of determining letters or letter complexes which are important factors in producing word form. But he differs from them in concluding that certain syllable complexes are clearly perceived and then the rest of the word is supplied associatively.

Also on the basis of tachistoscopic reading, Messmer (180) considers that the total word form is determined principally by the length of the word and by its vertical profile but, in addition, to some degree by its relative number of vertical letters, e.g., u, i, m, n, t, l, and curved letters, e.g., o, e, c, s. However, if the word is made up mainly of one of these types of letters, for example "surcease," it will be less readily perceived than if it contained some of both kinds, or several letters which have both vertical and curved lines (b, d, p, q, h): examples are "consonant" and "dappled." Both Zeitler and Messmer used very short tachistoscopic exposures which Dodge (66) criticizes severely. He demonstrated that under such conditions the perception of a word must take place mainly from the afterimage because there is not time enough for the clearing up of the visual sensation itself. And he found that with the short exposures any prominent features, such as dominating letters, would tend to stand out and be remembered to the exclusion of other features of the word. He states that, in normal reading or with exposures of 100 ms. or more where the visual impression is ordinarily fully cleared up, the so-called dominant letters would stand out no more clearly than the rest of the word. Perception, therefore, would occur by means of the total word form. Other writers (Kutzner, Stein, Heimann, and Thorner) cited by Vernon (338) also stress the importance of form quality (properties of the whole) of the word, i.e., the total structure of the word. Dominant letters contributed greatly to this structure or word form.

Woodworth and Schlosberg (355) present an analysis of data on word perception. They point out that Erdmann and Dodge's "general word shape" probably meant the external configuration of the printed word, while Cattell's "total word picture" covers also the internal pattern of curves and vertical strokes. For instance, the external outlines of the words "consonants" and "commumfs" look alike but the internal patterns are different enough to prevent their being easily confused (page 101). Woodworth and Schlosberg also point out that, in Pillsbury's experiment (207) with mutilated words, the subjects frequently noted the wrong letter or missing letter although perceiving the word correctly. That is, the reader often sees details which he disregards in reading the word (as "fashxon," read "fashion"). "Now if such details are visible when he cannot use them, correct details must also be visible in an unmutilated word and help to make up the complete word picture. Therefore, the visual impression received during a brief exposure must be much more complete and detailed than is implied by the phrase 'general word shape.' " (Page 102.) In cited experiments, although each subject can report only a few of the letters shown briefly, he believes he has seen all of them clearly. Thus, during a brief glimpse of a word, either during a fixation pause while reading, or a tachistoscopic exposure so short that no eye movements during the exposure are possible, the word is not spelled out letter by letter even though all letters may be clearly seen. That is, without verbalizing the successive letters, the subject has all the cues he could desire for accurate perception of the word. This is what Woodworth and Schlosberg apparently mean in approving the "total word picture" as used for perception in reading. That is, *total word shape*, the bare outline of a word, may cease to function in the normal reading situation, but the *total word structure* or total word picture, which includes the details of the internal pattern, may still function as a cue. This may appear to be a minor distinction, but it has important implications as we shall see later in our discussion.

In an examination of the errors made in normal reading, Vernon (338) found a tendency to omit letters, especially from long words. Since ascending letters were rarely omitted in comparison with descending letters, there appeared to be an inclination among readers to attend to the upper contour line or shape of the word, but not the lower. This seems logical, since Huey (130) found that printed material in which the lower half of the words had been eliminated was read much more easily than a passage in which the upper halves of words had been deleted. This contrast is illustrated in Figure 1. Messmer (180) found that the long letters which projected above the line are usually the dominating ones. Apparently the reader's attention is focused largely on the upper half of the word. The descenders and the short letters are of less importance. But Huey (131) notes

18

that in the relatively long pauses of actual reading (in contrast with tachistoscopic exposures), many if not all parts of a word can affect consciousness somewhat and give clues which help in recognition. This would tend to prevent errors in the filling out from the dominating letters such as may occur in words exposed briefly. Thus, while dominating letters may play the main role in word perception, the others have an important part as well.

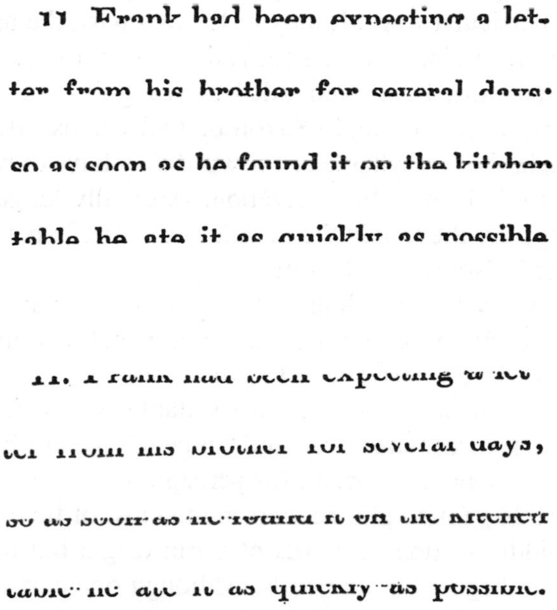

11. Frank had been expecting a let-

ter from his brother for several days.

so as soon as he found it on the kitchen

table he ate it as quickly as possible

11. Frank had been expecting a let-

ter from his brother for several days,

so as soon as he found it on the kitchen

table he ate it as quickly as possible.

Figure 1. Examples showing that the upper half
of a printed line furnishes more cues for word
perception than the lower half. Adapted
from Paterson and Tinker (197).

This view is somewhat like that of Woodworth and Schlosberg cited above. The role of ascenders and descenders in giving characteristic shape to words printed in lower case is shown in Figure 8 in Chapter 11. This figure also emphasizes the fact that all-capital printing provides fewer word-form cues to perception than words in lower case.

Possibly note should be taken of Huey's conclusion (131)

that the first part of a word is more important for its perception than the last part. Actually, Huey's demonstration was far removed from normal reading. On the average, his subjects identified 29 words per minute when only the first half of each word was visible, and 20 words per minute when only the last half was seen. The rate in normal reading would be 250 to 300 words per minute. In criticizing Huey's view, Vernon (338) notes that the part of a word that is most important for perception depends upon the particular word. It may be the first part, the middle, or the last part. Ordinarily, the root is the most important part of a word and must be apprehended to recognize the word. In many short words of Anglo-Saxon or Old English derivation, the root is in the first syllable or the word may have only one syllable. But words of Latin derivation, especially longer words, frequently have the root in the middle with a prefix before and a suffix after it. Note the following:

Anglo-Saxon: whaling, toothless, home, name

Latin: unsuccessful, inflammation, subservient

In words of Latin derivation, the root (success, flame, serve) must be apprehended and the last syllable is also important. Thus for the words "subserve" and "inflame" the last half of the word becomes most important for perception. In her own work, Vernon (336) found that readers made most of their mistakes on the middle section of words of Latin origin but also made mistakes on beginnings and ends. Although one part of a word may seem more important than others, in normal reading, perception appears to be achieved by a simultaneous view of the entire word.

What then is the relative importance of individual letters, determining letters and letter complexes, vowels, syllables, and total word form in word perception?

Obviously, a clear view of some letters of a word is required to enable the reader to reconstruct enough of the whole word to recognize it. Certain letters in a word are more likely to be seen clearly than others when glimpsed briefly, as during a short exposure or during a fixation pause in reading. These include initial and final letters, ascenders and descenders, and the relative distribution of vertical and curved letters in the word. Identifying vowels and syllables helps the reader to arrive at the correct pronunciation. As noted by many of the writers cited above, the nature and distribution of letters in the word give it a characteristic total shape which has strong cue value in its perception. A single aspect of letters, such as determining letters, or ascenders and descenders, or distribution of vertical and curved letters, or consonants and vowels, does not lead to ready perception of a word. Apparently several of these aspects of letters and their grouping, working together, produce for the reader a characteristic word form which tends to be readily recognized or perceived.

In the normal reading situation it is doubtful if many words are perceived correctly when the cue is merely the word shape as determined by the bare outline of the word. It appears that the process of perception is begun by the visual appearance of the outlined word shape and then is completed when enough details, such as initial consonant or consonant blend, a vowel or syllable, or the final letter, are apprehended to permit recognition of a word that fits the verbal context in which it appears.

This procedure for perception in reading, in which the external outline of the word shape has an important cue value, *operates only for sight words,* those words which have become thoroughly familiar to the reader from meeting them often in his reading. From the time a person begins to learn to read and throughout his life if he continues to read, he is constantly adding to his "bank" of sight words. The visual structures of these words have become so familiar that they are recognized at a glance. All adults who are fairly mature readers have a large store of sight words in their word banks. This is fortunate for otherwise reading would remain a slow, laborious procedure of analyzing each and every word in a sentence. The more familiar a word, the greater is the cue value of its shape.

Perception of unfamiliar words, or words not familiar enough to have become sight words, is a different matter. They can be perceived only by a process of analysis. The amount of analysis depends upon the degree of unfamiliarity. Words which have been met in one's reading may have a wide range of familiarity, from hardly any to enough to be a sight word recognized at a glance. Any degree of familiarity less than that which produces a sight word means that some analysis is necessary for perception. This is where the total word structure, which includes details of the internal pattern in which the reader gets an adequate simultaneous view of all its parts, functions in word perception. In this viewing, the reader apprehends whatever details (letters, both consonants and vowels, with their organization) are needed, with the help of verbal context, to achieve correct perception. But in the case of new words which are completely unfamiliar because they have not been encountered before, an exception must be made. Analysis of them requires rather complete visual scrutiny of the word elements to sound out the word mentally or perhaps subvocally. Having identified the pronunciation, the reader, through use of the verbal context in which the word appears and association with whatever past experience he has had with the sound of the word, achieves meaning and perception. If his experience with the spoken word or its sound is meager, the reader must depend largely upon the verbal context in which it is used or even on a dictionary to discover its meaning. This verbal context may be a sentence, a paragraph, or a larger segment of the text. Thus, word form as such provides little or no help in perceiving an unfamiliar (new) word. As pointed out by Anderson and Dearborn (8), these facts may help to explain why authorities have not always seemed to agree on the cues which are most important in word perception. "The value which Zeitler and Goldscheider and Müller assigned to individual letters applies mainly to unfamiliar words. These writers conceded that word shape or structure is often sufficient to touch off the recognition of familiar words." (Page 199.) But, as demonstrated by Vernon (336), word structure fails as a cue to perception when words are unfamiliar and the exposure time is too short to allow clear perception of all details, i.e., letters.

Certain other factors influence the perception of words. Other things being equal, a word is perceived most readily when printed in an optimal typographical arrangement (see Part Three). Also, illumination must be adequate for the most effective perception of printed words (see Part Four). The role of verbal context in promoting accurate perception of words needs strong emphasis. As noted in the early part of this chapter, perception implies sensory impression plus meaning. For instance, if a person does not understand the Polish language but has learned to pronounce correctly the word "ksztaltsi" without understanding what it means, he does not perceive the word. He is merely pronouncing what for him are nonsense syllables. Proper use of verbal context can help greatly in the acquisition of a meaningful vocabulary. The verbal meanings in a sentence or paragraph frequently make it possible to infer the meaning of a new word. For example, suppose a reader comes upon this sentence, in which the italicized word is new to him: "The happy responses of the children to the puppet show revealed the *quintessence* of delight possible in youngsters." Here the context quite readily gives considerable meaning, and therefore perception, to the word "quintessence." McCullough (175) has pointed out that the verbal woods are full of contextual aids to the meaning of new words in reading. The proficient reader depends greatly upon clues in the verbal context, not only to recognize a relatively unfamiliar word, but also to infer its exact meaning, i.e., to achieve more adequate perception of the word. In fact, the person who has not developed skill in the use of verbal context has not become a mature reader.

To some degree, we perceive what we want to perceive. That is, meanings tend to be personal. Interpretation of word meanings is often in terms of the reader's related experiences. The extent to which this is true of mature readers varies, depending in large measure upon the content of what is read. Although involved only to a slight degree in grasping words that refer to concrete objects such as a house, turnpike, factory, or basket, personal interpretation does come into play prominently in attempts to understand words referring to more complex and abstract concepts. A reader will react in his own individual ways to the textual material and its wider references and implications in proportion as his background of experience is uniquely his own (320). Expectancy is also involved in perceiving word meanings. When one reads in a specific field or on a given topic, he anticipates to some degree the words he encounters. And this kind of anticipation is of course most highly developed among mature adult readers.

Mental set due to one's special interests (biology, geology, music, etc.), or induced by the context of what is being read at the time, influences the unitary perception of words. This is nicely illustrated in proofreading. The successful proofreader must constantly ward off the tendency to become absorbed in the meaning of the text. Crosland (55) discovered that proofreaders miss many errors when they attend too much to meaning. And untrained proofreaders have much greater difficulty in resisting this tendency. The professional proofreader, if he is to be an expert, must avoid attending to meaning so that he may be set specifically to discover typographical errors.

From the discussion above, it appears that perception of words by adults who are skilled readers varies considerably. Familiar words, the sight words in the reader's bank, are perceived primarily in terms of word form or total structure. The perception of unfamiliar words requires a visual survey of the detailed composition of the word, with perhaps a mental or subvocal sounding out of the syllables or letter complexes involved. In such a case, the meaning of the word may be derived from the context in which it appears plus association with any related experiences of the reader. In situations in which the word is somewhat familiar but is not a sight word, perception is achieved partly by noting the pattern of the word form and partly by enough attention to detailed parts of the word to bring recognition. The amount of detailed examination will vary with the degree of familiarity and the amount of help secured from the context. All this refers to word perception by skilled adult readers. The perception of words by children who are learning to read differs considerably from that of adults (see the next chapter).

3   *Perception in Reading among Children*

In the beginning, as they start to learn to read, children do not adopt proficient techniques for perceiving words. But as they progress at a normal pace in the developmental program they gradually acquire more and more skill in word perception. A few become fairly mature readers by the seventh- or eighth-grade level, others at the high school level, and still others while in college or later. Some, of course, never become mature readers. Those who do become skillful adult readers have acquired the proficiency in word perception described in Chapter 2.

Children's Approach to Word Perception

A brief statement on children's perception in general may help to explain how they perceive words. Vernon (338), after surveying the literature, deduced the following (pages 141–142): In any perceptual situation, the young child tends to respond in terms of those aspects which appeal to his interest and are within his comprehension. He does not attend to minute details of form and structure. He interprets simple stimuli as familiar objects, but with a complex stimulus, he will report the objects, activities, and situations familiar to him and may invent others which he associates with those actually seen. If the child is somewhat beyond the very young age, he may begin to show considerable powers of interpretation and subjective elaboration. And "if the stimulus object contains comparatively little of interest to him, as does, for instance, a single word or a collection of letters, his eye will rove round looking for something interesting, and ultimately he may invent some such thing if he cannot find it." In general, it appears that the types of percep-

25

tion occurring in young children are mainly subjective in nature, in that the role played by the objective stimulus is secondary to that of familiarity and interest.

It would seem that children may have difficulty in learning to read until they are able and willing to perceive the small dissimilarities of form that differentiate letters and words from each other. Apparently this occurs at about the time the average child begins to learn to read. If well motivated and therefore anxious to read, he will be ready to learn to differentiate the visual details presented in the printed words. According to Vernon's deduction (338), a child learns to read easily only if the meaning and significance of the reading material are comprehensible, familiar, and interesting to him. The words used must be among those commonly found in the child's vocabulary.

The ineffective techniques of perceiving words adopted by various children in the early primary grades seem to result in part from the methods of instruction employed. According to Anderson and Dearborn (8), investigators are inclined to agree that the start in reading is best made with the "word" or "look-and-say" method. Initially a word is learned by viewing it, perhaps with a picture, while it is pronounced. Presumably the visual total word structure is then associated with the spoken word and the heard sound. The words used are already in the speaking and understanding vocabulary of the child. When a few words are learned, they can be used in a simple story. Very soon the child is able to enjoy the experience of reading meaningful little stories. And Anderson and Dearborn state that the "word method is the quickest and most direct way to teach a basic reading vocabulary and to get the process of real reading under way" (page 256).

The word method would seem to receive strong support from Hildreth (118) who states that there is abundant evidence that young children learn to recognize (perceive) words as wholes. This evidence is alleged to come "from observations of parents, teachers, child psychologists, and others, from analogy with other types of linguistic learning, and from laboratory experiments and their implications for word perception" (page 135).

Hildreth gives additional observations based on primary reading instruction. She places emphasis upon the tendency of children to hear words as total blends of sounds, of auditory patterns conveying specific meanings. Hildreth considers that school beginners easily learn words as wholes, even large numbers of words. Her argument is largely concerned with teaching the beginner words by the look-and-say method rather than by teaching the separate letters or sounds first. As already indicated the consensus is that this method is a good procedure to get beginning reading under way. But if the method continues to be used beyond this initial stage, and especially if it is used without supplementation by other techniques for teaching word perception, problems are likely to arise.

The word or look-and-say method was introduced to get away from the tedious and irksome practice, common in the early nineteenth century, of drill on letter names and sounds for month after month before allowing children to attempt reading words and sentences. When the researches of Cattell (47) and Erdmann and Dodge (70) revealed that adults tend to read words as units rather than letter by letter, the word method received further impetus, for it was assumed, apparently wrongly, that young children perceive words in the same way adults do. For a time, teachers discarded all forms of word analysis. Each and every word was to be learned as a sight word by viewing it and repeating its sound many times. It was soon discovered, however, that use of the look-and-say method by itself is ineffective: it depends too much on guessing, which leads to many errors in word perception. Further, most writers now agree that only a few young children perceive and recognize words by the total word structure. As pointed out by Durrell (68), a part of a word often stands out and serves as a clue for recall of the whole. This, too, often leads to errors by children.

When phrases and/or sentences are employed in the teaching of beginning reading, the child must eventually learn to perceive words, but the phrase and sentence methods also have their hazards: there is a tendency for many children to memorize the materials in primers and then depend upon some incidental visual

27

cues for future "reading" of them. This may delay learning of word perception skills. Although words, for the most part, should be taught in meaningful context of sentences and stories, every child must learn to perceive individual words accurately if he is to be able to read.

The alphabet method of reading words by compounding letters was rightly discarded. The word or look-and-say method, while useful, has limitations, as have the phrase and sentence methods. If the teaching of reading to children is to be as effective as possible, there must be a more widespread understanding of how children start out in reading and how they progress to the adult stage.

Cues to Word Perception by Young Children

As noted above, the look-and-say method assumes that a child will learn each word as a unit by perceiving the word form as a total unified structure but, apparently, few children achieve this ability during the beginning stages of learning to read. In fact, Bowden (28) found that children in learning to read individual words pay little attention to the total word form or general contour. And characteristic aspects of the total word form, due to the presence of ascending and descending letters or an alternation of straight and curved letters, do not help children to perceive words correctly, as they do for adults. It appears that the reading of these children was a rather imperfect form of word perception in which recognition depended upon noting the presence or absence of certain familiar letters. The report of Gates and Boeker (89) also emphasizes the role of individual letters rather than total word form in perception of words by young children. And evidence presented by Meek (179) led to the conclusion that certain letters or small groups of letters, such as i, ll, g, o, and k, were the chief cues for word perception. According to Hill (119), the letters at the beginning and end of words are used by children most frequently as cues to perception rather than the middles of words. Young children, it seems, recognize words by remembering some small thing or special detail that characterizes the word for them. The detail hit upon varies

28

from child to child. For instance, according to Gates and Boeker (89), the word "monkey" was remembered by the "hole" (of o), or the "funny chair" (on k), or the "tall middle," or the "monkey's tail" (y) at the end. Again, "pig" was recognized by the dot over the i and "box" by the "funny cross" at the end. One child remembered "look" because it had two eyes it used to look at you. An extreme case is given by Durrell (68). After a child had successfully read the word "children" on a flash card, he was unable to read it in a book, insisting that he had never seen it before. He was then shown the flash card again and asked how he recognized the word as "children." The reply was "By the smudge over in the corner."

As Anderson and Dearborn (8) put it, young readers do not seem to have much of an eye for word shape or structure. Only an occasional bright and able reader among young children appears to make much use of word form. Most children, at least during the early stages of learning to read, search out some small detail of the word, usually a single letter or two, a prefix or suffix or some other letter group, which then comes to stand for the whole word. That is, some feature, a small detail that stands out, is selected as the cue for perceiving the word. The letter or letters used for word identification are not necessarily recognized as such. They only represent a specific detail that stands for the word. The result is inaccurate word perception, due to the lack of careful analysis of the words.

It should be clear from this discussion that children, at the time they begin to learn to read, have not yet developed an habitual tendency to attend to the total structure of objects, including words. Furthermore, the very method ordinarily used for teaching a basic sight vocabulary to children, the word or look-and-say method, is associated with a number of problems including inaccurate word perception. As a single technique, the word method imposes a strict limitation on the size of the reading vocabulary, avoids word analysis, and encourages word-by-word reading. Usually there is little or no attempt by teachers to give specific training in perception of word forms or total structure of words. In any case, we do not know how effective such training would be. Furthermore, too frequently the word method continues to receive undue emphasis beyond the time at which a basic sight vocabulary is acquired. There is need to employ at an early date teaching methods that make it possible for the child to discard as soon as he can the inadequate method of perceiving words by noting some minor detail rather than by observation of the whole word. This is possible, provided the teacher understands the problem and knows how to teach by a combination of methods. When this is done, most children will move along in the developmental program to the point where they perceive words as adults do.

Developing Word Perception

Most experienced teachers, about 96 per cent (18), prefer to introduce their pupils to reading through the use of sentences or very short paragraphs. Russell (226) reported in 1944 that expert opinion and practice were in favor of the sentence method alone or in combination with other methods. Incidentally, paragraph organization in primers is hardly noticeable and means little to the beginner. He reads a series of sentences that form a little story. While children are interested in reading such sentences, they are far from enthusiastic about drill on isolated words. This procedure of using sentences and short paragraphs from the first lesson on, however, does not avoid for long the task of learning to perceive accurately the individual words they contain. Even though it is the initial sight vocabulary that is learned ordinarily from the teacher's pronunciation of words in the look-and-say method, any teacher may occasionally and legitimately give the correct pronunciation of a difficult word in a similar manner with pupils at any grade level. However, little progress in beginning reading will be made until the look-and-say method is supplemented by other techniques in a combined approach to word perception. As stated by Tinker and McCullough (320), the combined approach is intended to furnish the child with the available techniques and to teach him to be versatile in applying them. When this is done, the child should be able to employ the clue or clues that will lead to quick and accurate perception of a word.

Basic to any program of word perception is emphasis on adequate visual and auditory discrimination. Word perception involves matching the visual symbol with the sound of the spoken word and the meaning represented by the printed symbol. Thus there must be correct discrimination of the sounds represented in a word and precise visual discrimination of both total word form and details of its structure.

It may be re-emphasized here that the term "word recognition" as used in the literature on reading means word identification, if it is a new word, or appreciating that it is a familiar word if it has been encountered before. In both instances, perception is involved. Because some writers use "word recognition" and "word perception" as synonymous terms, it should be kept in mind that the discussion here of developing "word perception" might also be called a discussion of "word recognition" methods.

Clues and Techniques in Word Perception

A detailed program for developing word perception or recognition is given by Tinker and McCullough (320). Only an abbreviated outline will be presented here. At the same time that a basic vocabulary is being taught by the look-and-say method, the words should be used in sentences as much as possible and emphasis placed upon meanings. There is little agreement on how many sight words should be taught before introducing supplementary techniques to aid word perception. Although some authors suggest that 50 to 100 be learned this way, it is difficult for most beginners to learn even 50 words well enough to remember them by their appearance alone. Fortunately the present trend is to depart from a strictly look-and-say method early in the first grade. As soon as words the child is learning have common characteristics, like the initial consonant in "boy," "bell," and "ball," he should be encouraged to note that such words begin with the same sound. It is not necessary, therefore, to wait until 50 or more sight words are learned before introducing supplementary word perception aids. Actually there is

31

little justification for permitting a child to identify a word by some such characteristic as the tail on the word "monkey." It is better to guide the child at an early date to use of more enduring and more dependable methods of word perception.

It has been emphasized that word form is seldom a clue to perception in beginning reading. The use of word-form clues without special training does not ordinarily occur until a child has made considerable progress in learning to read. Then, as a word becomes more familiar by frequent encounters, the visual clues from total word structure are more potent. This occurs most readily when a word has a distinctive shape or form. The presence of definite word form is illustrated in the left column and its absence in the right column below:

stopped	moraine
distinct	nervous
largely	amnesia
dictator	DICTATOR
agitate	AGITATE

Casual inspection of a few pages in a dictionary reveals that a large majority of words have characteristic word forms that are due to alternation of long and short letters. Also it is obvious that most lower-case words have more distinctive word forms than words in all-capital letters (see also Figure 8 in Chapter 11).

Since we now know that beginners while learning the basic vocabulary make little use of word form in perceiving words, the teacher might well direct attention to this kind of clue. At the same time, she will need to point out that some words have like shapes and may be confused, as "house" and "horse." To obtain effective use of clues to word forms in perceiving words, Tinker and McCullough (320) suggest that, in the developmental program, some emphasis be placed upon teaching pupils the characteristic shape of words, encouraging in them the habit of combining context clues with word-form clues, and helping them to recognize that closer visual examination of a word is sometimes necessary for complete and accurate perception.

When a child has caught on to this procedure, little or no further training in word-form clues to perception is necessary.

Although beginners do not learn quickly to employ word-form clues to perceive words, children use this kind of clue to an ever greater extent as they progress to more efficient reading in the developmental program. And, as a person becomes a fairly mature reader and continues his reading experiences, use of clues from total word structure becomes extensive for perceiving words at a glance. In fact, without this skill one cannot become a rapid reader.

Sight words added to the reader's word bank as he continues to gain experience in reading are not acquired by the look-and-say method used to build the initial sight vocabulary of the beginner. Words that are met frequently and become familiar enough to be recognized at a glance are the ones added to the reader's word bank. In the developmental educational program, extensive and rapid reading of materials free from difficulties with words tends to encourage use of word-form clues to develop perception of *well-known* words at a glance. And sight words are accumulated as long as a person continues to read widely, i.e., throughout life for some people.

Context clues constitute another aid to word perception. They consist of picture clues and verbal clues. Particularly in children's books, appropriate pictures can contribute a great deal to contextual meaning which provides clues to perceiving some of the words in the story (for details, see Tinker and McCullough, 320, pages 145–148). In factual reading material, maps, tables, and other graphic representations also provide context clues to word perception.

Verbal-context clues derived from meanings of known words in a sentence or paragraph make up one of the more important aids to word perception. In a class where reading is well taught, these clues begin to operate as soon as a child begins to read sentences in little stories. Verbal context may be used in word perception by inferring that a new written word is a word already in the reader's speaking or understanding vocabulary that would fit into the meaning of the sentence. (It is desirable to use the

33

word "infer" rather than "guess," if context clues are used properly. In this situation, the word "guess" is apt to imply a wrong meaning.) Suppose the new word is "ride" in "John likes to ride his bicycle." If the pupil knows all the words except "ride," it is not difficult for him to infer from the context that the new word is "ride." In many instances context clues operate quickly and effectively. But pupils need training in using context to aid in perceiving words. This training should continue throughout the elementary grades. A number of procedures for teaching the use of context clues are available (320). Bond and Wagner (27) state that in all probability context clues should be employed in the perception of every word occurring in a meaningful setting. The use of these clues limits the choice of words to the very few that could fit in with the meaning of the passage being read. One of these words is chosen. The reader then employs the proper analytical technique to check the accuracy of his choice (see below). He makes an increasing use of context clues as he becomes more and more proficient in his reading. Effectiveness of context clues for word perception depends almost always on using the clues in combination with other methods of perception. Ordinarily, the meaning-supplying clues derived from verbal context are most effective in aiding word perception when they are used with phonetic analysis and structural analysis. In fact, no person can become a proficient reader unless he acquires phonetic ability and knows how to use it properly in the combined approach to word perception. As Durrell (68) puts it, if a person were without phonetic ability, reading would becoming a guessing game, but if phonetics alone are used, reading becomes just nonsense-syllable analysis.

Phonetic analysis deals with identifying sounds in words, and progressing through words from left to right while saying the successive sounds aloud or subvocally to obtain clues to the pronunciation of the whole word. Correctly pronouncing a word ordinarily recalls its meaning if it is in the reader's speaking or understanding vocabulary. Coordination of the visual and auditory aspects of phonics is essential. Visual analysis and sounding are interdependent, for proper sounding of the word elements cannot take place in reading without visual analysis of the word occurring at the same time. The visual and auditory elements of a word correspond, as in mag-net-ic, or pos-si-bil-i-ty.

There are certain prerequisites to learning phonetic analysis. Instruction should begin only when a pupil is ready and able to profit by the teaching, i.e., he should possess phonic readiness. This means that the child must have adequate auditory and visual discrimination, be able to read with understanding, have acquired an adequate sight vocabulary, be able to use context clues for word perception with at least moderate effectiveness, and have acquired the habit of proceeding from left to right in reading. Accumulated evidence indicates that both mental age and perceptual knowledge are important for phonic readiness (320, page 154).

Learning to use phonics is a complex process, taking a long time to master. For some children acquiring skill in phonics is rather difficult. Once a child has identified the word elements and their sounds, he must blend the sounds in order to pronounce the word as a unit. In the learning program phonetic analysis of lists of isolated words is decidedly unprofitable and should be avoided. Soon after sounding out a word, the child should always use it in the context of a sentence. This provides an additional clue for accurate perception of the word, since help is had from the meaning of the sentence in which it occurs. The simplest phonetic technique (initial consonants) should be introduced first and fairly soon after the pupil begins to read. Then, in the developmental program progress to the more complex aspects of phonics should take place in the most sensible order. Programs for teaching phonics are given by Durrell (68), Bond and Tinker (26), Tinker and McCullough (320), and Sister Mary Caroline (242). The last is an excellent phonics handbook which may be employed advantageously with any basic reading program.

Structural analysis, which deals with identifying the parts of a word which form meaningful units and/or units of pronunciation, and phonetic analysis are two related aspects of word analysis and are frequently combined in word perception. In such a case, structural analysis precedes phonetic analysis in words of more than one syllable. The initial visual analysis reveals the pronounceable units and this is followed by whatever phonetic analysis is needed to achieve proper pronunciation of the units. Usually division into syllabic units indicates how the sounding is to be done, as with "ba-by" and "con-sti-tute."

Syllabification may be classified with structural analysis. Its use permits separation of the longer words into relatively large elements to be recognized and pronounced as units, i.e., each syllable pronounced in one breath. Skill in syllabification is a useful technique for identifying the pronunciation of polysyllabic words, for it is more effective than letter-by-letter phonics. Visual analysis identifies the syllables which are then synthesized in pronouncing the word to achieve perception. Dictionaries also may employ syllabification to indicate pronunciation of words. Units of meaning may be parts of a compound word, as in "backyard"; base words, as "speak" in "speaking"; suffixes (-ing in "speaking"); prefixes (re- in "recall"); the root word in the inflected form of a word ("play" in "played"). For polysyllabic words that are not compound words and are without prefixes, suffixes, or inflected endings, perception is best achieved by syllabification. Structural analysis, combined with phonics and context clues, becomes very useful in word perception. There is no satisfactory substitute for these techniques in arriving at the perception of new words.

How are the various clues to be used to perceive words? As they are taught, the child learns how to choose the most effective clue or combination of clues to identify, recognize, or perceive words in any specific situation. To take an example, suppose he meets the word "telescope" in this sentence: "One clear night Jim looked through the *telescope* and saw mountains on the moon." The child might employ the following methods to identify and perceive the word: He could use letter-by-letter soundings and blend the sounds. Or he could, through visual analysis, note the syllables "tel-e-scope" and blend the pronunciation of the syllables. Or he could use the contextual meaning of the rest of the sentence, note the initial consonant, and thus infer the

identity of the word. Ordinarily this last method, using a combination of context clues with phonics (for sound of initial consonant, or more if necessary) will be effective and most rapid.
If the pupil is skilled in syllabification, the second method may
be equally effective and fairly fast, especially if helped by use of
context clues. The first method is used only when perception
cannot be achieved by one of the other procedures. Letter-by-
letter sounding and blending is laborious, slow, and usually
more difficult to use. The word-form clue would be of little or no
help here since the word is new.

Training the child to progress from the ineffective cues to
word recognition hit upon while acquiring an initial basic vocabulary by the look-and-say method to efficient mature procedures
of word perception requires a developmental program of teaching and learning. In general, the pupil in his progress should
become familiar with the clues in all the word-perception techniques, understand their most appropriate uses, their limitations,
and the need of using a combination of clues in certain situations.

We may repeat, the skilled reader will employ the clue or
combination of clues that will be most effective and operate most
rapidly in any particular situation. Unless a person is versatile
enough to use a combination of clues when this would be most
effective for perceiving a specific word, he has not yet become a
skillful reader. Practice under guidance is usually necessary to
achieve such versatility. The skillful teacher will develop word
perception in situations meaningful to the pupil. At first she
teaches the use of a clue with known words, and later introduces
exercises using it with unknown words *in context*. It is essential that the pupil understand the meaning of the word he pro-
nounces, for otherwise he is only speaking nonsense syllables.
And the teacher will avoid drill on lists of isolated words. In
teaching word perception, the developmental program should
follow a logical sequence, progressing from the simpler to the
more complex techniques. In all this, the teacher will place special emphasis upon having the child move from left to right in

perceiving word elements and in coordinating visual with sounding analysis in perceiving words.

When a pupil reaches the higher levels of the developmental program at which he has become a relatively mature reader, he will be perceiving words in the adult manner described in the previous chapter.

4   *Comprehension in Reading*

Comprehension is the objective of all reading. At every grade level in school, from the introduction to reading in the first grade on, the teaching of reading is primarily concerned with developing comprehension. That is, the emphasis is upon reading-to-learn rather than learning-to-read. To become a mature reader, one must be able to comprehend all printed materials which will serve his purposes. And to achieve this ability, development of the thinking side of reading is essential.

In developing reading comprehension, the acquisition of mechanical skills such as left-to-right progression of perception, accurate return sweeps of the eyes from the end of one line to the beginning of the next, a sight vocabulary, perception (recognition) of words — the skills of verbal facility in general — is designed to promote the understanding and interpretation of the meanings embodied in printed symbols. Without these skills, the more advanced pupil or adult will be unable to attain his possible maximum comprehension. Although they are fundamental to reading, the mechanical skills must be relegated to their appropriate place. They must become automatic in their operation so that the reader is free to devote himself to comprehension and interpretation. To become a good reader, therefore, control of the mechanical aspects of reading must be adequate so that the meanings represented by the printed symbols can be clearly and accurately understood and interpretations achieved by the operation of the thinking side of reading. Any instructional program which overemphasizes the mechanical aspects of reading tends to lead to verbalism, a poor substitute for true reading.

The essential components of comprehension are many. The

extensiveness of the factors involved in reading comprehension is well illustrated by the detailed list of 22 such factors presented by Betts (20, pages 94–95). And Tinker and McCullough (320) have emphasized that, in addition to perception of words and the understanding of word meanings, other processes are necessary for comprehension. For instance, the constituent parts of a sentence need to be evaluated and their organization in relation to each other understood. Word meanings that are in harmony with the rest of the verbal context must be selected. In addition, to comprehend a paragraph or larger unit the relations among its sentences need to be understood.

What is the relation between listening and reading comprehension? Comprehending printed material involves much the same processes as understanding spoken words. That is, the perception of words arouses meanings which lead to comprehension. These meanings depend upon a person's whole background of experience as well as his facility in communication. According to Gates (88), if a pupil is not handicapped by difficulties in the mechanical aspects of reading, he should be able to comprehend in printed form as long and as complex a unit as he can comprehend in spoken form. Tinker and McCullough (320) in summarizing research on this subject, found certain trends: In the early elementary grades, auditory comprehension ordinarily was equal to or better than reading comprehension. Also, at all levels but particularly in the higher grades, pupils of lower mental ability revealed this same trend. But for skilled readers and for those of higher mental ability, reading comprehension ordinarily was equal to or superior to listening comprehension. By the time students reach college, listening comprehension tended to be better for easy material and reading comprehension for the more difficult. The experimental literature as a whole makes obvious that reading comprehension becomes more and more effective with advancing age among those who read widely, and eventually exceeds listening comprehension in the case of the more able readers.

This seems to be a logical and expected progression. In the primary grades, while much emphasis is placed upon learning the mechanics of reading, auditory comprehension tends to be superior. But when the mechanics have become pretty much automatic, which is achieved earlier by the more able children, reading comprehension and listening comprehension are at about the same level. And then, when the pupils reach a higher level of reading proficiency, reading comprehension may and usually does become more efficient than auditory. In other words, pupils tend to progress from superior listening comprehension in the early grades to equality with reading comprehension, which finally becomes best, owing to accumulated experience, greater maturity, and increased proficiency. This trend is especially prominent with superior readers.

What is the relation of speed of reading to comprehension? Much difficulty can arise from treating speed of reading and comprehension as separate aspects of reading. In general, there has been an overemphasis in the classroom on speed of reading as such. Tinker (277) has stated that the speed at which words can be identified has little significance for reading unless the printed material is comprehended. He suggests that it is better to use the term "speed of comprehension" rather than "speed of reading." This stresses the view that, when one thinks of speed of reading, he should be concerned with quickness of understanding. Here, two points should be emphasized. While children are mastering the mechanics of reading during the primary years, little or no attention should be devoted to speed. But during the intermediate and higher grades there will be some need to improve speed of comprehension. In general, however, throughout elementary school, the emphasis should be placed upon development of comprehension, word meanings, and concepts. If this program is properly carried out, there will be little need for specific training in speed of comprehension for most pupils. Any class-wide program for "whipping up" the speed of comprehension represents misplaced emphasis. When the program of teaching is adequate, speed will tend to take care of itself. "When material is within the child's capacity to understand, the more clearly he comprehends it the faster will his rate of progress tend to be" (320, page 172).

Factors in Comprehension*

The meanings in reading are built upon experiences. Hence the relations between experience and comprehension are intimate. As noted by Harrison (115), the meaning may be derived directly from past experiences, or it may consist of a newly constructed meaning which results from combining and reorganizing meanings already in a pupil's possession. This is well illustrated by an example given by Bond and Tinker (26, page 231). A fourth-grade child reads the following sentence: "The tired rider drooped in his saddle as his spotted horse walked along the mountain trail." Although the child has never seen such a rider, he may derive the meaning of the sentence from reorganizing a variety of remembered experiences, such as his grandfather napping with his head bent forward as he sits in an easy chair; a bridle path through the park; a mounted man who sat erect on his black horse; a spotted black and white dog; and the scenery during a trip through hilly country. By calling up these memories the pupil may well reach a close approximation of the meaning intended by the writer of the sentence.

A number of factors determine how readily readers comprehend. Among these are the following: individual differences in mental ability; wealth of experience; the degree to which the mechanics of reading have been mastered; and flexibility of approach in reading, for the person who uses the same rate and method to read all materials cannot become a proficient reader. Flexibility, or ability to adjust method and rate, is particularly important in reading different contents, such as literature versus science material (see below). McCullough (176) has drawn up a list of four conditions favorable to comprehension: First, such impediments as lack of confidence, meager vocabulary, poor understanding of sentence and paragraph organization, and inadequate critical evaluation skill should be removed. Second, the degree of difficulty of a particular content of material should be proper for the reader. Third, a pupil should be thoroughly prepared for what is to be read by assuring that he knows the correct

* This section is based partly on material prepared by M. A. Tinker for Chapter 8 in Tinker and McCullough (320).

pronunciation and meanings of difficult new words and by giving him an explanation of new concepts. Finally, motivation is of prime importance. To foster this, the teacher must provide incentives which will develop the pupil's interest in the subject. McCullough states that comprehension of material in any area of knowledge requires recognition of these four conditions.

Comprehension is a complex of skills which needs to be taught at successive grade levels. In addition to understanding words, a pupil must learn many other skills before he can comprehend meanings in sentences, paragraphs, and larger units of material. Sentences involve grasping the relations between words as well as groups of words, phrasing or reading by thought units, proper interpretation of punctuation, and understanding figures of speech and symbolic expressions. To comprehend paragraphs requires an understanding of sentences and the relations between sentences. Since any well-constructed paragraph is concerned with a single central idea, it is especially important that the pupil be able to identify the topical sentence which gives the key idea of the paragraph. Then the reader must interpret its relation to the separate explanatory or amplifying sentences in that paragraph. The topical sentence may be the first or second, or it might be a summary sentence at the end. Ability to comprehend a paragraph well as a unit is important in all reading. In longer units, the good reader comprehends the relation between the successive paragraphs. These give the explanatory details in logical sequence of what has been introduced in the initial paragraphs. And the final paragraph or two of an article or chapter or short story usually gives the outcome or conclusions, or perhaps summarizes what has been said. Techniques and sources of material for developing comprehension are given by Tinker and McCullough (320).

Specialized Methods of Comprehension*

Facility in the more complex comprehension skills identifies the mature reader. But these skills can be mastered only after a

* This section is based partly upon material written by M. A. Tinker in Chapter 9 in Tinker and McCullough (320).

firm foundation is acquired in the basic abilities of word, sentence, paragraph, and complete unit comprehension. And, as noted by Tinker and McCullough (320), the proficient reader will obtain from the printed material only what he is seeking, e.g., a football score, directions on how to assemble a power lawn mower, a description of the nature of photosynthesis, an explanation of visible electromagnetic light waves, the development of the plot of a novel, or an analysis of all the data upon which a scientific conclusion is based. In all such situations, the proficient reader makes use of his special comprehension skills to the degree required to attain his objectives.

In practice, the specialized comprehension skills and study skills operate together. That is, the study skills, such as using reference materials, locating information, organizing the material selected, and interpreting tables and graphs, are brought into operation when one or another comprehension skill is used. This is particularly true when reading science, mathematics, social science, or literature. The study skills will not be considered further here. Details of their role are given in Tinker and McCullough (320).

As pointed out in McCullough's survey (174), readers taught in our schools can ascertain facts but many have failed to become thoughtful readers who use specialized comprehension skills selectively and effectively. She also emphasizes the need for systematic teaching of these specialized comprehension skills. They not only are difficult to learn but are not sufficiently mastered for facile use at any one grade level. After the pupil achieves knowledge of these skills, it is necessary for him to learn to select the skill or skills appropriate for reading a particular selection. To do this, the reader also needs a clear understanding of the purpose for which the reading is to be done.

The main specialized comprehension skills may be briefly outlined. For a detailed discussion of them see Tinker and McCullough (320, pages 186–194).

Skimming is a specialized technique in which partial reading is done at a fast pace to obtain certain kinds of information. It is a highly serviceable method which must be properly used and not abused. Skimming should be done with a definite purpose to acquire certain precise and accurate information or ideas or points of view. Thus the information sought might be just a single item such as the name of a person or place, a particular date, or a germane fact. It might be the point of view developed in a magazine article, or a section of an article or book that is relevant to a problem at hand. Or the reader might skim a magazine article, a chapter, or even a whole book to acquire an overview or general impression of the contents. If a reader has sufficient background in a field, he should be able to skim new material in the area with ease and efficiency. Ordinarily, skimming involves ignoring the irrelevant parts and selecting those which are pertinent. The accuracy of what is obtained by skimming depends upon how well the reader uses his background of information in checking what he selects. In any skimming, the reader needs to know how to find a proper source of the information desired, i.e., a newspaper, a magazine, a book or part of a book, an encyclopedia, or other reference work. This means that the reader must not only be acquainted with source and reference materials but also be able to use properly the indexes in books and reference works. Skimming is not easily taught or learned. Grayum (107), working with six groups ranging from fourth-graders to college students and well-read adults, found marked differences among the readers at each level in ability to skim. All readers were of average or superior intelligence. Some of the adults were as poor in this skill as the fourth-graders. And a considerable numbers of readers of both average and superior intelligence were very poor skimmers. It seems that greater emphasis should be placed upon teaching skimming, for the proficient skimmer possesses a valuable asset. Skimming is a specialized skill that is different from other reading skills. It is very useful in many kinds of reading, particularly in study situations.

Another specialized comprehension ability is that of reading to *grasp and assimilate relevant details*. This kind of reading is characterized by relatively slow, step-by-step progress and at times some rereading. The aim is to grasp the relevant details, ignoring others. If this is properly done, the reader will understand the relation of these important details to each other and to the pattern of thought running through the unit of material read. Clear purpose and strong motivation are essential for best results. Precise attention to details is required in reading much of science and mathematics, and parts of social studies, geography, and history, as well as certain kinds of literature.

A different approach is needed for reading a unit of material to *grasp the main idea*. In this, the reader is concerned with the central theme, or general meaning of the text. The important meaning may involve an idea or it may concern the emotion expressed, i.e., the central thought or impression. By means of discrimination and judgment, the reader grasps the essential significance of the unit as a whole. This skill requires considerable training, for it is not easy to acquire. But it has wide application in the reading of newspaper articles, novels, short stories, and other materials. Much of one's everyday reading is of this type and should be done rapidly and accurately but not superficially. The common tendency to try to remember many details hinders reading for the main idea.

Reading of *printed directions* that must be followed in one or another operation bulks large in everyday life, e.g., directions for baking a pie, constructing a model, assembling an apparatus, conducting an experiment, playing a game, or solving a mathematical problem. Such reading is relatively slow and painstaking as pertinent details are grasped in proper sequence. Owing either to the inherent difficulty of the material or to lack of sufficient experience and training, many advanced students and adults are unable to follow printed directions properly. Many of the difficulties frequently encountered by students in science and mathematics appear to be due to lack of this skill.

Understanding and enjoyment of narrative material is enhanced by the ability of the reader to *follow a sequence of ideas* and to predict what is to follow. This requires grasping the main idea and appreciating cause and effect relations between successive events and what these mean in the unfolding of the plot. Since this skill is also used in listening, it begins to develop early as stories are read or told to the child, and continues to develop through training in the grades.

The thinking side of reading is necessarily involved in *drawing conclusions*. This requires judgment in selecting and coordinating relevant materials during the reading of one or more books, articles, or items. When the selecting and coordinating are done successfully, a general rule, a generalization, or a conclusion is suggested. Reading of this sort is purposeful and the purpose is usually derived from a question that points toward an inference, e.g., why does it snow on mountain tops in the southwestern United States when it rains in adjoining valleys? It should be kept in mind that any first generalization is tentative and should be checked for accuracy by referring to experience, additional reading, and perhaps discussion. Although school children tend to generalize readily, they frequently jump to conclusions which are inaccurate. They should have guidance in their selecting of relevant information and in evaluating their initial conclusions.

Critical evaluation of what is read is one of the special comprehension skills very difficult to acquire. And this skill is needed in many situations met in reading, especially the reading carried out in the upper grades and by adults. For instance, the material presented in an experimental report that leads to a conclusion needs to be critically evaluated. Gans (84) investigated the ability to determine whether a sentence or paragraph contained information relevant to a given question or topic. She found that the discrimination required for critical evaluation of what is read tended to be poorly developed, even among the more able pupils in the upper grades. Few students in the intermediate grades, high school, or even college possess adequate technique for critical evaluation in reading. This comprehension skill should be taught in the developmental reading program from the beginning of the fourth grade on through the upper levels.

The importance of critical evaluation in situations in school and out is illustrated by the following: Conflicting views are met with in discussions of specific topics in such publications as newspapers, magazines, scientific journals, and books. To reconcile or choose among these views frequently requires a high level of critical judgment. For this, the reader must make use of his whole background of related experience plus perhaps additional reading. Class discussion under competent supervision is helpful.

In contemporary life one is bombarded with propaganda in many forms — by radio and television and in speeches, advertisements, and other printed materials. It is desirable to learn not only to detect propaganda but also how to evaluate it. Although the task is not easy, teachers can do much by guiding pupils to recognize many of the more obvious propaganda techniques: name calling, statements by so-called prestige individuals, the term "scientific finding" attached to a promotion statement, or views expressed in editorials and columnists' writing. At higher levels, as in high school and college, additional and more sophisticated methods of training are needed to develop keen discrimination and critical evaluation of the more subtle forms of propaganda. It is surprising and perhaps alarming that such a large proportion of our adult population has not acquired a questioning attitude toward appealing generalizations as well as toward specific claims unsupported by factual evidence.

At this place, it may be well to re-emphasize the role of comprehension in reading. Beginning with the first lessons in reading, the understanding of printed material should be sought. Obviously the mechanical aspects of perceiving words accurately must be taught. But comprehension is fundamental to all reading. The goal in developmental programs is to help the reader acquire as rapidly as possible the ability to understand what the author is trying to convey. As the child is learning how to perceive words accurately, he is also progressing in vocabulary knowledge and sentence and paragraph comprehension. By the time he starts the fourth grade he begins to learn the specialized comprehension skills. Acquisition of these skills is slow and extends on through high school and perhaps into the college years for some students. The major skills of a mature reader include accurate perception of words plus adequate command of the basic comprehension skills and of the specialized comprehension skills.

Versatility in Reading

Since to comprehend effectively requires versatility in reading, the mature reader is also a versatile reader. In addition to having acquired mastery of the mechanics of reading, the basic comprehension skills, and the specialized comprehension skills, he is able to adjust his approach to each reading situation for most effective reading. Such a reader can turn with ease from one to another reading task, almost automatically choosing the method that will achieve in the most proficient manner what is required. For example, a different approach would be used for each of the following: skimming to find a name, a date, or a fact; reading for the general idea; reading to remember details; reading a mathematical problem; studying the explanation of a new concept in science. In general, the versatile reader knows how to select and use the proper attack for reading material in each of the content subjects.

A prime example of versatility in reading is flexibility in adjusting speed of reading to the kind and difficulty of materials read and to the purpose for which the reading is done. Thus the versatile reader is able to move along very rapidly or he can employ a moderate or a very slow rate, whichever is appropriate. Even rereading parts of material is in order when studying text requiring a highly analytical procedure for grasping the essential passages. Unfortunately, too few students even in high school and college have become truly versatile in their reading. A surprising number tend to read most or all material at about the same rate. For example, those accustomed to reading science material tend to read newspapers and novels at a relatively slow rate, and those who have concentrated on literature tend to read science too rapidly for adequate comprehension.

How does one become a versatile reader? He must develop this skill through practice under guidance. Few achieve versatility on their own. To gain the needed flexibility in rate of reading, the developing child can be helped to acquire the knack of choosing the speed appropriate for a particular situation and learning to read at that rate with understanding. As he progresses through the grades and into high school and college, he will necessarily read numerous kinds of material for many purposes. A program to develop the flexibility in speed needed to read materials for different purposes is a difficult one for the teacher to carry out. But unless this program to develop flexibility in reading becomes a continuing part of instruction throughout the school years, most students will never become versatile readers.

Part Two: Eye Movements in Reading

5 Nature and Measurement of Eye Movements

The oculomotor behavior involved in reading attracted the attention of scientists at an early date. With the accumulation of a considerable store of information and the publication of Huey's book (131) on the psychology and teaching of reading in 1908, the application of eye-movement findings to education became evident. Intensive programs of research were soon under way at several universities. In addition to investigations on the mechanical functioning of the eyes in reading, studies appeared on variation of oculomotor patterns with proficiency in reading, age of the reader, and reading in special situations such as interpreting formulas, learning to spell, and learning to read foreign languages. Fairly early in the programs of investigation, corrective reading instruction was instituted.

The study of eye movements in reading began about 1879 with the observations of Professor Emile Javal, the great French opthalmologist. But research activity became vigorous only after 1900. To date, several hundred investigations have been reported. Most of these have been reviewed in three articles by Tinker (280, 293, 312).

The traditional belief, one that is still held by many of the uninformed, is that a person reads as his eyes sweep uninterruptedly and smoothly along a line of print. Actually, in reading a line the eyes make several stops, each a *fixation pause*. The move from one fixation to the next is a quick jerk called a *saccadic movement*. Such movements are so fast that while they are in process no clear vision is possible. Fixation pauses are the periods of clear vision and it is during the pauses that perception occurs. Since in most situations about 93 to 95 per cent of reading time on the average is devoted to fixation pauses, the eyes are motionless for relatively long periods. During the reading of a line of print, the eyes sometimes move backwards toward the beginning of the line and make fixations to get a clearer view of material or to reread it. These backward movements are called *regressions*. When one line is finished, the eyes make a long *return sweep* to the beginning of the next line. The time relations of eye movements and fixation pauses will be considered in detail in the next chapter.

Experimental investigations of eye movements in reading have contributed much to an understanding of how children learn to read. These studies have also provided essential information about the nature of the reading processes of both children and adults.

Techniques of Measurement

The first published description of eye movements in reading appeared with Javal's report (135) of investigations completed in his laboratory. There is a fuller report in Javal's book (136). Direct observation revealed that the eyes move along a line in quick jerks, or saccades, with pauses between the moves. An attempt was made without much success to count the number of moves per line by means of a tiny microphone attached to the upper eyelid.

Mirrors have been used by several investigators (136, 70, 81, 183) to observe movements of the eyes in reading. A mirror is placed in front and a little to the right of the reader so that the experimenter, looking at the mirror from behind the reader, can observe and count the eye movements. Erdmann and Dodge (70) made direct observations of eye movements by viewing the eye through a telescope. They also developed a method using afterimages to determine the approximate location of the fixation pauses along a line of print. The reader looked at the apex of a small wedge-shaped piece of brightly illuminated red paper until the retina was well fatigued. Then as he read the experimental passage, there was a sharply defined green negative afterimage at the place of each fixation which the reader would report. The Miles (181) peephole technique of direct observation is simple and effective. The experimenter views the eye through a hole near the center of the reading copy which is held up in front of the reader. Eye movements are counted for reading the selection and the total is divided by the number of lines to obtain the number of fixation pauses per line. Both Tinker (267) and Robinson and Murphy (222) have demonstrated that in direct observation many of the small movements are missed even by well-practiced observers.

Research workers soon turned to other methods of recording eye movements. After noting the displacement of the cornea during reading, Schackwitz (231) devised a pneumatic arrangement for recording eye movements. A tiny rubber capsule was mounted on a spectacle frame so that the capsule rested on the slightly drooping eyelid at the edge of the cornea. The eye movements were recorded on smoked paper by changes in the air pressure through a tube connecting the capsule with a tambour. Others have employed modifications of the Schackwitz apparatus.

A first attempt to record eye movements by a device attached directly to the eye was made by Ahrens (2). Following this suggestion, Delabarre (61) made further improvements on the Ahrens method and finally the additional modifications made by Huey (130) led to successful recording of eye movements during reading. An aluminum marker was activated by a tiny lever attached to a cup on the eye. This marker was suspended over a smoked drum so that all horizontal eye movements were recorded. To record time, the marker was in circuit with an electric current which was interrupted regularly by a tuning fork so that a spark, jumping from the end of the marker to the metal drum, punctured the paper and displaced a spot of soot.

Researchers next turned to photographic methods of recording. A motion picture technique for studying eye movements was used by Judd, McAllister, and Steele (139). A small flake of Chinese white attached to the cornea was employed as a point of reference in recording the eye movements. Successive photographs were taken of the portion of the face about the eyes. The path of the eye movements was plotted by outlining on the reading copy the successive positions of the spots of Chinese white as recorded on the film.

All these methods of observing and recording eye movements have undesirable features. Afterimage reports are highly subjective. In direct observation, accurate counting and recording depend upon the memory span of the experimenter and his ability to detect minute moves of the reader's eyes. But they are useful for noting the nature of eye movements in reading and hence are of value as instructional devices. Since they are not accurate, however, they are not suitable for research use. All those methods which involve mechanical attachments to the eyes require a very careful and delicate technique to prevent harm to the eyes and to ensure satisfactory records. They are limited in their use, therefore, to a very small number of subjects. Also, they involve an unaccustomed load for the eye muscles in addition to other highly artificial conditions.

According to Dodge and Cline (67), any satisfactory method of recording eye movements must fulfill the following conditions: the eyes must be able to operate under normal conditions of binocular vision; the apparatus must be capable of registering the movements of both eyes simultaneously; the unit of measurement must be one ms. (millisecond) or less*; the registering medium may have neither momentum nor inertia, while the eye must perform no extra work during registration and be subjected to no unusual conditions; and the apparatus should be such as can be used to record the eye movements of a large number of subjects, without serious inconvenience to them either during or after the experiments.

The method developed by Dodge (67) seems to fulfill these requirements. A beam of light is directed into the reader's eye. On striking the eye the light is reflected from the surface of the cornea into a camera where a falling photographic plate records

---

* Although the results of Dodge and Cline are given in ms., their photographic records were in hundredths of a second, i.e., the hundredths were converted to ms.

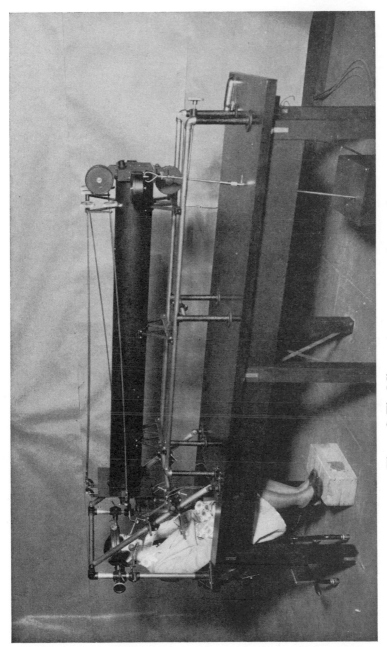

Figure 2. The Minnesota eye movement apparatus.

changes in the direction of the beam of light which occur with each movement of the reader's eye. Timing data are obtained by interrupting the beam of light at regular intervals, e.g., every fiftieth or hundredth of a second.

The Dodge technique was modified by others from time to time to make it more adaptable to reading research: see Tinker (280). Film was substituted for the photographic plate and devices were attached to the apparatus for photographing the movement of both eyes simultaneously, for photographing horizontal and vertical movements at the same time, and for photographing head movements along with eye movements.

One of these modern cameras incorporating the improvements mentioned just above was built under the direction of Tinker (275) at the University of Minnesota. It is illustrated in Figure 2. This camera is essentially a research device. The apparatus is flexible in that it may be used for studies of visual fixation and speed of eye movements in addition to investigations of reading.

The eye movements of a good and a poor reader are shown in Figure 3. Record 1 illustrates the progress of a good reader who made 5 fixation pauses per line of print with no regressions. Record 2 is that of a poor reader who made 10 fixations per line with two regressions. (B indicates the beginning of a line, E the end, and R represents regressions.) Each dot marks 1/50 second.

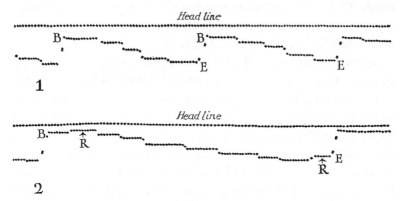

Figure 3. Eye movements of a good and poor reader.

The time per fixation may be obtained by counting the dots in each row between the breaks which show where the saccadic moves are made from one fixation to the next. The head line (reflection of light from a metal bead attached to a spectacle frame worn by the reader) makes it possible to differentiate between head movements and eye movements. Actually, a head line is seldom needed, for it is easy to note a head movement in the eye-movement record. The head moves relatively slowly and produces a curve in the eye-movement record which is different from the sharp break due to a saccadic move.

A relatively simple eye-movement camera that is portable has been devised and is described by E. A. Taylor (257). And an effective modification, the Reading Eye, is described by S. E. Taylor (259). The more elaborate apparatus has been employed mainly for research. But the Reading Eye may be used either for research or for clinical work. The corneal reflection techniques as described above have proved to be very useful and have been widely employed during the past 50 years to study eye movements in reading.

Various modifications of the corneal reflection method have been devised for recording eye movements in special situations such as simultaneous recording of eye movements and voice response in oral reading, the study of eye movements in viewing advertisements, and recording eye movements while reading music. Others are still more specialized, such as those for studying various aspects of visual fixation and speed of eye movements. See Tinker (280, 293, 312).

More recently several electrical apparatuses for recording eye movements have been constructed. Changes in the corneo-retinal potentials are closely proportional to the sine of the angle of rotation of the eye. With proper placement of electrodes and with an amplifying system, the eye movements may be recorded mechanically or photographically. According to the check made by Hoffman, Wellman, and Carmichael (122), the electrical records are about like those made by photographing the corneal reflection and therefore can be employed in reading studies. A detailed description and evaluation of electrical techniques are given by Carmichael and Dearborn (45).

An electrical recording has distinct advantages in some experimental situations. This is particularly true when continuous records must be taken for long reading periods. In such situations, the less restraint placed on the reader the better. In contrast to the electrical methods, the corneal reflection technique imposes rather severe restrictions upon the reader by head clamps and the necessity of elaborate apparatus in close contact with the subject. In general, recent trends have been to employ an electrical rather than a corneal reflection method, especially for research. But corneal devices such as the Reading Eye continue to be widely used. They are much less complicated than any electrical apparatus and relatively inexpensive in comparison. Furthermore, corneal reflection yields the more precise record of visual fixation and coordination of the eyes in reading.

Evaluation

Reliability. The reliability or consistency of eye-movement records has been considered by several workers. Imus, Rothney, and Bear (133), using 50-word samples of text, found that the measures had low reliability: $r = .59$ to .72. In another report, the same investigators (134) re-emphasized the unreliability of eye-movement records. Employing the same material, i.e., 50-word text, Anderson (6) and Broom (31) noted similar trends of low reliability. In a more extensive study, Tinker (282) found that reliability of eye-movement measures was low *only* when short samples of text (5 to 10 lines) were employed. When 20 to 40 lines were read the reliabilities were about .80. Thus eye-movement records will have adequate reliability only when a satisfactorily long sample of reading is used. When only group comparisons are involved, relatively short samples are adequate but, in the clinic where individual diagnosis is to be made, it is important to have records from the reading of at least 20 lines of text, and an even larger sample is desirable.

Validity. If eye-movement measures are to have meaning for validity evaluation, there must be adequate comprehension of the material read. Users of the ophthalm-o-graph for photographing eye movements have commonly employed short samples of text with questions on comprehension furnished with the apparatus. Imus, Rothney, and Bear (134) have found this check on comprehension to be useless. Authors such as Broom (31), Anderson (5, 6), and Imus, Rothney, and Bear (133, 134) have reported very low validity coefficients for eye-movement measures of reading when correlating these measures with scores on standardized reading tests as criteria. Such a comparison constitutes an unsatisfactory check of validity since it is well known that reading scores derived from different reading situations are not related or yield only low correlations. Tinker (282) has shown that when the material read before the camera is strictly comparable to that in the performance test (such as a different form of the test), the validity of fixation frequency and perception time (fixation frequency times pause duration) was very high, r = .80 to .99. Pause duration and regression frequency by themselves were found not to be valid measures of reading performance.

Is a reader able to give a typical reading performance in the apparently artificial laboratory situation where the photographing of eye movements takes place? Tinker (282) has checked this and found that the performance was the same before the camera as when working at a table. This finding has been confirmed by Gilbert and Gilbert (91). It should be noted, however, that it is important to adapt a reader to the laboratory situation before photographing eye movements.

It has been common practice, especially in the earlier publications, to plot the location of fixation pauses made while reading a line of print. The film record is projected onto the reading copy and the fixation points marked. This is illustrated for a good and for a poor reader in Figure 4. The plotting has ordinarily been done for a single eye, under the assumption that the two eyes coordinate in fixating on the text. When Stromberg (254) plotted the fixations for both eyes he found what appeared to be startling discrepancies in binocular fixation. That is, the fixation of one eye frequently did not coincide with that

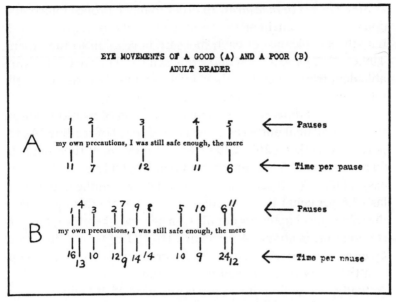

Figure 4. Location of fixation pauses. Location of the fixations is indicated by the vertical lines. Numbers at the top of these lines show the sequence of the fixations; those at the bottom show the time taken for each fixation in 50ths of a second.

of the other eye. Apparently there has been unwarranted optimism concerning the usefulness of plotted fixations to show exactly where the eyes paused during the reading. Since a reader fixates an area rather than a point, and because movement of the reflected beam of light does not correspond exactly to the visual angle of displacement, plotted fixations can only represent approximations to the correct place of fixation. One suspects that part of the binocular fixation discrepancy found by Stromberg was due to the reflected spot of light not being in corresponding locations on the two eyeballs, a condition which would prevent correspondence on the photographic record. Nevertheless, this study does raise an important question concerning interpretation of plotted fixations. Stromberg's findings, however, do not invalidate the usefulness of other aspects of eye-movement measures — fixation and regression frequency, pause duration, and perception time.

Significance of measures. In order to make proper interpretation of eye-movement measures in reading, it is necessary to evaluate the significance of each measure in relation to the others. Tinker (272) and Tinker and Frandsen (319) have made available data from several of their investigations in order to facilitate interpretation of the eye-movement measures.

Perception time, which is actually the sum of fixation pauses, is for all practical purposes a measure of speed of reading. As reported by Tinker (269, 279), the eye-movement time tends to fluctuate around 6 per cent in most reading. Only in reading very easy material (9.6 per cent) and in reading complicated formulas (2.8 per cent) is there much deviation from this figure (see the following chapter for details). In general, therefore, the perception time is about 94 per cent (16/17) of the reading time (pauses plus moves). Thus, in the practical situation, perception time may be employed as a criterion of speed of reading. Actually, perception time has a correlation of .90 with speed of reading (Tinker, 282).

The correlations of eye-movement measures with each other as given by Tinker (272) and Tinker and Frandsen (319) are summarized in Table 1. In interpreting the correlations in Table 1, one should keep in mind that the eye movements were photographed while subjects read a wide variety of material such as easy narrative, scientific prose, and objective examination questions. Fixation frequency quite consistently correlated highly with perception time irrespective of how specialized the reading situation was. Although there is a wide range in the correlations

Table 1. Interrelations of Eye-Movement Measures

Measures Correlated	Correlation Coefficients *	Median
Fixation frequency vs. perception time	.73 to .92	.85
Regression frequency vs. perception time	.47 to .88	.62
Pause duration vs. perception time	.18 to .88	.62
Fixation frequency vs. regression frequency	.67 to .91	.79
Fixation frequency vs. pause duration	−.31 to .71	.14
Regression frequency vs. pause duration	−.29 to .86	.02

* Data in each line are based on 16 correlations derived from 7 studies.

between both regression frequency and pause duration and perception time, the median coefficients are not high — only .62. The correlations between fixation frequency and regression frequency fluctuate considerably and the median is fairly high. The larger of these coefficients were for reading objective questions where the range was .79 to .91. The correlation of pause duration with fixation frequency and with regression frequency tended to be insignificant.

What may one conclude about these relationships? Both perception time and fixation frequency are satisfactory measures of reading ability when this is defined as speed of reading. In general, pause duration and regression frequency are not particularly good measures of speed of reading.

Many misinterpretations and unconvincing conclusions may be avoided by a more careful consideration of what each photographic measure of reading signifies. Writers should not infer that pause duration and regression frequency measure the same reading function as perception time, or pause duration the same as fixation frequency. But both pause duration and regressions play an important role in analysis of oculomotor patterns which are characteristic of particular reading situations. For details see later chapters.

The data presented in this chapter indicate that measurement of eye movements in reading can be done effectively. The obtained records are reliable and also valid. Perception time and fixation frequency are good measures of speed of reading. All the measures, as will be explained later, may be employed to good advantage in analysis of oculomotor patterns.

6 Time Relations for Eye-Movement Measures in Reading

Eye movements in reading involve rather complex motor adjustments. In the relatively brief discussions in most textbooks, the tendency is merely to indicate that a certain number of saccadic movements and fixation pauses occur. There is much more to the oculomotor behavior in reading. To describe more completely these motor adjustments of the eyes, one should take into account the nature of the saccadic moves between fixations, the convergence and divergence movements involved, movements within the fixation pauses, the accuracy and duration of the fixation pauses, and the relations among eye-movement duration, pause duration, and reading time.

Saccadic Eye Movements

The very rapid sweeping movements of the eyes from one fixation pause to another in reading are called saccadic because of their nature, i.e., jerky moves. This kind of movement is employed, not only in reading, but also in shifting the line of regard from one object to another in the field of view as when examining a picture or a landscape, or when inspecting factory products. As pointed out by Dodge (64), saccadic movements are fundamentally reactions to eccentric stimulation. There is a strong tendency to move the eyes so that the image of the new point of interest will fall upon the fovea, the area at the back of the retina where clearest vision occurs. In shifting the eye from one fixation to another, the initiation of the movement is a voluntary affair. But after the decision to shift is made, the speed of the movement that occurs apparently is not under voluntary control. Dodge's analysis of horizontal saccadic movements revealed three distinct phases: first there is a positive acceleration to the maximum velocity; this maximum velocity is maintained for considerable angle of movement and constitutes the second phase; this second phase gives way to the third phase, a negative acceleration as the eye slows down and comes to rest. For relatively short excursions of the eye, the second phase, the period of maximum velocity, is very short. But in the relatively long excursions, the second phase is conspicuous. Evidence presented by Dodge and Cline (67), and by Miles (182) shows that abductive (toward temple) saccadic movements are faster than adductive (toward nose) movements. For any individual eye, and for movement in the same direction (abductive or adductive) through a given angle, the duration of successive movements remains remarkably constant.

As stated in the previous chapter, saccadic eye movements are so fast that no clear vision is possible during the movement. Clear vision is possible only during a fixation pause when the eye is motionless. This is easily demonstrated. Look at the image of your right eye in a mirror. Now look over to your left eye and then back to the right. Try to detect movement of the eyes in the mirror image as the eyes shift from one fixation to the other. The eyes will appear motionless.

Holt (125), finding no perception during saccadic movements, concluded that this was due to central visual anaesthesia during the eye movements. Dodge (63), however, denied that this is necessarily true. And Woodworth (354) showed that an object which moves with the eye, at the eye's rate, is seen clearly during the movement. Thus the eye can be stimulated during saccadic moves. In a later report, Dodge (65) stated that we habitually ignore such stimulation in the ordinary life situation such as reading, probably because of attentional factors. If we did not ignore it, clear vision in reading would be disturbed. As noted by Huey (131), we habitually ignore stimulations and sensations which have no meaning for us. Any gray-blur sensation produced during interfixation movements in reading is

65

faint, of transient existence, and remains beneath the threshold of clear consciousness. Whatever the cause, there is no doubt that we are not conscious of the fusion of such sensations. We systematically ignore stimuli which would disturb our clear vision if given attention.

Accurate measurement of the speed of saccadic eye movements became possible with the development of the technique for photographing eye movements. Data derived from a few measurements on 3 subjects are reported by Dodge and Cline (67). In a later experiment, Tinker (287) reported a more comprehensive study on 14 subjects, 7 men and 7 women. Data from the two investigations are given in Table 2 for comparison. The

Table 2. Mean Eye-Movement Speeds in Milliseconds for
Various Angles Found in Two Studies

Visual Angles in Degrees	Tinker Study	Dodge and Cline Study
5°	26.4	28.8
10°	37.2	38.8
15°	47.7	48.2
20°	58.4	54.8
25°	66.3	*
30°	76.2	80.4
35°	87.3	*
40°	*	99.9

* Angles not used.

two sets of determinations agree quite well with each other. Note that an excursion twice the distance of another does not take two times as long. For example, 26.4 ms. (milliseconds) is the time for 5 degrees and 37.2 ms. for 10 degrees. The explanation is that the maximum velocity of the second phase endures for a different length of time as the angle of movement changes. As mentioned above, the period of maximum velocity is very short during relatively short excursions of the eye. Using the Dodge and Cline data, Shen (237) computed the estimated velocities for smaller angles: 9.9 ms. for 1 degree; 17.3 for 2 degrees; 22.2 ms. for 3 degrees; and 26.0 ms. for 4 degrees. Actual measurements correspond closely to these estimates. On the average, movements in reading range from about 1 to 4 degrees for moves to the right and about 14 to 16 degrees for moves to the left (back sweep). Tinker's measurements (269) for duration of reading movements were 10 ms. for 1°4′; 17 ms. for 2°3′; and 48 ms. for 14 to 16 degrees (back sweep). There were other relevant findings in Tinker's experiment. (287) There are no significant sex differences in speed of saccadic eye movements, although individual differences are significant. But for any single person, percentage variation (mean deviation / movement time) in speed of the saccadic eye movements through a given visual angle is small, viz. about 2.6 for 10 degree moves, 8.5 for 25 degrees.

As noted by Tinker (280), several investigators report minute movements of the eyes during fixation of a point. Apparently these moves are reflex in nature. Subjectively the point remains fixated. Photographic records reveal at times eye movements during a fixation pause in reading. Dearborn's (58) records show an unsteadiness or shifting of various amounts within a pause. And Miles and Shen (184) found that the eyes during certain pauses showed a tendency to glide in continuous curves. These movements within a fixation pause are readily distinguished from short saccadic moves. They appear on the photographic record as continuous curves while a saccadic move produces a sharp break in the record. If a fixation pause shows a continuous curve, this may be due to head movement which tends to be relatively slow, or to a "drifting" or shifting of the eyes during perception at that pause. These shifting moves are much slower than saccadic moves, slow enough for perception to occur during the shifting.

In reading, the eyes make convergence movements during interfixation shifts and divergence movements as the eyes adjust to the new fixation pause. Schmidt (232) and Clark (48) have reported these movements. And Stromberg (253) has made an analytic study of them in the reading performance of 71 good and 71 poor readers. There were no significant differences between groups in the average extent of the convergence and divergence movements, either in the interfixation shifts or in the back sweeps to the beginning of new lines. An empirical check of individual cases indicated that the pooling of the individual mean scores did not obscure any consistent differences that might have been present in the individual data. In a later investigation, Stromberg (252) showed that the amount of convergence and divergence movement of the eyes has no significant relationship to degree of lateral muscle balance of the eyes. Although no satisfactory basis for the convergence and divergence movements of the eyes during reading has been educed, it is possible that the different velocity for abductive and adductive moves (see above) are involved.

The Fixation Pause

Two aspects of oculomotor behavior in reading that have received considerable attention are duration and frequency of fixation pauses. As already noted, the fixation pauses are the periods of clear vision and hence of perception in reading.

What is the minimum pause duration used for seeing during binocular vision? Arnold and Tinker (9) determined the briefest possible pauses made in successively fixating dots and in successively fixating and identifying single letters. On the average, it took 172 ms. to fixate the dots and 157 ms. to fixate and identify the letters. These pauses are longer in duration than the exposure necessary for a well-cleared-up perception which, according to the results of Dodge (66), who employed a short exposure technique, is 100 ms. In the clearing-up process the effects of past stimulation fade out and the new sensory impression reaches its full maturity so that clear perception is possible. But when a succession of fixations is involved, as in Arnold and Tinker's experiment, the minimum pause duration is greater than 100 ms. When a readjusted fixation is needed, the initial part of the fixation pause takes about 70 ms. and the final part about 100 ms., or a total time of about 170 ms. Apparently perception begins in the initial part and is completed in the final phase of a readjusted fixation. These two parts of such a fixation may be considered to be phases of a unitary whole. In reading, as shown below, pause duration is considerably greater than that which is required for successively fixating dots or identifying letters.

The proportion of reading time taken by pause duration is relatively great in comparison with eye-movement time. Erdmann and Dodge's results as corrected by Tinker (269) show that 6.4 per cent of reading time was taken by the eye movements and 93.6 by pauses. In a later study, Tinker (279) examined the changes in eye-movement time produced by variation in reading material. The data are summarized in Table 3.

Table 3. Percentage of Movement Time and of Pause Time in Reading

Kind of Material Read in Various Line Widths	Percentage of Reading Time	
	Movements	Pauses
Very easy prose		
Silent reading (25 pica line).................	9.6	90.4
Oral reading (25 pica line)..................	6.2	93.8
Easy narrative prose		
9 pica line	6.4	93.6
19 pica line	8.1	91.9
40 pica line	8.5	91.5
Hard scientific prose (25 pica line)..............	7.3	92.7
Algebra problems with formulas (20 pica line)....	5.3	94.7
Easy speed of reading test (19 pica line)	7.9	92.1
Multiple-choice examination questions (25 pica line)	6.2	93.8
Over-all mean	7.3	92.7

The greatest proportionate time taken by eye movements, 9.6 per cent, was for reading silently very easy prose — fourth-grade difficulty read by college students. This is comparable to the 10 per cent obtained by Walker (341). The least time taken, 5.3 per cent, was for reading an algebra problem including formulas. As noted in Chapter 5, only 2.8 per cent of reading time was taken for formulas alone (269). The over-all average was 7.3 per cent for moves and 92.7 per cent for pauses. In general, the more careful and analytical the reading, the smaller the relative time taken by the moves. Apparently in the more complex kinds of reading in which the mental processes of apprehension and assimilation become involved, less proportionate time is devoted to movements and more to pauses, which are the periods of perception (and comprehension). In oral reading and in reading text in very short lines (9 picas) of narrative, there was also a tendency to devote relatively more time to pauses. These results suggest that no single figure can be given for the amount of reading time taken by moves or by pauses in reading. In most reading, however, movement time centers around 6 per cent and pause time, 94 per cent.

The degree to which pause duration is affected by the content of the material read and reading requirements is considerable. Basic data, cited by Tinker (299), are given in Table 4. Mean

Table 4. Pause Duration in Reading

Material Read	Number of Readers	Mean in Milliseconds	Percentage of Variability
Tinker experiment			
Easy prose	77	217.0	12.9
Easy reading test	57	217.8	12.6
Scientific prose	77	230.8	12.2
Sisson experiment			
Easy narrative	60	226.6	12.2
Scientific prose	60	236.4	12.8
Frandsen experiment			
Scientific prose	66	243.4	10.4
True-false test items	66	270.6	17.4
Completion test items	66	323.6	25.8
Multiple-choice test items . .	66	281.2	14.9
Analogies test items	66	296.6	13.3
Wrong-word test items	66	298.6	12.7

Sources: Tinker (282), Sisson (239), Frandsen (80).

pause duration for reading easy prose ranges from about 217 to 227 ms.; for scientific prose, 231 to 243 ms.; and for objective examination questions, 271 to 324 ms. These are average values. Examination of the original data reveals occasional pauses with durations as great as 500 to 600 ms.

Why are fixational pauses in reading of much greater duration than the time required for cleared-up vision? Oculomotor adjustment of the eyes gives rise to one set of factors. The mean reaction time of the eye to eccentric stimulation, according to Hackman (110), is about 173 ms. Furthermore, the eyes converge during saccadic interfixation movements and diverge at the beginning of the fixation which follows the movement. The overlapping of processes in a series of fixations, as for identifying letters or in reading, would tend to shorten reaction time in comparison with a single reaction to an eccentric stimulus. Thus the 157 ms. for fixating and identifying successive letters. Reading, however, consists of more than perceiving clearly the printed symbols. The reader must comprehend the ideas and relationships involved in the text. The more complex and difficult these are, the longer the pause duration to permit adequate comprehension before moving on to new material. This is well illustrated by the fact that so-called "reading" without attention to meaning (merely identifying successive words) is done with fixations of brief and constant duration, while reading to comprehend algebraic problems produces fixation pauses of long and varying durations.

It is frequently stated that pause duration is relatively constant. Evidence on this point is given in terms of percentage of variability in the last column of Table 4. For straightforward reading of easy and scientific prose, the percentage of variability or relative variability ranges from 10.4 to 12.9. Only in certain special reading situations, such as those involving objective test items, does the percentage variability fluctuate considerably, the largest percentage being 25.8. As properly pointed out by Huey (131), however, average pause durations are misleading. Examination of individual records reveals that pause duration varies greatly.

Various investigators have devoted attention to the location of fixation points along a line of print. The first and last fixations in a line are usually indented from the ends of the line (see Figure 4 in Chapter 5). And the easier or more familiar a text, the greater the indentations. Huey (130) reported that 78 to 82 per cent of the printed line was covered by the fixations. The findings of Dearborn (58) were similar. And Walker (342) reported percentages of 74.5 to 81.2 for his good readers. Tinker (271) found a variation in pattern with the requirements of the reading situation: 84 per cent of the line was covered by fixations in reading scientific prose; 89 per cent in algebra problems, and 99

71

per cent in lines of formulas. As reading and study become more analytical, therefore, more of a line is included within the fixation pauses. Contrary to earlier surmises, extensive analysis revealed that the correlation between extent of eye movements and duration of the succeeding pauses was negligible on the average. This is confirmed by Walker (342).

As soon as accurate recording of eye movements and fixations was possible, it was found that the exact point that is fixated may be in any part of a word or in the space between words. Actually, the eyes do not fixate a point in reading, but an area. The plotted points of fixation, frequently found in the literature, can only represent the approximate center of an area of fairly clear vision in and surrounding the fovea which extends over about 7 to 10 letter spaces. There is less distinct vision to the right and left of the fixated area. The mature reader has learned to devote more attention to material in peripheral vision to the right of the fixated area. Dodge (66) emphasized the very important role played by peripheral vision in reading. Extra-foveal vision, especially to the right of the fixation, yields premonitions of coming words and phrases as well as stimulates meaning premonitions. That is, word forms indistinctly seen in peripheral vision begin the perceptual process much in advance of direct vision. Good peripheral vision that is utilized tends to decrease the number and duration of fixation pauses and thus increase the speed of reading. Vernon (338) cites a case of disturbed vision in which the individual was quite unable to read when deprived of peripheral vision to the right of the fixation. There is need of training for the correct use of these marginal impressions in reading. In an unpublished study by Tinker, it was found that a moderate amount of training to increase useful peripheral vision to the right of the fixation produced an increase of about 40 per cent in speed of reading with no loss in comprehension.

The pattern of pause durations within a line is related to the above. Dearborn (58), in discussing rhythmic reading, states that there is a particular pattern of pause durations characterized by a relatively long initial pause followed by several pauses of decreasing duration and terminated by a somewhat longer end pause. The assumption is that during the initial pause the reader, by means of peripheral vision, perceives indistinctly the shapes of several succeeding words. This leads to several shorter pauses during which perception of these succeeding words is completed. Sisson (240) found little evidence for such a pattern in either short or long lines of print. Apparently Dearborn's statement needs to be modified. Examination of a large number of individual records from several investigations including Dearborn's fails to confirm the presence of such a specific pattern of pauses. The longest pause may occur anywhere in a line of print. But another pattern is present. Irrespective of where it occurs, a relatively long pause is usually followed by one or two shorter pauses. This frequently occurs more than once in a single line.

Also frequently quoted (uncritically) is Dearborn's concept of short-lived motor habits which he states are evidenced by a rhythmical series of the same number of pauses per line in two or more successive lines. This rhythmical reading is supposed to be facilitated by short lines of print and to be connected with good reading ability. In other words, the fast reader is said to be fast because he is able to establish readily rhythmical eye-movement habits. Unfortunately, the concept of eye-movement habit and rhythmical reading has become almost sacred in the reading literature. Most unwise are the endeavors to improve reading skills by training eye movements to establish regularity of fixations in successive lines of print.

Although a few writers have questioned Dearborn's concept of rhythmical reading, no experimental check was made until 30 years later when Sisson (240) reported a quantitative analysis of motor habits of the eyes in reading as related to length of the printed line, kind of material read, and level of reading ability. The tendency toward rhythmical motor habits was evaluated by means of a habit index, i.e., the percentage of successive lines having the same, or nearly the same, number of fixations. The habit index was higher for reading the shorter lines of print and slightly higher for the more efficient readers. However, this apparent relation may be accounted for in terms of probability rather than motor habit, for the fewer the fixations, the better the chance of two adjacent lines having the same number of fixations. The habit index favored neither easy narrative nor scientific prose in reading. In view of his results, Sisson concludes that the concept of short-lived motor habits is useless. The writer would add that this notion of rhythmic reading is not only a useless concept but a harmful one. From the publication in 1906 of Dearborn's report to the present, the view that rhythmical eye-movement behavior is characteristic of effective reading and is highly desirable has directed attention toward patterns of eye movements as causal factors in reading performance. This has led to an undue emphasis upon peripheral oculomotor mechanics and sacrifice of adequate attention to the more important central factors of comprehension and assimilation. The findings of Walker (342) are in line with these conclusions. He found "no evidence of a habit of moving the eyes any fixed distance or in any rhythm" in his analysis of eye movements of good readers. If rhythm is absent in the eye movements of highly skilled readers, as indicated in these studies, the view that rhythmical eye-movement patterns are desirable for effective reading becomes meaningless and should be abandoned.

Regressive Fixation Pauses

The role of regressions or regressive fixation pauses deserves special attention in any discussion of eye movements. After the first fixation near the beginning of a line of print following the back sweep, any fixations following backward movements (toward the left) are termed regressive pauses. Practically all reports of eye-movement studies list the frequency of these regressive pauses. Many writers offer an interpretation of their function.

Regressive pauses occur in the reading of all kinds of material irrespective of whether readers possess good or poor reading ability. In reading relatively easy narrative, printed in optimal typography (see the next section on legibility), good readers make few regressions while poor readers make many. For instance, in his study Walker (342) found that even good readers averaged .70 regressions per line. When material includes difficult and complex ideas for any reader, the number of regressions increases. Walker's results lead to the conclusion that comprehension is a very significant determiner of eye-movement patterns. And Judd and Buswell (140) note that complexity of eye movements, indicated by regressions, appears to be directly correlated with mental processes. As the processes of comprehension and assimilation become more difficult, regressions increase in number and complexity of arrangement along the line of print. In other words, when a reader meets a difficult concept, an unfamiliar word, or an elaborate formula, the customary eye-movement habits which operate in reading familiar prose are abandoned. Fixations are spaced close to one another and ordinarily many regressive pauses occur.

Tinker (271) classified regressive fixations into two general categories. Type I are those which occur at the beginning of a line and serve to rectify inaccuracies of judgment or motor coordination in the back sweep from the end of one line to the beginning of the next. Regressive pauses of Type II occur within a line and help to correct inadequate perception which often happens with too long an eye movement within the line. This kind of regression also happens when a difficult word, phrase, formula, or concept is encountered, interfering with comprehension. When this type of regressive pause occurs, the pause duration frequently becomes much longer. The two types of regressions are illustrated in Figure 5. Note that the first and last lines are read smoothly with uninterrupted sequences of pauses. In lines 2, 3, and 4, regressions of Type I appear. Also in these three lines, regressive pauses of Type II show up, particularly on formulas and the word "hydroxyl."

An excellent analysis of regressive pauses in the reading of ninth- and tenth-grade pupils is given by Bayle (14). She found that regressive pauses tend to fall into five patterns: adjustment after the first fixation in a line, readjustment within a line when the span of vision has been overreached in a too long forward move, regressive pauses for verification, regressive pauses for phrase analysis, and regressions with pauses to re-examine a whole line. It became apparent that regressive pauses were

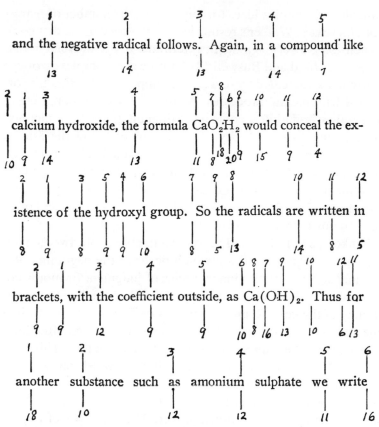

Figure 5. Location of pauses in reading chemistry by an adult subject. Vertical lines show the location of pauses. The numerals at the top of the vertical lines show the sequence of pauses; those at the bottom indicate duration of the pauses in 50ths of a second. Adapted from Tinker (271).

caused by a need to complete perception and by difficulties of interpretation due to a failure to recognize the meaning of a word or to connect the meaning of a word with the context. Bayle correctly points out that regressive pauses are necessary aspects of the reading process in analytical reading. Buswell (42) gives a cautious approval of this view but many writers ignore it. Too frequently writers hold that all regressive pauses are symptoms of inefficient reading and should be eliminated. Recognition of the fact that regressive pauses are legitimate and even essential in certain kinds of reading would avoid some of the misconceptions involved in training eye movements (see Chapter 9).

Oculomotor Efficiency in Reading

The role of oculomotor behavior in reading has received considerable emphasis ever since the pioneer observations of eye movements were made nearly a century ago. Soon after 1900, writers in the field began to stress the need for so-called efficient eye-movement coordination as essential in good reading performance. This has led to two fundamental assumptions: that oculomotor control is an important factor in reading; and that possession of "proper" patterns of saccadic or reading movements will automatically result in improved reading skills. Apparently, oculomotor control is considered to be an important determinant of reading proficiency. Certain writers have attempted to give experimental support to these assumptions.

Vernon (340), employing 9 readers, made an extensive examination of individual eye-movement records. She states that "those whose ocular-motor ability, as constituted by steadiness of voluntary fixation and accuracy of voluntary movement in reading was great, made a small and regular number of fixation pauses of long, irregular duration, while those whose ocular-motor ability was relatively small made a large number of fixation pauses of short and regular duration." In a later discussion of the same topic, Vernon (338) states: "But whatever the origin, it seems clear that the use of frequent short pauses, or less frequent long pauses, and the tendency to overrun the word and then regress to it, are permanent ocular-motor habits, unconnected with perception and assimilation of the reading content."

Gilbert (94) photographed the eye movements of pupils in grades 1 through 9. Subjects in each grade group read series of digits and two easy prose selections. Eye movements in digit reading were classified as simple motor activity of the eyes. The number of fixations and regressions and pause duration in reading digits were correlated with like measures in reading easy prose. The correlations ranged from .31 to .71, with an average of .55. It is claimed that simple motor activity (reading digits) is substantially related to oculomotor performance in reading connected (easy prose) material. A further analysis is warranted. The pupils were shown how to read the digits before photographing their eye movements. Obviously, digits are symbols for words. Except for the space required for printing, *9* is the same as *nine*. The series of digits were read, not just fixated. The prose samples must have been extremely easy reading for all except the first- and perhaps the second-grade pupils. The following is a sample (p. 167): "Early in the spring a mother hen came to live in the schoolroom. The boys built her a house. The girls brought her corn and water." Eye movements in reading such material should be little influenced by comprehension factors. So it is not surprising that oculomotor patterns (fixation and regression frequency, pause duration) for reading the digit series and the easy prose turned out to be somewhat similar. Undoubtedly they are to some degree similar reading situations. Gilbert's conclusion that oculomotor ability is substantially related to eye-movement performance in reading connected material cannot be accepted as valid, for oculomotor patterns in reading digit series is not a measure of motor coordination. All that Gilbert has shown is that fixation and regression frequency and pause duration in reading digit series are correlated about .55 on the average with fixation and regression frequency and pause duration in reading very easy prose. The literature concerned with eye movements in reading indicates that this is to be expected.

Other conclusions based upon the correlations cited above are also invalid: Eye movement patterns do not reflect efficiency of central processes of comprehension. There is plenty of evidence to the contrary in the literature. If the author had presented both easy and difficult materials to his readers, he would have obtained evidence that variations in difficulty of comprehension are reflected in eye movements. Another conclusion of Gilbert is that eye-movement records do not predict reading test performance. They would, if taken while reading the same or very similar test material (Tinker, 293). Gilbert also states that poor oculomotor coordination is a handicap in learning to read well. Since no satisfactory measure of this coordination was used, this conclusion does not follow.

Tinker (281), using 64 adult subjects, studied the relation of oculomotor coordination to reading efficiency. First, he obtained speed of reading scores on a standardized test and the eye-movement records for the reading of a prose selection. He also recorded the number and amount of ocular adjustments during shifts in fixation. Finally he obtained speed of convergence-divergence movements. The scores for ocular coordination were correlated with speed of reading and with fixation and regression frequence, pause duration, and perception time in reading the prose. There was the expected small correlation (.27 to .53) between the eye-movement scores in reading prose and speed of reading. And the correlations between the number of readjustments and the amount of readjustment were substantial, .58 to .74. That is, individuals who are most frequently inaccurate in their fixations in numbers and dots are also inaccurate by a greater amount.

When accuracy of fixation (motor coordination) was correlated with eye-movement measures in reading prose, the coefficients ranged from —.19 to +.35 with an average of +.09. A similar trend was found for the relation of motor coordination and speed of reading. And the correlations between speed of convergence-divergence and both speed of reading and eye movements in reading prose were insignificantly small. The correlations given above indicate clearly that there is no significant relation between oculomotor coordination and proficiency in reading.

When only the extremes of Tinker's group (15 with best and 15 with poorest motor coordination) are considered, there appears to be a slight advantage in speed of reading for those with markedly greater motor coordination. This applies to a few extreme cases, not to readers in general.

The data by Tinker presented above seem to refute the claims of Vernon (338, 340), and Gilbert (94) that variation in motor control of the eyes in terms of steadiness of fixation or accuracy of movement to a new fixation is significantly related to reading ability. Stromberg (253) agrees with Tinker that there is no difference between fast and slow readers in speed of convergence-divergence movements during reading.

7 Variation of Eye Movements in Reading

The materials reviewed in the two preceding chapters indicate that eye-movement records can be employed to good advantage in studying reading performance. Such a utilization of eye-movement measures permits a kind of analysis which is not possible by use of other techniques. And, as noted earlier, perception time is virtually a speed of reading measure. Furthermore, an analysis of the oculomotor patterns as revealed by variation in pause duration and frequency and distribution of fixations and regressions furnishes a wealth of information not obtainable by other means. Although the study of eye movements provides a unique type of information about reading, it should be used to supplement rather than to replace other methods of investigation. For instance, standardized and other performance tests may yield reliable and valid measures of comprehension and speed of reading.

Eye-movement patterns indicate and reflect the nature of the central processes of perception and assimilation during the reading. That is, they provide information as to why the reading is slow or fast and give clues as to which parts of the reading material (a word, phrase, concept) are easy or difficult to comprehend. The following sections of this chapter will indicate the value of eye-movement records in reading investigations.

Variations Due to Age and Maturity of Reader

The most cited study of changes in eye-movement behavior with age is that of Buswell (39). He investigated stages of growth in eye movements of 186 readers represented all grades from the first to the college level. All read the same text except the first-graders who needed easier material. The line width of all materials was 21 picas (3.5 inches).

In the silent reading, fixation frequency decreased rapidly during the first four school years; it remained about constant from the fifth grade through the freshman year of high school; it then again decreased through the middle high school years only.

The number of regressions dropped off rapidly during the first four grades; no material change occurred through grades 5, 6, and 7; but there was another reduction during the early high school years.

Pause duration also showed a rapid decrease up to the end of the fourth grade, followed by a slower drop off to the end of the sixth. Thereafter there was no decrease except for high school juniors. The results suggest that a pause duration of about 240 to 250 ms. (milliseconds) satisfies the perceptual demands for reading easy material by mature readers and that this level may be reached by the end of the fourth grade. Considering the trends for fixations, regressions, and pause duration, it would appear from Buswell's results that eye-movement habits in silent reading have become fairly stable by the end of the fourth grade. A more accurate statement of trends, however, must take into consideration the results of two more recent investigations.

Ballantine (13) photographed eye movements for readers in grades 2, 4, 6, 8, 10, and 12 to obtain growth curves for the various eye-movement measures. All material was printed in a 25 pica line width. That for grade 2A was in 14 point type; that for 2B and for all other levels was 11 point. Ballantine used the em as his unit of linear measurement. The em is defined as the width of the capital M of the size of type used. It is difficult to see any advantage in employing the em rather than the full line, for the former is a constant small fraction of the line when the size of type remains the same and the lines are all the same width, 25 picas in this study. Furthermore, the data for grades 2A and 2B, printed in 14 and 11 point type respectively, were combined.

Only if one were computing the number of words read per fixation would the em become useful. This was not done by this author. In any case, most readers of material in the eye-movement field are familiar with fixations per line, and not with the em.

All subjects, 20 in each grade, read an easy selection of second-grade difficulty, and another selection appropriate to their own grade in difficulty. The experiment was carefully controlled in all respects. Fixation and regression frequency improved (i.e., decreased) rapidly from grade 2 to 4, less rapidly from 4 to 8, and only slightly or not at all from 8 to 12. Refixations at the beginning of lines decreased steadily from grade 2 to 8 but not in the higher grades. There were no important differences between the easy selection and the at-grade selections in oculomotor performance as to either rate or pattern of growth. Pause duration was not measured in this study.

Gilbert (94) photographed the eye movements of pupils in grades 1 to 9. The same relatively easy material was read by all subjects. The average number of fixations decreased rapidly to the fifth grade and quite slowly from the fifth to the ninth grade. Regression frequency decreased rapidly from the first to the fourth grade and then more slowly to the eighth grade. The drop in size of pause duration was rapid up to the fourth grade with little change thereafter except for a decrease from the eighth to ninth grade.

What may one conclude from the results of these three studies? All the investigations reveal that the greatest amount and the most rapid rate of improvement in oculomotor behavior in reading occur during the first four grades. Buswell found no important changes in eye-movement patterns from the end of grade 4 to the high school level where some further improvement occurred. Although Ballantine obtained continuing improvement from grade 4 to 8, it was at a slower rate than in the lower grades. And the changes from grade 8 to 12 were small and of little significance. Gilbert's results are similar to those of Ballantine. Possibly the differences between these studies are due in part to sampling errors which are more likely to occur with small groups. None of the three studies was longitudinal, i.e., the same pupils were not measured in successive years. Therefore, the results do not reveal the amount of growth in eye-movement patterns for the same pupils as they progress from grade to grade. Probably Ballantine's data come closest to what might happen in a longitudinal study. In any case, it seems safe to conclude that the mechanical aspects of oculomotor behavior in reading become fairly stable by the end of the fourth grade and become fully stabilized somewhere between the fourth and eighth grades. Any apparent improvement at the high school level or in college could be due to selective factors, for many students drop out of school or do not go to college. An example may be noted in the data from the Educational Developmental Laboratories, cited on page 112 by Spache (248). Eye-movement records were obtained from 12,143 subjects, first grade to college. Fixation and regression frequency improved at a rapid rate in grades 1 to 6 and 1 to 4 respectively; pause duration decreased mostly from grade 1 to 4. There was, however, gradual improvement in all measures up to the college level. This gradual improvement in the higher grades and college is best explained in terms of improved reading ability of the more able pupils who remain in school rather than to further stabilization of the mechanics of eye movements.

Oral and Silent Reading

Oral and silent reading are related. Most of the techniques and skills employed in proficient silent reading are also used in oral reading. Buswell (39) found that the trends in eye movement in oral reading were similar to those in silent reading but on a less efficient level. From the second grade to the college level, average fixation frequency was always at a more efficient level for silent than for oral reading; the levels for regressions fluctuated from first to sixth grade but, from grade 7 to college, silent reading was at a higher level of efficiency; pause duration was more efficient at all levels, grade 1 to college. These differences between oral and silent reading in eye-movement measures are to be expected from the nature of the two processes.

The eye-voice span in oral reading is related to eye movements. Ordinarily the eyes travel along ahead of the voice when reading aloud. The number of words by which the eyes are ahead of the voice at any moment is called the eye-voice span. With mature readers the eyes tend to lead the voice by a relatively wide span. At times this may be as much as seven or eight words. The immature reader, especially the one who has not learned to phrase in his reading, has a very narrow span. Such a reader does not move his eyes from a word until he has spoken it, i.e., he is a word-by-word reader. His eye-voice span is reduced to a minimum. As pointed out by Buswell (38), the eye-voice span is of real significance in the reading process. A span of considerable width is necessary for proper interpretation of a passage. A very narrow span prevents use of contextual clues to meaning and pronunciation. And adequate attention to punctuation is also prevented.

A rough measure of the eye-voice span may be obtained by suddenly covering a page from which a student is reading aloud. The number of words he is able to read after the page is covered indicates his eye-voice span. An average of several trials should be taken. More exact methods of measuring the eye-voice span are now available. Gray (101) devised a technique by which the eye movements were photographed simultaneously with the recording of the voice on a dictaphone. The two records were synchronized so that the eye-voice span could be readily determined. An additional improvement in method was made by Tiffin (264). He installed a sound wave recorder in an eye-movement camera so that it was possible to record the eye movements and the sound waves from the voice simultaneously on the same film while reading aloud. The spoken words were recorded on a phonograph record. These words were matched with the photographic records so that the eye-voice span was readily obtained.

Quantz (214) found, for a mature reader, an average eye-voice span of 7.4 words at the beginning of a line, 5.1 words in the middle, and 3.8 near the end. The most extensive investigation of the eye-voice span has been reported by Buswell (38). His subjects ranged from grade 2 to the college level. All reading material was printed in a 27 pica line (4½ inches). Elementary school pupils read easy prose; the high school and college students, more difficult prose. There were 4 to 6 subjects at each grade level. For the elementary school pupils, the eye-voice span increased from the second to the fifth grade and the span for good readers was 58 per cent wider than that of the poor readers on the average. Marked individual differences were present. In high school there was no improvement in eye-voice span from year to year. But on the average, the span for the good readers was 36 per cent better than that for the poor readers. The trend was similar for college students.

Although Buswell did not find, like Quantz, variation of the eye-voice span within lines of print, he did discover that the span was longest at the beginning and shortest at the end of sentences. The average spans for his group of 54 readers were 15.9, 13.4, and 10.9 letter spaces for the beginning, middle, and end of sentences. According to Buswell, the eye-voice span is shortest near the end of sentences because this indicates the end of a thought unit. The good oral reader hesitates at the end of a sentence so that his voice may express one thought clearly before he starts the next sentence with a new thought. This hesitation results in a narrowing of the span near the end of sentences. Poor oral readers, who tend to neglect proper phrasing and consequently pay less attention to meanings and punctuation, reveal less variation in span from the beginning to the end of sentences. Their eye-voice span tends to be short and of relatively constant width throughout a sentence and from sentence to sentence.

To a large degree, variation in the eye-voice span is due to changes in the difficulty of the material read, especially for the good readers. Smooth and rapid comprehension produces the widest span. But when the reader meets a difficult word or concept, the span becomes narrower. There is hesitation while the reader cogitates, trying to clarify the meaning. Regressions may occur at such a place. This brief period of hesitation allows the voice to catch up with the eyes. The resulting variation in width of span characterizes the skillful oral reader.

A relatively large eye-voice span is a valuable asset whether reading aloud to give others pleasure or information, reading a notice at a club meeting, or reading in school. When reading to a group one should look up at his audience occasionally to keep in rapport with the listeners. The good oral reader with his wide eye-voice span is able to do this without interrupting the continuity and smoothness of his delivery. Such a reader is able to continue talking because his eyes are several words ahead of his voice. As noted by Anderson and Dearborn (8), some oral readers employ their eye-voice span so effectively that it is often hard to determine, unless the textual material is in sight, whether they are reading or just talking.

A wide eye-voice span is needed for effective comprehension by the reader. Interpretation of a passage is difficult or almost impossible for the word-by-word reader. Buswell (38) emphasizes the need of a wide eye-voice span for proper interpretation of passages and for reading aloud with good expression. For instance, a wide span permits the correct phrasing necessary for satisfactory comprehension. Also it makes it possible to look ahead, note a question mark, and use the appropriate rising inflection of the voice which signifies a question. A further advantage of a wide span is that the advance of the eyes beyond the voice permits use of context to achieve the right pronunciation and meaning of words that are spelled alike but have different meanings. For example, note the following: "A little boy came running out of the woods. He had tears in his coat and tears in his eyes."

Proficiency in oral and silent reading is related. From the above it is clear that a good quality of oral reading and a wide eye-voice span go together. Buswell (38) points out that both are due to a general attention span wide enough to hold a large number of words or reading elements in the mind at one time. For the poor reader, the attention span, just as the eye-voice span, may be confined to the word or even part of a word on which the eyes are fixated. More proficient readers have both wider eye-voice spans and larger attention spans. Since in silent reading there is little or no attention devoted to verbalization (there may be some inner speech) consciousness can be focused upon the eye and the meaning. In silent reading, however, the size of the attention span is not limited to a part or the whole of eye-voice span. For efficient reading the attention span must be great enough to cover the reading material by complete thought units. It now becomes obvious that phrasing or reading by thought units is just as important in silent as in oral reading. Furthermore, in silent reading, the whole sentence as a thought unit must be kept in mind at times for most efficient grasping of the meanings involved. When a difficult word, frequently the label of an unfamiliar concept, is encountered in silent reading, the attention is narrowed so that the attention span is cut down to the word on which the eyes are fixated just as it would be in oral reading. It appears that a wide eye-voice span is intimately related to a wide attention span and that the latter is necessary for good silent reading. It is important, therefore, that a wide eye-voice span be developed so that an appropriate attention span is made available for effective silent reading. According to Buswell (38) this should be done during the first four grades, the period during which oral reading predominates.

Reading Ability and Individual Differences

Before 1917, research workers in the field of eye movements were interested primarily in an analysis of the reading process. Little attention was devoted to individual differences. Nevertheless, examination of their data reveals marked individual differences in fixation frequency. In fact, it has been shown again and again that there are marked individual differences in all eye-movement measures in reading. The better readers tend to make fewer fixations and regressions per line and to have shorter pause durations. However, pause duration tends to be less variable than the other measures. In silent reading, Gray (101) noted two types of rapid readers: those who reduced the number of pauses to a minimum; and those who employed relatively short pause durations. But in general the rapid readers made shorter as well as fewer fixation pauses. An excess of regressions was a feature of slow as well as immature readers (lower grades). In comparing the oculomotor patterns of 50 good and

50 poor readers, Anderson (4) found that all eye-movement measures distinguished good from poor readers.

A few citations will emphasize the role of individual differences in eye movements. Morse (188), studying seventh-grade pupils, found a range of 8 to 28 fixations per line, and of .026 to 8.01 regressions per line. Mature readers also show marked individual differences. For example, the results of Dixon (62) for college of education professors reveal a range of 5.4 to 14.3 fixations per line, and zero to 3.3 regressions per line. In a group of university students, Tinker (271) found a range of 5.8 to 10.3 for fixations per line, of 0.2 to 1.8 for regressions per line, and 210 to 276 ms. for average pause duration. All these values are for reading material well within the comprehension of the subjects.

Nature of Reading Material

Ordinarily, a reader encountering a change in difficulty of reading material modifies his eye-movement patterns. Thus eye movements reflect the difficulties of the reader when he comes upon a word that is hard to recognize or understand, or a concept that is difficult to comprehend. Apparently good readers are more versatile in adapting eye movements to changes in difficulty than poor readers. After noting that comprehension is a very significant determiner of eye movements, Walker (342) states that the eye movements of good readers are symptoms of the ease or difficulty in the ability of the reader to comprehend the material. And Anderson (4) found that the eye movements of poor readers do not adapt to changing conditions such as variation in difficulty as well as those of good readers.

Employing fifth- and seventh-grade pupils, Morse (188) failed to find significant differences in eye movements while material differing in difficulty by two grades was being read. The most satisfactory interpretation (not given by Morse) is that this lack of flexibility in adjusting to changes in difficulty was due to lack of maturity in reading skills and to the tendency of such pupils to read all material with the same mental set. That is, to some degree his results may well have been strongly influenced by the careful control of the reader's attitude through directions on how to read. Furthermore, the differences in difficulty of the texts were not marked. In studies where the change is such that it produces more severe difficulty in word perception or concept understanding or comprehension, eye movements are affected. Apparently Morse's subjects had not been taught successfully to vary their pace to fit the difficulty of the material.

A large number of other investigations have been concerned with the effect of changes in readability or difficulty on eye movements. The trends of research on this point may be stated without citing the specific studies. As the difficulty of the material increases, the number of fixations and regressions increases and pause duration becomes greater. Analysis of the results indicates that eye-movement patterns reflect the efficiency of the central processes of perception and comprehension of the proficient reader. Lack of flexibility in adapting eye movements to the difficulty of the reading material indicates that the readers have not yet acquired the versatility which is the hallmark of maturity in reading. The importance of flexibility in oculomotor adjustment at the college level has been demonstrated in a convincing manner by Laycock (146a). The flexible, in contrast to the inflexible, group of subjects were able to adjust rate and eye movements to fit the reading task.

For some time it has been recognized that variations in subject matter and purpose produce changes in eye movements. In an early study, Judd and Buswell (140), using four high school students, found striking variation in fixation and regression frequency, pause duration, and perception time in reading seven kinds of material. Seibert (236) made an analytical study of eye movements of eighth-grade pupils while they read mathematics, biography, adventure, physical science, history, and geography. Although not statistically significant in most instances, differences in all eye-movement measures occurred in going from one subject matter to another. But some children manifested inflexible reading habits since they maintained a definite pattern of eye movements throughout all materials. A similar investigation was completed by Stone (251) with college freshmen as subjects. They read arithmetic, biology, English, educational psychology, physical science, and social science. As with the preceding study, differences were obtained for eye-movement measures in going from one kind of material to another. Some were significant. In Ledbetter's investigation (147), eye movements were photographed while eleventh-grade pupils read selections in English, mathematics, natural science, and social science. Significant differences in oculomotor patterns were found for reading in the various subject-matter fields. The eye movements for reading a poem and mathematics were considerably more complex than in the other areas. Examination of all the literature available suggests that variation in eye movements occurring with variation in subject matter is due largely to differences in difficulty of the material or to changes in the purpose for which the reading is done, rather than to differences in subject matter as such. For instance, in Dixon's study (62), the more efficient reading (fewer fixations and regressions) of materials that were familiar to the reader may only mean that the familiar material was easier even though equated to the other subject-matter materials for difficulty by a formula.

Eye Movements and Fatigue

Eye movements in reading, along with other measures, have been employed in the search for an adequate measure of visual fatigue. Dearborn (59) presents some tentative data which suggest that eye movements may reveal visual fatigue. After a long day of visual work consisting of proofreading and study, speed of reading was reduced and saccadic movements through relatively long angles were retarded. Since only two readers served as subjects, these trends need checking. According to Clark and Warren (49), during a 65-hour vigil there was no consistent trend in variation of fixations, regressions, or pause duration for eye movements in reading. Although sporadic and temporary changes in binocular behavior occurred for certain individuals, there was no uniform tendency as the period of wakefulness increased. The most thorough examination of eye movements in reading as measures of visual fatigue has been made by McFar-

91

land, Holway, and Hurvich (177). Thirty minutes of either a rapid saccadic exercise or rapid convergence-divergence movements failed to produce any significant changes in eye movements while reading following the exercises. However, the authors consider that a more sensitive recorder which would yield a more precise measure of fixation and of binocular coordination might have given positive results. But fixation and regression frequency and pause duration, the oculomotor measures of reading performance, would have remained the same.

In general, these investigations suggest that eye movements in reading are insensitive indicators of visual fatigue. Only when the visual task is extremely severe and extended is there a hint that eye movements are modified. Two factors apparently prevent visual fatigue from affecting eye movements in reading. All the investigators cited above used only 10 to 12 lines of text to be read before the camera. It is well established that the visual mechanism can compensate enough to give normal performance for the short periods of time required to read such materials. Furthermore, there is no satisfactory way to evaluate precisely the degree of comprehension in the short paragraphs of text ordinarily used. The reader, since there is a tendency to maintain one's oculomotor pattern, may read two paragraphs with similar eye movements but with different degrees of comprehension. In fact, a good reader can maintain his normal oculomotor behavior with little or no comprehension of what is read. An adequate check of eye movements as a measure of visual fatigue can be obtained only with long samples of reading material and with an experimental design so arranged that comprehension is maintained constant or is satisfactorily measured. To meet these requirements, two experiments which involved long periods of reading were undertaken.

Hoffman (121) had 30 college students read a light historical prose selection continuously for 4 hours. Eye movements were recorded electrically for 5 minutes at the beginning and during the last 5 minutes of each 30 minutes of reading during the 4 hours. There were no interruptions for comprehension checks during the reading period. After the first half hour there was a decrease in the number of lines read per 5 minutes. However, length of reading period had relatively little influence on number of fixations per line, i.e., there was no significant increase until the very end of the 4 hours when there was an average increase of 0.430 of a fixation in comparison with the first 5 minutes of reading. Similarly, there was no important change in regression frequency until at the end of 4 hours when there was an average increase of 0.175 per line. As the author recognizes, the decrement in the number of lines read on successive measurements may only mean a lessening of motivation on the part of the readers. However, the increase in fixations and regressions discovered at the final measurement suggests that fatigue was beginning to operate by the end of 4 hours of reading; experimental confirmation is needed.

In a comprehensive investigation, Carmichael and Dearborn (45) set themselves the task of determining how long a normal human subject can continue to read before there are significant changes in his reading behavior. Twenty subjects read an interesting historical novel for 6 hours continuously and for another 6 hours read an economic treatise. Another 20 subjects read the same materials reproduced on microfilm (and projected) for similar periods. Short comprehension tests were interspersed during the reading to maintain motivation and a long test was given at the end of the 6 hours. Eye movements were recorded electrically at the beginning and during the last 5 minutes of each half hour. Oculomotor measures considered were fixations per 5 minute period, and regressions per line. The results, considering all oculomotor measures, indicated that the subjects read as well at the end of the 6 hours as at the beginning, i.e., the eye-movement patterns did not change significantly. This was true both for reading the books in regular print and for reading them in microfilm reproduction. Except for a few reports of mild discomfort, it was not found that reading for the 6 hours was done at any "cost" to the organism. The practical educational inference that seems justified is that there is no basis for the belief that requiring high school and college students to read for long periods may be injurious to their visual mechanisms, if their eyes are in fair condition to start with.

The reading in Carmichael and Dearborn's experiment was done under optimal or near optimal conditions of print and lighting. And motivation was maintained throughout the six hours of reading. The trend of evidence in this and all other well-designed experiments is that eye movements in reading do not reveal visual fatigue from long periods of uninterrupted reading or by use of a reading test following stress-producing exercises or loss of sleep. Under such conditions, no significant alteration in oculomotor patterns occurred. It is worthwhile to note that severe stress on the visual mechanism can cause deterioration in fixation time, velocity of movement, and accuracy of fixation when a subject makes continuous saccadic movements (not in reading) as fast as possible for 4 minutes through an arc of about 14 degrees (33, 34).

When conditions for reading are not optimal or near optimal, eye movements in reading are altered significantly. Print of poor legibility or inadequate illumination does modify oculomotor behavior. Although such changes are not signs of visual fatigue, it seems probable that long periods of reading under such adverse conditions might result in visual fatigue. Details on legibility of print and illumination for reading are given in later sections.

8 Eye Movements in Special Reading Situations

A number of investigations have dealt with oculomotor behavior while reading such materials as foreign languages, formulas, and numerals. Since eye-movement patterns in reading such materials deviate considerably from those in ordinary reading, they are here considered separately.

Foreign Languages

Before 1900, Landolt (145) and Erdmann and Dodge (70) had noted that a foreign language, in comparison with one's own language, was read with an appreciably greater number of fixation pauses and sometimes with a greater pause duration also. Judd and Buswell (140) compared eye movements in reading French and Latin with each other and each in turn with those in reading English which was the native language. The high school readers were good third-year language students. The eye movements indicated a labored type of reading in the French. The records tended to resemble those made in reading rather incomprehensible English prose. The average fixation frequency per line for 9 subjects ranged from 9.6 to 14.4, and pause duration from 240 to 272 ms. (milliseconds). Regressions were rather numerous. The records for Latin indicate that no pupil exhibited even a labored type of reading. There was an aimless looking at the Latin words with numerous irregular eye movements which indicated an unsuccessful attempt at analysis. In fact, these eye movements took on the character of mere helpless wandering. No attempt was made to correlate complexity of oculomotor behavior with amount of meaning present in reading either the French or Latin.

A comprehensive investigation of eye movements in reading English (vernacular), French, German, Spanish, and Latin has been made by Buswell (41). The eye-movement records showed that, at the end of two years' training, elementary school pupils had not reached the maturity in reading a foreign language attained by high school and college students after a like period of study. The so-called direct method of teaching produced desirable reading habits but the translation methods did not. At the end of two years, high school and college students exhibited similar and fairly efficient oculomotor habits in reading French, Spanish, and German but less efficient eye movements in Latin. It was quite evident that the average student, either in high school or college, does not achieve a level of final maturity (as gauged by the reading of experts, adults skilled in the use of the language) in reading performance by two years' study of a foreign language. But certain individuals in the groups studied did reach this degree of maturity at the end of two years and, in a very few cases, at the end of one year. It is estimated that the oculomotor performance of the groups as a whole fell below that of the expert readers by an amount represented by a year of additional study. These experts were able to read relatively rapidly and comprehend well. The findings of Futch (83) are somewhat similar in his comparison of eye movements in the reading of English and Latin. Both beginners and advanced Latin college students revealed less oculomotor efficiency in reading Latin than English but the difference was greater for beginners. Although there was an improvement in reading Latin, the advanced students were still on a word-by-word recognition level. Comparison of teaching methods revealed that emphasis on grammar and translation without abundant reading of easy material hindered the development of efficient eye-movement patterns.

These investigations of reading foreign languages provide an indictment of the indirect or translation method of teaching foreign languages. Buswell (41) suggests that, with a more careful selection of students and perhaps a further revision of teaching methods, presumably toward more emphasis on direct methods, students of a foreign language might achieve mature reading performance in the advanced classes. (More recent eye-movement studies are not available. Use of language laboratories, which is now fairly common, may produce more efficient eye movements.)

Reading Numerals and Formulas

At an early date, attention was directed to eye movements in reading numerals. Landolt (145) noted that in reading series of numbers, the eye movements were so short and followed one another so rapidly he could not count them. There seemed to be one move for almost every digit. And in Dearborn's study (58), photographic records showed that in reading numerals the attention is concerned with much smaller printed units than in reading words. When the digits were in small groups of two to four items, the fixation frequency was relatively less than when a continuous series of numbers was read. For instance, there were as many as 30 fixations in reading a group of 24 digits.

In an extensive investigation, Terry (263) analyzed the eye movements made in reading numerals in arithmetical problems and numbers arranged in lines. He found that the numerals in problems made greater demands on the attention of the reader than the accompanying words, in use of more fixations and regressions as well as in longer pause durations. Marked individual variation in all of these measures occurred. Because Terry's subjects read arithmetical problems and isolated numerals with more complex oculomotor patterns and consequently more slowly than ordinary prose, he concluded that they are more difficult types of reading than the prose. The application of this conclusion to the reading of numerals per se may not be valid since the digits in such numerals are symbols and involve a larger amount of abbreviation than words. Numbers are a compact way of printing. Their very compactness probably requires more fixations per unit printing space than words do. For instance, compare thirty-seven with 37, or nine hundred twenty-eight with 928.

Tinker (267) obtained consistent results demonstrating that the compactness of printing achieved by employing numerals rather than words produces faster reading of simple arithmetical problems when other conditions remain constant. The materials with numerals were read with fewer fixations, the same number of regressions, slightly longer pause duration (by 20 to 72 ms.), and shorter perception time (by 760 to 1160 ms.). In Terry's study, the greater complexity of the eye-movement patterns in reading the problems must have been due to solving the problems rather than to reading the numerals per se. In a photographic study of reading familiar numerals, Rebert (215), found that, in general, such numerals tended to be read in the same manner as words of the context although in several cases detailed readings involving two or more fixations on the numerals occurred, especially with 3.1416. Pauses on numerals were longer than on words of the context.

Eye movements of adults during the addition of digits in columns of varying length and difficulty were found by Buswell (40) to be characterized by regular progress of fixations either up or down the column, relatively short and uniform pause duration, about one fixation per digit although at times two digits were read with one fixation, and fairly uniform progress of fixations along the column of numbers. With younger children, however, the eye movements involved regressions at the beginning and within the column, marked variation in pause duration, a tendency toward mature oculomotor patterns (like adults) by good adders but irregular and often random eye movements along the column by children with poor arithmetical skills, and longer pause duration than in ordinary reading. Buswell concluded that the eye movements are adapted to mental processes and that the complex oculomotor patterns and very long pauses denote confused central processes of apprehension and assimilation.

As with numerals, eye movements in reading formulas are influenced by the task or purpose for which the reading is done. Tinker (271) found that algebraic formulas in the context of a problem produced a greater fixation and regression frequency than the reading of scientific prose. The mature students read chemical formulas about like the algebraic ones. But the eye movements of high school students in elementary courses showed that these pupils read some formulas and omitted others. The eye movements in reading isolated formulas (no problem context) were essentially the same for readers with various amounts of training in mathematics. This reading was mainly analytical in nature and was characterized by a high fixation and regression frequency, long pause duration, and concentration of fixations about fractions and compound exponents. In a later investigation, Rebert (216) found that formulas in context were read like words with unitary fixations only when the formulas were quite familiar, very simple, and merely contributed to an understanding of the text. In general, formulas tended to be read by both experienced and naive subjects in an analytical manner and in detail, especially when the context directed attention to relationships between characters in the formulas. Rebert's conclusion that "familiar chemical formulas tend to be read as units in the same manner as words are read, although analytical readings occur" may be somewhat misleading since only the more simple of such formulas, as HCl, were read with single fixations.

The eye movements in reading both numerals and formulas show what may be inferred logically. Familiar numerals and formulas in context, such as 1776 and HCl, are usually read like words with a single fixation. But when in isolation (no context) the situation is quite different. Here each digit in a numeral and each character in a formula is a condensed symbol representing a unit word (HCl is hydrochloric acid and 1776 is one thousand seven hundred seventy-six) and tends to be read as such with an appropriate number of fixations. Just as with words, two or three items occasionally may be read with one fixation by the more mature reader.

Learning to Spell

Eye movements in studying spelling are analogous to those in other kinds of reading according to Abernethy (1). The more

99

mature spellers have a broader recognition span (i.e., fewer fixations), briefer pauses, and fewer regressions. The eye movements of good spellers tend to be systematic. Although adults (presumably good spellers) tend to survey words as wholes, children exhibit random eye movements to a considerable degree in studying spelling. In a more comprehensive study, Gilbert (92) compared the oculomotor and perceptual habits of good and poor spellers from grade 3 through senior high school. At every grade level, the good spellers employed fewer fixations and regressions, a shorter study time, briefer and less variable pauses, and a broader study unit than the poor spellers. The study of spelling seems to be characterized largely by forward progression of fixations across a word with interruptions at times by regressions, then another cross-passage of the fixations, etc., until the word is learned. The oculomotor behavior indicated that younger learners tended to explore each word minutely, while the more mature students apprehended parts of a word in larger units and were inclined to concentrate on hard sections. The eye-movement patterns of the poor spellers were in marked contrast to those of efficient spellers. Gilbert failed to emphasize the fact that efficient or inefficient oculomotor performance in learning to spell is merely symptomatic of efficient or inefficient central processes of perception and apprehension. However, data he derived from an analysis of individual records of study procedure furnished important suggestions for teaching and remedial work. In a follow-up study of spelling, Gilbert (93) obtained records for six children over a three-year period. Although there was little change in pause duration with age, fixation and regression frequency decreased and there was evidence of a more effective method of attack in studying the words. Gilbert and Gilbert (95) recorded eye movements of fourth-, fifth-, and sixth-grade pupils before and after training them for speed and accuracy of perception in learning to spell. At each grade level, the training resulted in fewer fixations and regressions per word but no change in pause duration. In a later study, these authors (96) by analysis of eye-movement records of college students found that spelling is learned more effectively when words are studied in isolation than when encountered as critical words in reading.

Consideration of all investigations indicates that eye movements in the study of spelling adapt to more efficient patterns with increased age and experience and with training for speed and accuracy.

Other Situations

Among the numerous eye-movement studies reported in the literature (280, 293, 312), many are of minor import to most reading situations. Only a few of the more important of these will be considered here.

According to Butsch (44), oculomotor behavior during typing from copy revealed a greater fixation frequency and pause duration than in ordinary reading. The eye-hand span was found to vary directly with the speed of typing, ranging from zero to 13 letter spaces. Most of the typists tended to keep the eyes about 1 to 1½ words ahead of the hand so that there was about one second between seeing a letter and typing it. There was little evidence, even for expert typists, that typing is frequently done by phrases. The records indicated that during typing the eyes do not read at all at their maximum rate, which is determined by the requirements of comprehension, but instead read only fast enough to supply copy to the hands as needed.

A quantitative and qualitative analysis of eye movements in reading prose and objective examination questions differing in type and by measured amounts of difficulty has been made by Frandsen (80). The rank of increasing perception time was as follows: true-false, completion, multiple-choice, and wrong word. For frequency of fixations and regressions, the ranks were approximately the same as for perception time. Average pause duration, however, varied little from one type to another. Although there was a fair relationship between the eye-movement measures for the various types of questions, the correlations between prose and the questions were all low. And little relationship was discovered between eye-movement measures for the five levels of difficulty. However, increase in difficulty increased fixation and regression frequency and perception time. Characteristic differences in oculomotor patterns occurred with the various types of questions. In contrast to the reading of prose, the objective questions produced an analytical sequence of movements and a striking variety of procedures. In each instance, the mode of proceeding adopted for a particular kind of question appeared adequate.

Lofquist (149) studied the eye-movement patterns in reading clerical test items (pairs of names and pairs of numerals) as compared with eye movements in reading prose. Response to the test required detection of likeness or difference of the two parts of an item. Reading the test items required a more analytical procedure than in reading prose, i.e., more fixations and more regressions. The numeral items were read with more fixations and regressions and longer perception time than the name items. A similar trend was found for long (more complex and difficult) versus short items. The results in this and the above investigation by Frandsen provide additional evidence that oculomotor behavior in reading is subordinated and flexible in its responses to the central processes of apprehension and assimilation. Versatility in adjusting reading habits, including eye movements, to variation in purposes and materials is one hallmark of maturity in reading.

Proofreading is a highly specialized reading task. Ordinarily, the mature reader in general reading makes maximum use of word forms so that he tends to read familiar words as single units. In contrast with this, the trained proofreader needs to perceive every letter of every word with enough clearness to discriminate deviations (poor spacing, irregular alignment, etc.) and typographical errors such as misprints and omissions. At an early date, Erdmann and Dodge (70) noted that proofreading required many more fixations and a longer reading time than for reading either familiar or unfamiliar material. In a comprehensive investigation, Vernon (337) through analysis of photographic records pointed out the chief characteristic of oculomotor behavior by comparing nonprofessional (controls) versus professional proofreaders in a normal situation and in proofreading materials with misprints. During normal reading, the records showed that the average reading time per line and the number and duration of pauses of the professional proofreaders were much the same as those of the other subjects. However, the number of regressions of the former were considerably fewer than those of the controls, and also the variability of reading time and fixation frequency was much less for the proofreaders.

In reading material containing typographical errors (proof-reading), the reading time per line and the frequency of regressions increased considerably less and then remained more constant for the proofreaders than for the controls. And this advantage was maintained by the proofreaders but not by the other subjects during the subsequent reading of material containing no misprints. Vernon concluded that the professional proofreaders were able to adopt and maintain a mental set toward reading material containing misprints so that the recognition of small details of the structure of letters and words occupied the center of consciousness, while meanings of the context were relegated to the background. But the non-proofreaders were unable to adopt this attitude with the same degree of efficiency and permanency.

At this place, brief mention may be made of eye-movement studies concerned with the unit of perception in reading. Analysis of their records led Munoz, Odoriz, and Tavazza (189) to conclude that the natural form of reading is not by spelling or syllabification but by grasping word wholes, i.e., word forms or configurations constituting the units of perception in reading. Gray (105) also arrived at a similar conclusion based upon analysis of eye-movement records of mature readers in 14 different languages. The data indicated that the general nature of the reading act is essentially the same among all mature readers. As such a reader seeks the meaning of a passage, he follows along the lines with an alternation of short eye movements and pauses. At each fixation pause he recognizes words as wholes, usually two or three at a time, and by means of their configuration and striking characteristics. A study of eye movements by Waterman (343) is in agreement with Gray. In addition, Waterman noted that there is no apparent change in eye-movement habits when a native speaker of one language learns to read well in another language. Apparently, although there will be some variation due to form and structure of a language, the teaching of the basic skills in all languages can be similar to some degree.

Two investigations of similarities between twins in eye-movement patterns in the reading of prose have been reported. Morgan (187), comparing eye-movement measures for members of pairs in a well-controlled experiment, found very low correlations (.04 to .24) between artificial pairs, higher (.24 to .53) for fraternal twins, and still higher (.61 to .72) for identical twins. These coefficients indicate more fundamental bases for individual differences in eye movements in reading than is furnished by a "habit" concept (see Chapter 6). The underlying processes of perception and assimilation provide a more logical explanation of the results. Apparently hereditary factors play a significant role as indicated by the correlations. It is noteworthy that pause duration, which is least susceptible to training, showed the highest correlations for the twins. Morgan correctly infers that, in treating cases of poor readers, consideration should be given to capabilities of the individual rather than exclusively to certain ideal motor sequences characteristic of oculomotor patterns of efficient readers. In the other study, Jones and Morgan (138) report additional evidence on twin similarities in eye-movement patterns. Median correlations for eye-movement measures in reading revealed a trend similar to that in the earlier study: artificial pairs, $r = .11$; fraternal twins, $r = .44$; and identical twins, $r = .53$. Three judges had considerable success in identifying on the basis of general appearance the eye-movement photographs of identical twin pairs when they were mixed with photographs from fraternal twins. Considering the many factors that may modify oculomotor patterns, it is significant that this identification was better than chance. These results, therefore, support the earlier conclusion that eye-movement patterns in reading are not determined wholly by training. Genetic factors appear to be involved to an appreciable degree.

9   Role of Eye Movements in Improving Reading

As studies of eye movements in reading accumulated in the early years of the present century, it became clear that many factors influenced the patterns of these movements. It was discovered early that proficient readers make relatively few fixation pauses and few regressions per line of print. This contrasted with inefficient readers who show a relatively high frequency of fixations and regressions. Researchers also found that young pupils tend to make a large number of fixations and regressions in reading. And as the pupils develop and become more mature readers, they make fewer and fewer fixations and regressions. Thus the patterns of eye movements provide clues to the level of one's reading proficiency. This relationship of oculomotor behavior to reading performance eventually led to photographing eye movements to aid diagnosis in reading clinics and in other reading improvement programs. The next step was to train eye movements by means of a variety of pacing techniques in an attempt to improve reading. To discuss and evaluate these programs properly requires careful analysis.

Eye Movements in the Reading Clinic

Views vary concerning the usefulness of eye-movement records in the reading clinic. Certain writers claim they are indispensable, others state that they serve as a valuable objective auxiliary to other techniques of diagnosis, and still others are convinced that such records lack both reliability and validity as a clinical tool. These viewpoints continue to the present. A critical look at the literature is needed.

As early as 1920, Freeman (82) found that eye movements of an alexia (severe reading disability) case were so irregular and uncoordinated that it was frequently impossible to tell which positions on the record corresponded to the beginnings or the ends of the lines of print. This indicated a lack of orderly progress of perception along the lines and sentences. After remedial training, the subject's eye movements revealed fairly well-organized patterns which were correlated with considerable progress in reading ability. At about the same time, rather extensive use of eye-movement records was made by Gray (103, 104) as an aid in completing the diagnosis of cases requiring remedial training in reading. The photographic records revealed an unusual number of fixations and regressions which indicated confusion in word recognition, lack of orderly perceptual progress along lines of print, and inaccuracy of the return sweep from the end of one line to the beginning of the next. The extra long pause durations denoted a slow rate of recognition. Oculomotor patterns became more orderly and efficient after remedial training. Similar findings are reported by Hincks (120). Several others have employed eye movements for diagnostic purposes, including Miles and Segal (183), Pressey (211), and Pollock and Pressey (208). Among those writers who have strongly emphasized the role of eye movements in diagnostic and remedial reading are Pressey (210), Sievers and Brown (238), Hamilton (113), and Broom, Duncan, Emig, and Stueber (32).

Having noted the apparent relation between disorganized eye movements and reading disability, several writers have concluded that such eye movements are important causal factors producing the deficiency, i.e., peripheral motor habits are determinants of central perceptual and assimilative processes. It is true that reading deficiency, immature reading habits, and improvement of reading efficiency are readily detected by photographing the reader's eye movements. And considerable use has been made of this technique in diagnosing reading disability and checking improvement. It is questionable, however, whether eye-movement records contribute materially in diagnosing reading disabilities in the clinical situation. We know from published research reports that the eye movements of the nonreader or the retarded reader are characterized by many fixations and regressions and by aimless wandering. And because eye-movement habits readily adapt themselves to changes in reading ability, we can predict that improvement in reading will be accompanied by more orderly oculomotor performance. The research evidence indicates that in practically all cases faulty eye movements are merely symptoms rather than causes of poor reading. It appears, therefore, that measurement of eye movements may be dispensed with in the reading clinic without any appreciable loss either in diagnosis or remedial instruction. Eye movement recording should be considered a research rather than a clinical procedure.

Training Eye Movements

The stress on training eye movements to improve reading became a correlate to the use of eye-movement records in diagnostic and remedial programs discussed above. Because good readers made few fixations and regressions per line of print, attempts were soon made to improve reading performance by training eye movements. The necessary assumption is that eye movements are important determinants of reading proficiency. For example, if the retarded reader is trained to use eye-movement patterns similar to those which characterize efficient reading, his reading proficiency would presumably improve. In practice, this emphasis upon the mechanics of eye movements has tended unfortunately to direct the attention of both teachers and students to peripheral factors as determinants of reading performance rather than to the more important central or underlying processes of perception, comprehension, and assimilation.

Techniques of training eye movements in reading vary. On the one hand are those, represented by Pressey (210) and Sievers and Brown (238), who try to train subjects to pace three fixations at three regular intervals along a line of print. It seems naive to assume that, if a line of print is separated into three

107

groups of words, paced eye movements will result in reading each group with one fixation. In fact, Dearborn and Anderson (60) have demonstrated that such an arrangement, even after practice, results in more than three fixations. Buswell (43) also noted that few subjects ever achieve as few as three fixations per line. At the other extreme are those who attempt to increase the fixation span by employing techniques which to some degree approximate the normal reading situation. Thus, Dearborn and Anderson (60) have devised a flexible film projection method (the Harvard Films) for teaching phrasing to increase the size of the fixation span. Approximately the same principle is involved in the still-film projection technique developed by Buswell (43) to increase the span of recognition or the fixation span. Successive phrases of text are exposed in proper sequence and spacing to lead the eyes along in normal perceptual sequences. Timing and nature of textual material are flexible in both techniques. Between these extremes, a variety of methods have been employed to train eye movements. A commonly used one is the Metron-o-scope (or modifications of it) designed to develop "controlled reading." It is described by Taylor (257). This is a mechanically operated machine for exposing each line of print in three successive sections. Taylor states that the fundamental idea of the Metron-o-scope is to develop the mechanical, i.e., eye-movement and interpretative processes simultaneously. As noted above, such techniques do not reduce fixations to three per line.

Numerous reports, cited by Tinker (280, 293, 312), consider experimental results or statements of the value of training eye movements. A survey of a few studies will suffice here. Published experimental results are rather uniform in showing considerable improvement in speed of reading following eye-movement training. Certain other investigators have attempted to evaluate the role of eye-movement training as such. Sisson (241), using matched groups of adult readers, found that reading with intent to improve produced significant changes in eye movements comparable to the changes from eye-moving pacing. Employing matched groups of school children, Cason (46) found no significant differences in improvement in reading for the students trained in phrase reading or in eye movements by means of the Metron-o-scope in comparison with those who did motivated library reading. That is, free library reading resulted in the same gains as programs stressing the oculomotor mechanics of reading. Glock (99) studied the effect upon eye movements of three methods of training: using the Harvard Films which expose phrases in succession and thus train eye movements, using a new film exposing three successive lines of print simultaneously, and using printed material with subjects motivated to read fast and to comprehend. Training for four weeks was given to six sections of college students. The students made similar significant improvement in eye movements (fixations, regressions, pause duration) under all three methods of training. The technique that paced eye movements was no more effective than the others in modifying eye movements or improving reading. Although all his college students made significant gains in speed and comprehension, Westover's group (351) with controlled eye-movement training did no better than those without it.

All well-designed experiments which have attempted to evaluate the role of training eye movements to improve reading have failed to find that such training is either necessary or desirable. Eye-movement training may be evaluated in the following manner:

Many so-called procedures for training eye movements or for controlled reading result in improved reading efficiency, either in speed or in both speed and comprehension. This improved reading status is reflected in modified oculomotor patterns. But the improvement obtained by eye-movement training, with or without elaborate apparatus, is no greater than that resulting from well-motivated reading alone. Furthermore, there is no adequate evidence that training eye movements as such improves reading. Examination of experiments concerned with pacing eye movements and controlled reading reveals that they usually involve other training techniques as well and are never divorced from increased motivation. Buswell (43) flatly states that "training eye movements does not increase reading ability."

Unfortunately, the training of eye movements too often becomes a ritual and tends toward an overemphasis upon oculomotor mechanics with sacrifice of adequate attention to the more important processes of perception, comprehension, and assimilation. This training may also result in a decrease in the flexibility and adaptability of reading habits which characterize good readers. According to Buswell (43), writing in 1939, "The exploiting of machines and gadgets (to control reading) by persons who do not understand the psychology of reading seems at present to be adding greatly to this mechanistic folly." And Traxler (335) has "difficulty in seeing any justification for purely mechanical attempts to train pupils in better eye movement habits." In examining the literature on mechanical methods of improving reading, Spache (247) in 1958 found little evidence to contradict earlier views of Tinker (293) and Traxler (335) that "so-called eye-movement training does not actually affect eye movements nor does such training apparently contribute to general improvement in the broad act of reading."

A number of writers, after admitting that similar gains in reading skill may be attained by other means, state that the use of mechanical apparatus and other pacing techniques is justified because they provide the incentive that generates strong motivation in the learner. And Traxler (335) suggests that controlled reading and pacing techniques "need not be used in a purely mechanical way but that they might well be used to supplement, in a way that would have strong motivating force," a program in which reading comprehension is emphasized. This is all very well if it could be done. If pacers and controlled readers were used properly, i.e., as one aspect of training without neglect of all or most of the other aspects of developmental and remedial reading, there would be no objection to their use. But the writer of this book firmly believes that as long as machines and gadgets are used by those with an inadequate understanding of the psychology of reading, we shall continue to have an undesirable emphasis upon oculomotor mechanics. Unfortunately, many teachers have not had the opportunity to gain a sound foundation in the psychology of reading. Furthermore, they are often exposed to convincing sales propaganda on the wonderful gains in reading achieved by use of some particular mechanical device.

The question of training eye movements is intimately related to the problem of whether eye movements are causes or symptoms of reading proficiency. Those who hold that eye movements are causes of reading proficiency soon progressed to the position where they claimed that the good reader is good because he uses few fixations per line of print and rarely makes a regression. This view gradually developed into a strong emphasis upon peripheral factors of oculomotor mechanics, especially among the large group of writers with insufficient knowledge of the reading process. Such views are unfortunate and unnecessary. As early as 1922, Judd and Buswell (140) stated that "Eye movements are but external manifestations of an inner condition which is set up in the central nervous system." A similar view has been emphasized by Tinker in many of his publications. Eye-movement patterns are very flexible and apparently adjust themselves readily to any changes in the perceptual and assimilative processes involved in reading. It appears that eye movements merely reflect, or are symptoms of, efficient or poor reading performance.

Actually, there is no evidence to support the view that eye movements determine reading proficiency. As shown above, results obtained from training eye movements do not support the view that peripheral factors are dominant in reading although such training is based upon the assumption that they are. On the other hand, there are numerous experimental reports which indicate that the central processes are the important determinants in reading performance. These are cited by Tinker (293). It is noteworthy that every writer who may be considered a leader or well versed in the reading field emphasizes central processes as dominant in reading. All experimental evidence derived from well-designed studies shows that oculomotor reactions are exceedingly flexible and quickly reflect any change in reading skill and any change in perception and comprehension.

Careful consideration of the field should indicate that there

111

need be no conflict in assigning proper roles to peripheral (mechanical) and central factors in reading. To read well, one must perceive words in proper sequence and in doing this the eye fixations progress along a line in an orderly manner. In other words, eye-movement sequences accompany the perceptual sequences necessary in effective reading. The particular eye-movement patterns employed are conditioned by the nature of the central processes. Clear perception and rapid assimilation of the textual material are reflected in relatively few fixations and regressions when no comprehension difficulties occur. But ineffective perception and confused comprehension, accompanied by difficulties in assimilation, characteristically produce many fixations and regressions. The latter, however, should not be confused with the oculomotor pattern occurring in highly analytical reading where it is necessary to re-examine the text to work out and clarify relationships. In such a case, the complex eye-movement pattern may indicate an effective procedure in reading, rather than inefficient reading due to mental confusion. Real progress in programs of teaching reading and remedial reading would be achieved if the term and concept of "rhythmical eye movements" were abandoned, if eye-movement photography were confined to the research laboratory, and if the use of gadgets and other techniques to train eye movements were discarded.

Part Three: Scientific Typography: Printing for Easy and Efficient Reading

10   *Nature of Legibility*

Although some attention has been given to legibility of print for more than a century, only a few studies based on scientific research had appeared by 1900. Before scientific research, printers and type designers were concerned mainly with the esthetic appearance of the printed page. This preoccupation with esthetics, together with considerations of economy and tradition, dominated all typography until about 1920. As a result of these obstructive emphases, a scientific typography has been slow in developing. Indeed, the printing industry continues to resist procedural changes suggested by experimental findings. Even though type designers, printers, and publishers have at times achieved fairly satisfactory legibility by their approach, application of the results of research would lead to marked improvement.

At first in discussions of factors influencing easy and efficient reading, the term "legibility" was used. Beginning about 1940, "readability" came to be regarded as a more descriptive and meaningful word than "legibility," and it was commonly adopted. However, with the advent of "readability formulas," devised to measure the difficulty of reading material, an entirely different meaning developed for "readability." To avoid confusion, it seems best to employ "legibility of print" to designate the effects of typographical factors on the ease and efficiency of perception in reading.

Author's note: Part Three is based partly upon *Legibility of Print* by M. A. Tinker (Ames, Iowa: Iowa State University Press, 1963). The reader will find there details which cannot be covered here. The Iowa State University Press has granted permission to quote and paraphrase materials from *Legibility of Print*.

In any comprehensive discussion of legibility of print, it is desirable to state just what is meant by the term. That is, a practical definition of legibility is needed. This must take into account the various experimental methods which have been employed in this field, ranging from studying the relative perceptibility of the letters in the alphabet to measuring speed of reading continuous meaningful text. Each of the several research techniques used has contributed something of value to the understanding of legibility, and examination of them will provide the basis for a specific definition of legibility.

Discussions of legibility necessarily rely on certain vocabulary terms which are specific to the field of typography or the process of printing with types. The meanings of the most common terms should be established at the outset. *Size of type* is measured in points, such as 8 point type or 10 point type. The unit of measurement, a *point*, is approximately 1/72 inch. The size of a particular type is determined by the number of points in height of the type body (that part below the raised portion or face). This may be considerably different from the height of the faces (letters). Thus, 10 point Scotch Roman appears smaller than 10 point Garamond. The *pica*, about ⅙ inch, is the unit of measurement for line width (line width rather than line length is used by printers). Thus, a line width of 24 picas is four inches. *Leading* refers to the additional space inserted between successive lines of print. For instance, with 2 point leading the interlinear space is 2/72 of an inch more than set solid (no leading). *Style of typeface* refers to the particular design of a type, as Scotch Roman, Bodoni, Garamond. Each typeface has various forms: *Roman lower case* is the ordinary small letter printing customarily employed in most materials; *italic* printing may be either in lower case or capitals and is readily recognized, for the letters slant to the right and employ a thinner stroke; *boldface* is merely a heavier printing face utilized in both lower case and capitals; *all-capital* printing refers to the use of capitals for all letters. *Paper quality, color, margins, intercolumn space* and *rules*, and other terms, will be defined as they are used.

Only a brief description will be given for each method of

measuring legibility. For more details and additional materials on legibility than can be given here, see Tinker (317).

Luckiesh and Moss (157) invented and made wide use of the Visibility Meter to measure *visibility of print*. This meter yields, by means of a system of filters varying in density, a measure of threshold visibility, i.e., the apparatus is manipulated until a word, letter, or other symbol can just be recognized. The meter was calibrated so that the scale value of "1" represents threshold vision for a test object whose detail subtends a visual angle of one minute; a scale value of "2," two minutes; and so on up to a value of "20" for twenty minutes. The Visibility Meter can be employed to measure the relative visibility of typefaces, type forms, and size of type, and the effects of varying brightness contrast between print and paper. Although this method yields a precise measure of threshold vision, it has limited value for studying legibility. For example, one does not know what scale value corresponds to optimal legibility when investigating the effects of varying sizes of type, leading, or line widths. Although visibility measurements may be used to advantage to determine the influence of brightness contrast between print and paper, and the relative legibility of letters of the alphabet, of digits, and of other isolated symbols, application of the results to the normal reading situation is strictly limited. Visibility scores are related to those obtained in the two methods discussed next: the *distant method* and the *short exposure method*.

The distant method, which measures visibility or perceptibility at a distance, has found considerable use in studies of legibility of isolated symbols and symbols in groups and in words (Tinker, 273). The stimulus material, starting at a distance, is moved by small steps toward the subject. At each step the subject reads as much of the material as possible. Responses, together with distance from the subject, are recorded at each step. The score for each symbol is the farthest distance from the eyes at which it can be read correctly. This method has been employed advantageously to investigate the relative legibility of letters, digits, and specific letters in different typefaces, and the effects of brightness contrast between print and paper, but again application of results obtained by this method to the normal reading situation is somewhat hazardous.

The short exposure method (270) measures legibility by determining the quickness, i.e., speed, of accurately perceiving printed symbols. The printed material (a letter, a numeral, a word, or other symbol) is exposed briefly (1/10 second or less) in a short exposure apparatus (tachistoscope). The subject reports verbally or writes down what he perceived. This method has the same limitations as visibility measurements and the distant method for investigating the legibility of print.

Luckiesh (154) and Luckiesh and Moss (162, 164) have promoted *involuntary blink rate* in reading as a measure of legibility. The method is based upon the assumption that any factor which reduces ease of seeing will increase frequency of involuntary blinking. The reports of Luckiesh and his co-workers seem to substantiate this assumption. But all other researchers, such as Tinker (295), Bitterman (21), Carmichael and Dearborn (45), and McFarland, Holway, and Hurvich (177) have obtained only negative results even though Luckiesh's technique was duplicated. Apparently rate of blinking is a questionable criterion of legibility.

Some variation of a *speed of reading method* has been most used and most generally accepted as valid to measure legibility of printed material: Pyke (213), Ovink (192), Baird (12), Tinker and Paterson (326), and others (see Tinker's *Legibility of Print*, 317).

It may be helpful to describe one speed of reading method in some detail. Tinker and Paterson and Tinker (Tinker, 317) in numerous experiments over a period of 30 years used a controlled speed of reading technique to measure legibility. In certain experiments they employed the Chapman-Cook Speed of Reading Test (326) which consists of two equivalent forms. Each form has 30 items of 30 words each. In each item, one word spoils the meaning. This word is to be crossed out by the reader as a check on comprehension. The following is an item similar to those used: "If father had known I was going swimming he would have forbidden it. He found out after I returned, and made me promise never to skate again without telling him."

In this item, the word "skate" is to be crossed out by drawing a horizontal line through it. Use of this test permitted measurement of speed of reading as a single variable since comprehension is constant. With high school seniors and college students the average percentage of accuracy is 99.7. Thus the test is uncomplicated by a comprehension factor. And the median reliability of the test is high, i.e., .85. The "face validity" is in terms of measuring speed of reading as a single variable — the conditions of measurement require the subject to read as rapidly as possible and not make mistakes. As stated by Pyke (213), a type can most properly be tested for legibility by actually being read and when maximum speed of reading is desired it can be maintained more easily for a short time than over a long period. Hence a time limit of 1¾ minutes was used with the Chapman-Cook Test.

For longer testing periods the *Tinker Speed of Reading Test* (307) was constructed with two equivalent forms of 450 items each. It also has 30 words in each item with one word spoiling the meaning of the item. The median reliability is approximately .90. Any time limit up to 30 minutes may be employed on each form of the test. Tinker, in two studies (306, 313), has evaluated the effects of prolonged reading time in measuring legibility. He found that as brief a reading time as 1½ minutes may be safely used in most situations, i.e., the same results are obtained by short and long reading periods. But when legibility differences are marginal, as with italics vs. Roman lower case, a small difference (retardation for italics) becomes larger and statistically significant if the reading time is increased from 1¾ minutes to 10 minutes. However, the results for 30 minutes of reading were the same as for 10 minutes.

Most researchers employ speed of reading performance in continuous text (sentences and paragraphs) or in special reading situations (telephone directory, mathematical tables) to investigate legibility. The task in such studies is to discover the pattern of typographical factors that affects speed and thus, presumably, ease of reading. Although it is unsafe to claim that there are no legibility differences when two typographical arrangements are read equally rapidly, legibility must be a factor of importance when one arrangement is read significantly faster than the other.

Reader judgments of relative legibility and pleasingness must also be considered because it is likely that the criteria of speed and efficiency of performance will be challenged by those inclined to stress esthetic values in printing. Therefore, Tinker and Paterson (329) undertook a comprehensive study of reader preferences as to the pleasingness of various typographical arrangements. Judgments with regard to apparent legibility had been obtained and reported previously by Paterson and Tinker (197), who presented printed samples to college students with instructions "to arrange them in order from most to least legible." Legibility was defined as "ease and speed of reading." In a similar manner pleasingness judgments were obtained from a different group of college students who were told to rank the same samples in order from most pleasing to least pleasing. "Pleasingness" was not defined.

The results shown in Table 5 for ordinary lower case vs. boldface and for lower case vs. all capitals are typical of the findings in all the other comparisons that were made. The data in the up-

Table 5. Legibility and Pleasingness Ratings of Two Contrasting Typographical Arrangements

Typographical Arrangement	Speed of Reading		Judged Legibility		Judged Pleasingness	
	No.	Mean Score *	No.	Mean Rank	No.	Mean Rank
Ordinary Lower Case vs. Boldface						
Lower case	100	18.38	224	1.3	106	1.1
Boldface	100	18.38	224	1.7	106	1.9
Lower Case vs. All Capitals						
Lower case	320	18.83	224	1.1	99	1.1
All capitals	320	16.61	224	1.9	99	1.9

* Mean score equals the mean number of paragraphs of 30 words each that was read.

per portion of the table reveal that readers believed lower case
to be considerably more legible and at the same time more pleasing than boldface, although both kinds of printing were actually
read at the same rate. Note particularly the close agreement between the ranks for judged legibility and pleasingness. The results in the lower portion of the table show that lower case is read
much more rapidly (11.8 per cent) than all capitals and that
readers rank the lower case well ahead of all capitals with respect to both apparent legibility and pleasingness.

These two arrangements, lower case vs. boldface and lower
case vs. all capitals, were selected to illustrate two situations:
one in which judgments were not in agreement with the speed of
reading measures, and another in which there was agreement.
Among the other typographical variables studied were styles of
typeface, colored print on colored paper stock, leading, size of
type, line width, paper surface, lower case vs. italics, and space
and lines between columns. In all such investigations, where important differences in speed of reading were found, the judged
legibility agreed closely with speed of reading trends. Where no,
or only slight, differences in speed were found judgments of legibility varied, i.e., a definite preference for one or another arrangement often occurred. Examples: Roman lower case over
boldface; Roman lower case over italics; one typeface over
another; eggshell paper over English (moderately glossy) and
enamel (very glossy); and a rule with ½ pica space on each side
over other intercolumn arrangements.

In this study of reader preferences, the main point to be emphasized is the striking agreement between judged legibility and
pleasingness. These results provide a suggestion to those inclined
to believe that esthetic values should have greater weight than
efficiency (speed of reading) in determining the printing specifications. To some degree the publisher, editor, advertising
agent, and printer should be guided by the facts regarding the
speed with which particular typographical arrangements can be
read and also by reader judgments of legibility. Readers are con-
sumers of printed material. Publishers and printers, therefore,
should follow reader preferences when this can be done with-

out loss of legibility. Readers seldom prefer a typographical arrangement of less than optimal legibility. Furthermore, judged legibility may be accepted as equivalent to pleasingness.

Obviously there are other factors besides legibility as such that publishers and designers consider in specifying typographical arrangements. Although some may argue that readers regard as more legible and pleasing that which is familiar and that these readers must be educated through experience to accept new arrangements, such an argument is not entirely valid as shown by the detailed results cited by Tinker (317). For example, readers prefer much more leading in newspaper print and a larger size of type than they are accustomed to in their reading. Also they prefer a rule with a ½ pica space on each side or a 2 pica space between columns of print. As noted by Ogg (191a), such modern forms as sans-serif typefaces must be considered in the same light as any other contemporary fad — not as a basic letter design until time approves or disapproves.

Although much scientific experimentation on legibility has been done in the four decades after 1920, the findings are not necessarily good for all time. A new and more satisfactory technique of investigation might be devised which could lead to new developments in typographical arrangements. In any case, the basic experimental findings on legibility up to 1963 are presented in the following six chapters.

To achieve a valid measurement of legibility by the reading performance method, the following requirements must be fulfilled: The reading materials employed in comparisons must be of equal difficulty and not complicated by comprehension problems. Comprehension must be checked, for "reading" without understanding *is not reading*. And actual printing practice must be duplicated, i.e., photographic enlargements or reductions must be avoided. Obtained differences are unimportant unless they are statistically significant.

A controlled speed of reading method which fulfills these requirements is probably the most satisfactory technique for studying legibility of print in the customary reading situation. Occasionally, supplementary data obtained by other methods are helpful, such as eye-movement records or visibility and perceptibility scores.

To use the eye-movement method for studying legibility, the eye movements must be recorded during reading. Two commonly employed techniques of recording eye movements are the photographic and the electrical. For details, see Chapter 5. The four measures of eye movements are perception time, fixation frequency, fixation pause duration, and regression frequency. The first two are highly reliable and valid measures of speed of reading, but all of the measures provide valuable supplementary information for investigators of legibility. Explanation of variation in reading speed from one typographical arrangement to another is based upon an analysis of eye-movement patterns. For example, a slower reading rate in one setup may be due to increased duration of pauses; in another to an increase in fixation frequency; in still another to changes in more than one eye-movement measure.

Certain additional points concerning measurement of legibility of print should be noted. Is it better to employ a time limit or work limit method of administering speed of reading tests? The investigation of Paterson and Tinker (193) demonstrated that the two procedures yield equivalent results when the requirements for valid measurement of legibility outlined above are fulfilled. A second point is concerned with practice effects in test administration. In a methodology investigation, Tinker and Paterson (326) found that equivalence of test forms was upset by a variety of conditions including practice. Therefore they decided that there must be in each study a check for equivalence by means of a control group with corrections being made in the experimental groups where necessary, i.e., by adding or subtracting the amount of difference in the control group. Some investigators fail to do this. A third point is mental set. Certain critics have suggested that a change in mental set in going from the standard (first form of test) to a changed typography in the second form might be responsible for a lower score in the second. The results obtained by Tinker and Paterson (325) in an experimental check showed that mental set does not produce the differences obtained when typographical variations are introduced, i.e., the obtained differences can be safely assigned to the typographical variation. Finally it has been assumed that continuous reading of relatively illegible printed material will produce "visual fatigue." Although extensive research has been undertaken to discover a satisfactory method of measuring visual fatigue, all attempts to date have failed. For instance, visual fatigue is not necessarily indicated by a reduction in rate of work such as occurs in reading text in large type (14 point) or in all capitals. Hence, legibility of print is not necessarily concerned with visual fatigue as such.

In general, the measurement of legibility of print is a delicate and painstaking job. Adequate tools of measurement, proper experimental design with proper controls, and standard statistical evaluation of obtained data are all essential. Lack of any one of these may well lead to false conclusions.

A definition of legibility may now be formulated. Any inclusive definition must take into account the procedures of investigation described above. In one or another situation, therefore, we are dealing with speed of perception, perceptibility (i.e., visibility) of symbols, speed of reading, or analysis of eye-movement patterns. A typographical arrangement that significantly reduces speed of reading in comparison with another setup can be considered less legible.

Optimal legibilty of print, therefore, is achieved by a typographical arrangement in which the shape of letters and other symbols, distinctive word form, and other factors such as size of type, width of line, and leading are coordinated to permit easy, accurate, and rapid reading with understanding. Stated briefly, legibility deals with the coordination of the factors inherent in letters and other symbols, words, and connected textual material which affect ease, accuracy, and speed of reading (317).

11 *Legibility of Type for Adult Books*

As mentioned in the previous chapter, the dominant guides to typography until rather recently were esthetics, economy of printing, and traditional practice. But Tinker's survey (317) reveals that experimental studies of legibility began to appear during the last quarter of the nineteenth century and have continued up to the present. Various typographical factors that have been investigated include legibility of letters of the alphabet, kinds of type, size of type, width of line, and leading. Still other factors will be considered in a later chapter.

Letters of the Alphabet

The subjective opinions of type designers and typographers as to legibility of letters prevailed throughout the nineteenth century and have carried much weight even up to the present day. But, beginning in 1885 and continuing to the present, numerous experimental investigations have been reported. A large majority of the studies have dealt with the relative legibility of the letters, with an analysis of factors which appear to produce good, as contrasted with poor, legibility of each of them. These analyses led to suggestions for improving those letters which were difficult to identify or were frequently confused with others. Both upper-case letters and lower-case letters were investigated.

According to Tinker (270), at least 10 reports on the relative legibility of capital letters had been published by 1928. There is little agreement from one study to another, due probably to variation in experimental method and/or kind of type used. A survey of all reports revealed that A and L tended to rank high in legibility while B, G, and Q were consistently low. Many letters of low rank were confused with others, such as B with R; G with C and O; Q with O; M with W.

Investigations of the comparative legibility of capital letters probably contribute little that is useful in ordinary reading. One possible exception is the attempt to obtain letters of nearly equal legibility for use in tests of visual acuity. Perhaps the most helpful suggestions for improving legibility of capital letters are derived from Ovink's investigation (192). Employing a distance method, he studied the effect on legibility of varying the thickness of the constituent parts of the letters. Analysis of the results led Ovink to suggest the following: clear and simple definition of characteristic parts of letters, as the curve at the bottom of J; avoidance of too narrow a width in forming such letters as A and V; refraining from use of extremely contrasting hairlines in obliques, horizontals, and verticals, as in Y, N, and F; avoidance of heavy and long serifs; avoidance of too close verticals in such letters as U; keeping bifurcation about halfway from top to bottom in such letters as M. Such modifications would be useful in printing display cards and advertisements rather than in book typography.

The printing in books, newspapers, and magazines is limited mostly to lower-case letters. This is fortunate since words in lower case are more legible than in all capitals (see the following sections). Lower-case letters have more "character" in terms of variation in shape and in the differentiation of ascenders and descenders from the short letters in a word, producing distinctive word forms which are easier to recognize than words in all capitals. This holds even though the sheer visibility of capital letters as letters is greater than that of lower-case letters.

The research on legibility of lower-case letters has been summarized by Tinker (270). The findings from study to study agreed fairly well (correlations of .48 to .88) considering that different methods of measurement and different typefaces were used. Data from the seven investigations reveal the following fairly consistent trends:

> Letters of high legibility . . . d m p q w
> Letters of low legibility . . . c e i n l
> Letters of medium legibility . . . j r v x y

The legibility rank of the other letters varied to a greater degree from study to study.

Letters low in legibility tended to be confused with other letters — c with e, for example. Analyses by Roethlein (224), Sanford (230), and Tinker (270) provide information on factors which influence legibility of the lower-case letters: size is important (w versus i); simplicity of outline improves legibility (w versus a); heavy and long serifs reduce legibility; inappropriate use of hairlines in certain letters hinders accurate discrimination; the greater the enclosed white space of a letter, the greater the legibility; identification is aided when part of a letter serves as a distinguishing characteristic, as with b and k. Of all these factors, emphasis upon differentiating parts is most influential in promoting legibility of lower-case letters. White areas within a letter and size appear to be next in importance with simplicity of outline, proper serifs, and avoidance of hairlines exerting lesser but appreciable effect. Attention to these factors by type designers could improve legibility of individual letters. However, as demonstrated by Vernon (336), the mutual confusion of individual letters is a very minor factor in the ordinary reading of meaningful materials (sentences) that are comprehended by the reader.

To what degree, then, does the relative illegibility of certain lower-case letters interfere with efficient reading? Individual letters are not confused with each other enough in the reading of *mature* readers to cause any concern or to suggest marked changes in letter forms. With children beginning to read and with retarded readers the situation is different. The relatively illegible letters can become a real stumblingblock for them. These readers must distinguish between similar word forms by discriminating between certain letters. Examples: "these" and "there"; "draw" and "drew." Hence, children's books and books used by severely retarded readers should be printed in a typeface that employs letters of high legibility.

Typefaces

"Kinds of type" and "type forms" refer to styles of typeface, lower-case printing, all capitals, italics, and boldface type. Although traditional practices and "artistic appearance" often dictate what typography will be employed, presumably the alert publisher will want to have his books or magazines printed in an optimal typographical arrangement. Since readers tend to prefer such arrangements — ranking them most legible and most pleasing (see Chapter 10) — there need be no conflict between an effective printing setup and esthetics. To choose proper type forms, the printer must know the characteristics of type that affect legibility.

Information on printing practice may well serve as a point of departure for discussing the legibility of kinds of type. Soar (245) surveyed the printing practices in 18 psychological journals published in 1920 and in 1950. Soar followed Paterson and Tinker's specifications (197) for legible printing. All the journals followed optimal practices with respect to use of italics and boldface in both years. There was, however, widespread and even increased use of all capitals (less legible than lower case) during the 30 years. Using the same criteria of legibility, Nelson (190) appraised the typography in 36 employee handbooks. She also found extensive use of all-capital printing. In addition, she found medley arrangements, a mixture of words, phrases, and sentences in italics or in all capitals or in boldface introduced within paragraphs randomly along with lower-case printing — an arrangement difficult to read. A survey of print in comic books by Tinker (288) revealed wide use of all-capital printing (lettering). It may be noted that there is a rather extensive use of italics in a few books that have been listed among those of a given year's books judged to have the most artistic typography. It would seem that much printing practice fails to conform to specifications for optimal kinds of type.

Judged by the space devoted to description of typefaces and their uses, one might conclude that printers, publishers, and advertisers believe that styles of typefaces are far more important than other typographical factors. When the subject of legibility is mentioned in most books on typography inadequate data dealing with visibility are referred to (160, 224). To identify more legible typefaces, one must determine which permit most rapid reading in the normal reading situation.

In 1932 Paterson and Tinker (195) selected for study the seven typefaces most frequently mentioned by 37 publishers and printers in answers to a questionnaire: Scotch Roman, Garamond, Antique, Bodoni Book, Old Style, Caslon Old Style, and Cheltenham. In addition, Paterson and Tinker included three typefaces which differed radically from these seven, namely Kabel Light, American Typewriter, and Cloister Black (Old English). Samples of these typefaces are shown in Figure 6. The speed of reading technique described in the previous chapter was used to determine relative legibility of the typefaces. The reading material was printed in 10 point, set solid, on a uniform paper stock in a 19 pica line width. Scotch Roman was used as the standard, and the speed of reading each of the other typefaces was compared with the speed of reading for it.

The data in Table 6 reveal that typefaces in common use in 1932 do not differ significantly in legibility. But American Typewriter and Cloister Black retarded rate of reading significantly. Tinker and Paterson's (328) analysis of eye movements while reading showed that the 13.6 per cent retardation in read-

Table 6. Relative Speed of Reading and Judged Legibility of 10 Typefaces

Typeface	Percentage of Difference from Standard in Amount Read	Rank Order of Judged Legibility
Scotch Roman (standard)	0.0	7
Garamond	+0.4	5
Antique	−0.2	2
Bodoni Book	−1.0	3
Old Style	−1.1	4
Caslon Old Style	−1.3	8
Kabel Light	−2.2	9
Cheltenham	−2.4	1
American Typewriter	−4.7*	6
Cloister Black	−13.6*	10

* Statistically significant differences at the 1 per cent level.

129

ing Cloister Black is due to a marked increase in fixation frequency and a small increase in pause duration. These changes indicate difficulty in discriminating Cloister Black print and in reading by word units. In other experiments with other typefaces, perceptibility (224) and visibility (160) measurements of lower-case letters which are not valid techniques for determining legibility in ordinary reading do not agree with the trend of the findings above.

The column at the right side of Table 6 gives the ranks for apparent legibility as judged by 210 college students. First note that there are marked differences in reader preferences — as these are revealed by judgments of legibility among typefaces that are read at approximately the same speed. An examination of Figure 6 reveals that the top three in rank, Cheltenham, Antique, and Bodoni Book, are the typefaces that appear heavier or darker, i.e., show a tendency toward boldface. Obviously, readers do not consider Kabel Light, the ultramodern face without serifs, and Cloister Black to be legible. These data on "consumer response" suggest that editors and printers can follow reader preferences without decreasing legibility.

Pyke's (213) extensive study in 1926 of eight commonly employed typefaces led to conclusions that agree with the investigation discussed above. Legibility differences between faces were small. He concluded that differences in typefaces would have to be radical indeed in order to produce appreciable differences in legibility in everyday reading situations. And one part of Roethlein's (224) investigation yielded similar results. She found that the legibility of eight typefaces was "reduced to a common level" (no significant differences appeared) when the letters were in groups, i.e., when 4 to 13 letters formed nonsense combinations.

Table 7 compares ranks for judged legibility of the 10 typefaces used by Paterson and Tinker (195) with those for speed of reading, perceptibility at a distance (Webster and Tinker, 345), and visibility (Tinker, 290). Certain cautions are relevant in interpreting the data in this table: only American Typewriter and Cloister Black are read significantly slower than the other faces, which are grouped close together; some of the ranks

Table 7. Visibility, Perceptibility at a Distance, Speed of Reading, and
Reader Judgments of Legibility Compared for Ten Typefaces (Rank Orders)

Typeface	Visibility	Percepti-bility	Speed of Reading	Reader Judgments
Antique	1	3	3	2
Cheltenham	2	2	8	1
American Typewriter	3	1	9	6
Cloister Black	4	10	10	10
Bodoni Book	5	7	4.5	3
Garamond	6	6	1	5
Old Style	7	4	4.5	4
Caslon Old Style	8	5	6	8
Kabel Light	9	9	7	9
Scotch Roman	10	8	2	7

for other measures are not widely separated. However, a few trends should be noted: in general, there is little agreement from one rank order to another; American Typewriter is high in visibility and perceptibility but very low in speed of reading and fairly low in apparent legibility; Cloister Black is at the bottom in all but visibility; typefaces that are not significantly different in speed of reading (all but American Typewriter and Cloister Black, Table 6) receive widely differing ranks by the other measures; readers tend to rate higher in legibility those faces that appear darker and larger even though read at the same speed as less "bold" faces.

These data provide additional evidence that speed of reading is the most valid measure of legibility of typefaces. It yields measurement in a normal, ordinary reading situation. In contrast, visibility and perceptibility measures are obtained in abnormal and artificial reading situations. Furthermore, such measurements could lead to invalid conclusions. For example, large type, 16 point and larger, and all capitals yield high visibility and perceptibility scores but retard speed of reading seriously. Editors and printers, therefore, should not emphasize visibility and perceptibility measurements alone in choosing legible typefaces.

The Paterson and Tinker study (195) of typefaces, reported in 1932, is the latest available. And Pyke's extensive investiga-

Scotch Roman

3. This morning my mother asked me to find out what time it was. I therefore ran just as rapidly as

Garamond

3. This morning my mother asked me to find out what time it was. I therefore ran just as rapidly as I

Antique

3. This morning my mother asked me to find out what time it was. I therefore ran just as

Bodoni

3. This morning my mother asked me to find out what time it was. I therefore ran just as rapidly as

Old Style

3. This morning my mother asked me to find out what time it was. I therefore ran just as

Caslon

3. This morning my mother asked me to find out what time it was. I therefore ran just as rapidly as

Kabel Light

3. This morning my mother asked me to find out what time it was. I therefore ran just as rapidly as I could to

Cheltenham

3. This morning my mother asked me to find out what time it was. I therefore ran just as rap-

American Typewriter

3. This morning my mother asked me to find out what time it was. I therefore

Cloister Black

3. This morning my mother asked me to find out what time it was. I therefore ran just as rapidly as

Figure 6. Ten typefaces. Adapted from
Paterson and Tinker (197).

There is an appropriate type face for every printing need. Type style can help project character, reflect feelings and develop moods in the reader. It can suggest solidity and strength of manufactured items; it can enhance the frailty and beauty of finer things.

abcdefghijklmnopqrstuvwxyz

ABCDEFGHIJKLMNOPQRSTUVWXYZ&

1234567890$fifffflffiffl,.:;?()*

ABCDEFGHIJKLMNOPQRSTUVWXYZ&

Times Roman

There is an appropriate type face for every print ing need. Type style can help project character, reflect feelings and develop moods in the reader. It can suggest solidity and strength of manufactur

abcdefghijklmnopqrstuvwxyz

ABCDEFGHIJKLMNOPQRSTUVWXYZ&

1234567890$fiflffffiffl,.:;?()*

ABCDEFGHIJKLMNOPQRSTUVWXYZ

Janson

There is an appropriate type face for every print ing need. Type style can help project character, reflect feelings and develop moods in the reader. It can suggest solidity and strength of manufac

abcdefghijklmnopqrstuvwxyz

ABCDEFGHIJKLMNOPQRSTUVWXYZ&

1234567890$fiffflffifffl,.:;?()*

ABCDEFGHIJKLMNOPQRSTUVWXYZ&

Caledonia

There is an appropriate type face for every print ing need. Type style can help project character, reflect feelings and develop moods in the reader.

abcdefghijklmnopqrstuvwxyz

ABCDEFGHIJKLMNOPQRSTUVWXYZ&

1234567890$fifffflffiffl,.:;?()*

ABCDEFGHIJKLMNOPQRSTUVWXYZ&

Scotch No. 2

Figure 7. Four typefaces popular in contemporary use, printed in 10 point.

tion (213) was published in 1926. Although some of the typefaces used in these investigations are not now representative of
current publishing practice, they can serve to illustrate general
principles. Since certain of the typefaces that presently bulk
largest in book and magazine publishing were not studied in the
1926 and 1932 experiments, it may be useful to note how the
characteristics of typefaces now in wider use compare with those
in the Paterson and Tinker 1932 investigation.

Three characteristics of the faces used in the 1932 study may
be noted: a face that appears small for the point size of the body
(Scotch Roman); faces that produce relatively light-appearing
print (Caslon and Old Style); faces that approach the appearance of boldface type, i.e., look darker (Cheltenham and Antique). See Figure 6 for these characteristics.

Among the typefaces now much used are Times Roman, Janson, Caledonia, and Scotch No. 2. See Figure 7 for samples.
The following analysis is based upon examination of print in 10
point type, the same size as that used in the Paterson and Tinker
study. The Times Roman is relatively dark appearing and would
undoubtedly rank high for legibility if rated by readers. Print in
Janson appears lighter and would probably not be rated as high
as Times Roman. Caledonia appears slightly lighter than Janson. The print in Scotch No. 2 looks smaller and somewhat
lighter than Times Roman. These characteristics, therefore, are
similar to those for the typefaces used in the 1932 study. Examination of the typefaces of the print in currently published magazines, scientific journals, and books reveals the same trend for
variation in appearance of the typefaces now in common use.
Therefore, it seems safe to assume that currently used typefaces,
all printed in the same point size, leading, line width, and paper
stock, would be read with approximately the same speed (be
equally legible) but that readers would rate some to be more
legible than others.

Italic Print

Italic print is used for various purposes: to emphasize a word,
phrase, or sentence within a paragraph of Roman type; for titles

to statistical tables and chapters; for headings within scientific reports and book chapters; in bibliographical items; for some quotations, as at the head of book chapters; and occasionally for whole paragraphs or even for several pages in a book. This practice continues even though many typography "experts" consider that italic type is far less legible than regular Roman lower case. In 1923, Starch (250) after informal experimentation, stated that italic print is read more slowly than ordinary lower case. An experiment by Tinker and Paterson (321), employing very short time limits, resulted in 2.7 per cent slower reading for the italics. In a more elaborate experiment with relatively long time limits for reading, Tinker (306) found that italic print was read 4.2 to 6.3 per cent slower than lower case for 10 minutes of reading, and 4.9 per cent slower for 30 minutes. This represented a retardation of about 14 to 16 words per minute. Although this difference does not seem large, other considerations must be taken into account. Readers dislike italics. When 224 college students were asked to rank samples of ordinary lower case and italic printing according to apparent legibility, 94 per cent agreed that the lower case would be read more rapidly (197). Furthermore, when italic print is combined with other marginal conditions in which there is slight but not highly significant illegibility, the cumulative effect is markedly deleterious (Tinker, 297). These findings indicate that it would be wise to use italics sparingly. *In fact, the use of italics should be limited largely to those rare occasions when added emphasis is desired or to brief headings in textual material.*

Boldface Type

Boldface printing is frequently resorted to as a means of emphasis or to set off sections in a book by headings. The degree to which such a practice affects legibility in the normal reading situation was ignored in early studies (224, 235). In an experiment reported in 1940, Paterson and Tinker (197) discovered no difference in speed of reading boldface and ordinary lowercase type. In a supplement to this experiment, they found that 70 per cent of 224 college readers preferred the ordinary lower case over the boldface. As one might suppose, boldface type has greater visibility than ordinary lower case.

Since about two-thirds of readers judge it to be relatively illegible, boldface should not be employed for printing entire pages or books. The results cited indicate, however, that boldface type can be safely and advantageously employed without loss of legibility for contrast and emphasis in such positions as book and chapter titles, and section headings of various kinds, and in advertising material. Although some designers may have a strong esthetic objection to boldface for headings, this does not mean that readers react the same way.

All-Capital versus Lower-Case Type

As early as 1914, Starch (249a) reported that material set in Roman lower case was read somewhat faster than similar material printed in all capitals. In 1928, Tinker and Paterson (321) employed their speed of reading technique for a more accurate check on this trend. They found that all-capital text was read 11.8 per cent slower than lower case, or approximately 38 words per minute slower. And nine-tenths of adult readers consider lower case more legible than all capitals. Pleasingness ratings showed the same trend. Since critics considered the reading time of 1¾ minutes inadequate to measure legibility trends, Tinker (306) in 1955 reported an investigation with longer reading times. Sixty college students read material in lower case for four successive 5 minute periods and text in all capitals for similar periods. Scores were obtained for 5, 10, and 20 minute periods. The all-capital text retarded speed of reading from 9.5 to 19.0 per cent for the 5 and 10 minute time limits, and 13.9 per cent for the whole 20 minute period. Obviously, all-capital printing slows reading to a marked degree in comparison with Roman lower case.

There is an explanation for the poorer legibility of all-capital printing. Tinker's (276) investigation revealed that capital letters and words in all capitals are perceived at a greater distance than those in lower case; words in all capitals are perceived at the same distance as single capital letters; lower-case words are perceived at a greater distance than individual lower case letters. *All this suggests that total word form is more important in perceiving words in lower case* than in all capitals, where perceiving occurs largely letter by letter. It is well established that reading by word units is a characteristic procedure of mature readers. Distinctive word form facilitates reading by word units and contributes to the faster reading of lower case type.

Figure 8 illustrates the fact that word form is more distinctive when words are printed in lower case than when printed in all capitals. The word "stopped" has a distinct configuration in the Roman, italic, and boldface lower case that is lacking in the all capitals where letters are all the same height and are in straight horizontal alignment.

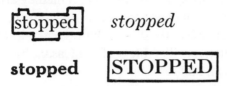

Figure 8. Block outlines of a printed word that illustrate how Roman, italic, and boldface in lower case exhibit a characteristic word form whereas such a definite shape is absent when the word is printed in all capitals. Adapted from Paterson and Tinker (197).

Other factors are involved in the slower reading (poorer legibility) of all-capital printing. Text in all capitals covers about 35 per cent more printing surface than the same material set in lower case. This would tend to increase the reading time. When this is combined with the difficulty in reading words in all-capital letters as units, the hindrance to rapid reading becomes marked. In the eye-movement study by Tinker and Paterson (327), the principal difference in oculomotor patterns between lower case and all capitals was the very large increase in number of fixation pauses for reading the all-capital print.

Although there is a tendency in certain publications to avoid excessive use of all-capital printing, it is employed widely in journals, pamphlets, and books for table titles, chapter and section headings, titles of articles, and in some instances in news-paper headlines. Considering the evidence that all-capital print-ing retards speed of reading to a striking degree in comparison with lower case and is not liked by readers, it would seem wise to eliminate such printing whenever rapid reading and con-sumer (reader) views are of importance. Examples of this would include any continuous reading material, posters, bus cards, billboards, magazine advertising copy, headings in books, busi-ness forms and records, titles of articles, books and book chap-ters, and newspaper headlines (see Chapter 14).

Mixed type forms are mentioned in the chapter on newspaper printing. Here it should be noted that inserting within para-graphs of lower-case type, words, phrases, and sentences printed in all capitals, italics, and boldface in a medley arrangement (a mixture of heterogeneous type forms) is unfortunate. Such ma-terial is read significantly slower than Roman lower case and is considered relatively illegible and unpleasant by readers (Tink-er and Paterson, 334).

Size of Type

Literature in the field reveals a lack of agreement as to the ef-fect of type size on the legibility of book print. According to Huey (131), the size of type is perhaps the most important fac-tor in legibility. Other writers tend to minimize the importance of type size by emphasizing the greater role of interlinear space, i.e., leading. In 1940, Paterson and Tinker (197) published a survey of printing practice. The data for type size are in Table 8. Certain questions may be raised by the diversity of practice re-vealed in this survey: do scientists and students require larger

Table 8. Printing Practice for Size of Type

Kind of Publication	Type Size in Points		
	No.	Range	Median
American nonscientific journals	100	7–11	10
American scientific journals	200	8–12	10
Foreign scientific journals	200	8–12	11
College textbooks	1000	8–14	11

sizes of type than the reader of nonscientific material and are all the type sizes used equally legible? The answers are found in research.

The early investigations by Griffing and Franz (109) and Gilliland (97) did not have satisfactory designs or controls. And the visibility study by Luckiesh and Moss (157) was not concerned with reading as such.

In two preliminary studies, using the speed of reading technique, Paterson and Tinker (197) determined relative speeds for reading material set in 6 to 14 point type. It appeared that 6, 8, and 14 point type were read considerably slower than 9, 10, 11, and 12 point. The 11 point was rated as most legible by 224 readers, with 10 and 12 point close behind. The eye-movement analysis reported by Paterson and Tinker (200) revealed that, in comparison with reading text in 10 point, fixation frequency, pause duration, and regression frequency increased significantly for the 6 point type; and pause duration decreased, while fixation and regression frequency increased markedly (12.6 to 21.1 per cent) for the 14 point type. The results suggest that the reduction in efficiency for the 6 point was due largely to discrimination difficulties in reading the small type. With the 14 point, however, the less effective oculomotor patterns seem to be caused by the increased amount of printing area (about 30 per cent) to be covered in reading a given amount of material.

These preliminary investigations by Paterson and Tinker employed material set solid in a 19 pica line width. No final conclusion concerning the most legible size of type for adult reading can be reached until certain other typographical factors are taken into account. Line width and leading are involved and must be coordinated with type size. That is, all three factors should be studied under conditions where simultaneous and systematic variation of all three are made.

As will be described in the next two sections of this chapter, numerous investigations of line width and leading have been made. In addition, optimal amounts of leading and line widths were determined for each of the following type sizes: 6, 8, 9, 10,

11, 12 point. With this information at hand, it was possible to design the crucial experiment to discover the relative legibility of materials printed in various type sizes (197). All material was set in Granjon typeface with 2 point leading, which was an optimal amount. The type sizes employed were 6, 8, 9, 10, 11, and 12 point, each set in an optimal line width as previously determined. The standard was 11 point, set in a 22 pica line width, with 2 point leading. The typographical arrangements and the results of testing 504 readers are shown in Table 9. These data reveal that 9, 10, 11, and 12 point type are equally legible (read equally rapidly) when each is printed in an appropriate line width with 2 point leading. The speeds for reading text in 8 and 6 point type are significantly slower than the rate of the control group reading text in the standard 11 point. These findings, plus the fact that 11 point type is rated over all others as most legible by readers, with 12 and 10 point close behind, appear to justify the trend toward using 11 point type more and more in printing practice.

To discover how the oculomotor patterns for reading the non-optimal and optimal type sizes compared, Paterson and Tinker (201) photographed the eye movements of subjects reading material printed in 6, 8, and 11 point type, each in the optimal arrangements given in Table 9. The 6 point text was read with more fixations and regressions than the material in 11 point and there was a significantly longer pause duration. For the 8 point,

Table 9. Relative Legibility of Six Type Sizes Set in Optimal
Line Widths and Leading

Type Size	Line Width	Leading	Percentage of Difference from Standard Amount Read
6 point	14 picas	2 point	−5.0*
8 point	16 picas	2 point	−3.4†
9 point	18 picas	2 point	−0.3
10 point	20 picas	2 point	−1.7
11 point	22 picas	2 point (standard)	0.0
12 point	24 picas	2 point	+1.0

* Significant at 1 per cent.
† Significant between the 2 and 5 per cent level.

there were significant increases in fixation frequency and pause duration over the 11 point. The regression frequency increased but not significantly. The eye-movement patterns for the 6 and 8 point are essentially alike. In comparison with those for the 11 point, they represent less efficient reading. Reduced visibility of the two smaller types appears to be the cause for the less efficient oculomotor behavior.

To obtain satisfactory legibility, the printer of materials for adult reading may employ 9, 10, 11, or 12 point type, provided he uses an optimal line width and leading. If he also wishes to satisfy reader preferences he will use 11 point type or perhaps 10 or 12 point.

Width of Line

For nearly a century, there has been a lively interest in the effect of line width upon legibility of print. Pyke's 1926 review (213) reveals a wide diversity of opinions about line widths for 11 and 12 point type. The recommended line widths from 1906 (Dearborn, 58) on were relatively short, i.e., 13 to 22 picas. These recommendations were made on the basis of opinion and inadequate experimentation, and without regard to the use of leading. In their survey of 1940, Paterson and Tinker (197) found that, for double-column printing of magazines and journals, there was a large range of widths (11 to 24 picas), the median being 17 to 18 picas. The figures for single-column printing of journals were 25 to 28 picas at the median interval in a range of 16 to 30 picas; for 1000 college textbooks, the median interval was 21 to 22 picas in a range of 16 to 30 picas. For the single-column printing of journals, line widths were concentrated around 24 picas; for textbooks, around 21 picas. The tendency to employ rather short lines was in accord with the expert recommendations prevailing from 1906 to 1927. Experimental results from 1929 to the present time reveal that highly legible printing is not in fact limited to relatively short line widths.

In their initial investigation of line widths for 10 point type set solid, Tinker and Paterson (322) found that materials set in 19, 23, 27, and 32 picas were all read significantly faster than text in 14, 36, 40, and 44 picas.* In a second study of 10 point type set solid, Paterson and Tinker (197) varied line width by one pica steps from 17 through 27 picas. No differences in legibility were found within this range. A 30 printing unit arrangement was employed in these first two experiments. In a third study (197) of 10 point set solid, a six printing unit arrangement was used — the sections of the Chapman-Cook Test were combined into paragraph form, with five 30 word sections in each of six units (326). The line widths were varied by relatively large steps: 9, 14, 19, 31, and 43 picas. In this study, which by use of the six unit arrangement closely approximated regular printing, line widths of 9, 14, 31, and 43 picas retarded speed of reading significantly in comparison to the text in a line width of 19 picas.

The introduction of leading modifies legibility. In a fourth investigation of 10 point type (197), the same line widths were used as in the study just cited but 2 point leading was employed throughout. The results appear particularly important, for 10 point book type is frequently printed with 2 point leading. Here texts in line widths from 14 to 31 picas were equally legible. Only the very short 9 pica and very long 43 pica lines retarded speed of reading significantly. Obviously, leading increases the range of line widths that may be used without loss of legibility. An analysis of eye-movement patterns (198) of subjects reading 10 point texts in 9, 19, and 43 pica line widths revealed that, in comparison with the 19 pica, the 9 pica material produced more fixations and a longer pause duration. Presumably, the subjects were unable to make maximum use of peripheral vision in reading the material in very short lines. And the 43 pica line width yielded increases in fixations, pause duration, and regressions (the latter by 56.7 per cent). In reading the very long lines, the major difficulty was to locate accurately the beginnings of successive lines following the back sweep from the end of the pre-

* In all the investigations by Tinker and Paterson reported in this chapter, 80 or more readers were used in each comparison, i.e., 10 comparisons would mean that at least 800 readers were employed.

viously read line. When this difficulty is experienced, it tends to upset the normal reading process so much that re-establishment of the most efficient oculomotor patterns in reading successive lines becomes difficult or impossible.

The next three investigations deal with the effects of line width on legibility of 12 point type (197). In the first of these, materials in 17, 21, 23, 25, 29, 33, and 40 picas were set solid in the 30 item arrangement. No significant differences in speed of reading the seven line widths were discovered. The six unit (paragraph) arrangement set solid was employed with line widths of 17, 21, 25, 29, 33, 37, 41, and 45 picas in the next study of 12 point type. The material in 17 through 37 picas was equally legible but the longer lines of 41 and 45 picas retarded speed of reading by significant amounts. In the third experiment, the 12 point type was set with 2 point leading in line widths of 9, 17, 25, 33, and 41 picas. Only the short and long lines of 9 and 41 picas slowed rate of reading appreciably.

Paterson and Tinker (197) conducted one study of the effects of line width for 8 point type set solid and another for 8 point with 2 point leading. In the first (no leading), 9, 29, 33, and 37 picas retarded speed of reading while 13, 17, 21, and 25 pica lines were equally legible and read fastest. The second investigation (2 point leading) revealed equal legibility for lines of 14 through 36 picas, while the text in the 7 pica line was markedly illegible.

In the same report (197), Paterson and Tinker describe two experiments dealing with line widths for 6 point type, one set solid, the other with 2 point leading. The material with no leading was equally legible for lines of 9 through 25 picas but text in 5 and 29 picas was read significantly slower. When 2 point leading was used, the 7 and 36 pica lines retarded speed, while lines of 14, 21, and 28 picas were read fastest. The eye-movement patterns for reading 6 point printing (199) revealed an increase in fixations and pause duration but fewer regressions for very short lines (5 pica) and an increase in pause duration and many more regressions (67.7 per cent) in the reading of text set in 36 picas.

143

The prevalent opinion seems to be that line width should vary somewhat with type size. Although type sizes of 9 point and smaller tend to be printed in relatively short lines, there is no consistent tendency to vary line width with 10, 11, and 12 point type (197). If there is an optimal line width for each size of type, it is not evident in printing practice.

Obviously, the area covered by print increases when size of type becomes larger. Thus, 10 point takes nearly twice as much area as 6 point; and 14 point more than three times the area cov-

6 point, 16 picas

28. On Sunday Mr. Jones never reads anything but good books for he is a very religious man. Each

8 point, 17 picas

28. On Sunday Mr. Jones never reads anything but good books for he is a very religious man. Each

10 point, 19 picas

28. On Sunday Mr. Jones never reads anything but good books for he is a very religious man. Each

12 point, 23 picas

28. On Sunday Mr. Jones never reads anything but good books for he is a very religious man. Each

14 point, 27 picas

28. On Sunday Mr. Jones never reads anythir but good books for he is a very religious man. Eac

Figure 9. Variation of line width with type size when set
solid with line for line printing. Adapted from
Paterson and Tinker (197).

ered by 6 point. Having noted this, Paterson and Tinker (197) had material printed line for line in 6, 8, 10, 12, and 14 point type. A sample of this is shown in Figure 9. Line widths varied from 16 picas to 27 picas as shown in the figure. The results of this experimental study with this material indicate that there is no direct relation between this variation in line width for type sizes and speed of reading. The 8 point type in a 17 pica line and 10 point in a 19 pica line were read equally fast and both were read more rapidly than the texts in the smaller and larger sizes.

It is noteworthy that 6 point type, even when printed in a relatively short line, is markedly illegible.

These investigations seem to indicate that the printer has considerable leeway in choice of line widths that are equally legible. A final decision, however, must take into account the role of leading.

Leading

Although there has been little agreement concerning the effect of leading on legibility, writers tend to voice opinions as to its value without reference to any experimental foundation. Before 1926, about 25 per cent of writers believed leading to be unimportant in printing, while some others were uncertain (Pyke, 213). A survey (197) reported in 1940 showed that most nonscientific magazines employed no leading or only 1 point. The trend for scientific journals was to use 2 point leading — 50 to 68 per cent. Only a few printed their material solid or with more than 3 points leading. Obviously there is need for experimentation in order to determine what effect leading has on the legibility of print.

Experiments before 1932 served only to point up the need for well-designed studies of the application of leading to the ordinary reading situation. At first thought, it might seem to be a relatively simple task to determine the effect of leading on legibility. Paterson and Tinker (197), however, discovered that one experiment led to another until 11 investigations involving over 11,000 subjects were completed (317). In the first experiment, material was set in 10 point type in a 19 pica line width. One point leading proved to be no better than set solid, 4 point improved legibility somewhat, but the fastest speed in reading was recorded with 2 point. Furthermore, readers judged text in 2 point leading to be more legible than the other arrangements. When 12 point type in a 25 pica line width was printed with 0 to 8 point leading, the results failed to reveal any significant effect on legibility.

The finding that leading was unimportant for 12 point but was effective with 10 point type naturally raised a question concern-

145

ing its influence on the legibility of text printed in sizes smaller than 10 point. Therefore, materials in 8 point type with a 17 pica line width were set in 0, 1, 2, 4, 6, and 8 point leading. Although any leading improved legibility, the text in 2 point was read fastest. Materials with 1 and 8 point leading were read almost as rapidly. Thus in printing practice, legibility of 8 point type in a moderate line width is definitely improved when 1 or 2 point leading is utilized.

In a letter from a printer to the writer, it was claimed that a smaller type size with double or triple leading is more legible than a larger type set solid. And in another letter it was stated that a page of 10 point text set solid is far more difficult to read than a page printed in 8 point type with 2 point leading. Paterson and Tinker (197) put the latter view to experimental check. The speed of reading text set in solid 10 point type in a 19 pica line width was compared with the speed for 8 point type in a 19 pica line width with 2 point leading. These two printing arrangements were equally legible for the 200 readers tested. Any assertion, therefore, that leading will make a smaller type size more legible than a larger size set solid is false. But since 8 point type tends to be less legible than 10 point, when other things are equal, these results give added emphasis to the value of 2 point leading for 8 point type. Apparently, type size and leading as well as line width are factors which affect legibility of typographical arrangements.

Leading and Line Width in Relation to Type Size

To obtain data most useful to printers, editors, and publishers, investigations which vary line width and leading for each of the commonly used sizes of type must be carried out. Such a program requires large numbers of readers. For instance, to study four degrees of leading and five line widths for a single type size necessitates 20 printing arrangements and about 2000 readers. Paterson and Tinker (197) next investigated 6 type sizes: 6, 8, 9, 10, 11, and 12 points. On the basis of the results, it is possible to direct attention to safety zones for the printing of each size of type. By "safety zone" is meant the limits of variation in line width and leading that may be used for a given type size without appreciable loss of legibility. The safety zones for the six type sizes follow.*

6 Point Type:
   14 pica line width with 2 to 4 point leading
   21 pica line width with 1 to 4 point leading
   28 pica line width with 2 to 4 point leading

8 Point Type:
   14 pica line width with 2 to 4 point leading
   21 pica line width with 2 to 4 point leading
   28 pica line width with 1 to 4 point leading
   36 pica line width with 2 to 4 point leading

9 Point Type:
   14 pica line width with 1 to 4 point leading
   18 pica line width with 1 to 4 point leading
   30 pica line width with 1 to 4 point leading

10 Point Type:
   14 pica line width with 1 to 4 point leading
   19 pica line width with 2 to 4 point leading
   31 pica line width with 2 point leading (marginal)

11 Point Type:
   16 pica line width with 1 to 2 point leading
   25 pica line width with 0 to 4 point leading
   34 pica line width with 1 to 2 point leading

12 Point Type:
   17 pica line width with 1 to 4 point leading
   25 pica line width with 0 to 4 point leading
   33 pica line width with 1 to 4 point leading

With these data available, it was possible to determine the relative legibility of the 6 type sizes set in an optimal line width and leading as described in the section on type size above. If the printer or publisher or editor is to cater to the preferences (judged legibility and pleasingness) of readers, he will employ a moderate line width with appropriate leading selected from those typographical arrangements within the zone of safety for that type size. Readers dislike very short and very long lines, as well as material set solid.

* Adapted from Paterson and Tinker (197) and also printed in Tinker (317).

Combining Nonoptimal Typographical Arrangements

In the discussion above the effect of combining nonoptimal printing arrangements as such was not emphasized. Presumably, when two or more of these arrangements are combined, the deleterious effect on legibility would be greater than the influence of any one acting alone. If so, are the adverse effects due to the nonoptimal conditions cumulative, or is the combined effect less than the sum of the separate effects? This problem cannot be solved by inference or by guessing.

Instances of combinations of nonoptimal printing are fairly common and easily discovered. To cite a few: some pamphlets, government and others, are printed in relatively small type in excessively long lines without leading on too thin paper stock; or dark colored print in all capitals is used on a dark colored paper; or white print in a very small type size appears on a black background.

The results obtained by Paterson and Tinker (197) in studies of three type sizes (6, 8, and 10 point) demonstrate that the progressive introduction of nonoptimal variations in two or more typographical factors is accompanied by ever greater loss in legibility. But the combined effect of two or more such factors is not strictly cumulative. That is, the nonoptimal factors operate together but their combined effect cannot be predicted exactly from a knowledge of their separate effects. And as shown by Paterson and Tinker (202), a combination of nonoptimal factors produces a severe disorganization of oculomotor behavior in comparison with such behavior when an optimal setup is used.

In view of these experimental results, it is suggested that nonoptimal arrangements should never be combined. To do so will only enhance to a striking degree the illegibility of the print.

It may be concluded that the material now at hand derived from research and practice, though not complete in all particulars, is sufficient to permit a high level of printing practice which will meet the demands both of legibility and of esthetics.

12 *Typography for Children's Books*

The legibility of the typographical arrangements utilized in printing books for children should be optimal, of course. Teachers and parents, as well as publishers, will want to know all the factors involved in printing that may affect the ease and quickness with which letters, words, and sentences can be discriminated and read in these books. This implies an emphasis upon providing reading material which will not cause any unnecessary strain on the eyes of children in perceiving the printed symbols. In selecting new books for children, the typographical arrangement of printed pages must be considered.

Print for adult books and magazines has optimal legibility only when all typographical factors are properly coordinated, as we have seen in the preceding chapter. In practice, the typography for young children differs somewhat from that for adults. At what age level do children read enough like adults so that it is unnecessary to differentiate between the two in specifying print for optimal legibility? A fairly definite answer is provided by research results. In an investigation of eye movements of children during reading, Buswell (39) found a definite stabilization of the oculomotor patterns by the end of the fourth grade. This result was verified in a later experiment. Ballantine (13) discovered rapid gains in eye-movement efficiency from the second through the fourth grade and then considerably slower improvement up to the eighth grade. Since oculomotor behavior represents degree of proficiency in the mechanics of reading, one may conclude from these studies that the mechanics of reading

Author's note: Part of the material in this chapter has appeared in a report by Tinker (314).

(word-recognition techniques, perceptual skill, use of context) becomes well established, or like that of adults, somewhere between the fourth and eighth grades. Further data on this subject are derived from a series of experiments by Tinker (316a). Children of two school levels were tested: fifth- and sixth-grade pupils together at one level and seventh- and eighth-grade pupils together at the other level. Using the speed of reading technique, seven investigations were carried out to obtain data on the legibility of several varieties of typographical arrangements: size of type; width of line; simultaneous variation of line width and type size; leading for 10 point and for 12 point type; optimal versus nonoptimal printing; styles of typeface. The data revealed that the reading by both groups of pupils showed essentially the same trends as that of adult readers when some aspect of typography was varied, such as size of type or line width.

The fact that children, by about the fifth grade (or at 10 years of age) and later, react like adults to variations in typographical arrangements and also have nearly, or even approximately, achieved a stable level in development of eye-movement patterns while reading provides an answer to the question posed above: When children reach about the fifth-grade level, they read enough like adults so that it is not necessary to differentiate between the two in specifying print for optimal legibility. This means that the conclusions reached in the previous chapter on print for adults are valid for children who are between 10 and 11 years of age and older. The rest of this chapter, therefore, will deal with print for books to be read by younger children.

There has been relatively little research done on legibility of print for young children. The following discussion will be based upon the available research plus a consideration of classroom experience and publishing practice.

Size of Type

McNamara, Paterson, and Tinker (178) report an extensive investigation of the effect of type size on speed of reading in the three primary grades. An experimental design which fulfilled the specifications in Chapter 10 was used with 3050 pupils in grades 1A, 2B, 2A, and 3B. A survey of children's books revealed that type sizes from 10 to 18 points were used. In order to cover this range and to extend somewhat beyond it, the test materials were printed in 8, 10, 12, 14, 18, and 24 point type. The results revealed no differential effect of type size in grades 1A and 2B. There was a slight advantage for 14 point type in grade 2A. But in grade 3B material in 8, 18, and 24 point retarded speed of reading by significant amounts, while text examples in 10, 12, and 14 point were read most rapidly, with a slight advantage for the 14 point type.

The results reported by Buckingham (36) showed that 12 and 14 point were slightly better than 18 point in grade 2, but the differences were small. In the Blackhurst (22) studies, variations in size of type between 14 and 30 point in grade 1 and between 10 and 24 point in grade 2 were unimportant. And in grades 3 and 4, text in 18 point was read fastest, that in 14 and 12 next, while 10 and 8 point examples were read much slower. This lack of important effects of the type size variations upon speed of reading in the early grades is probably a function of growth factors in reading proficiency.

The results cited above are based upon speed of reading tests. One should note that reading rate is not, or should not be, an issue in the early primary grades, particularly in grade 1 and probably in grade 2. These are the years devoted largely to developing discrimination of visual symbols, word recognition, vocabulary knowledge, and comprehension. A type size that makes possible easy visual discrimination should be chosen for printed material to be read by children at these early age levels. Experience based upon some research results suggests that type size for grade 1 should be 14 to 18 point, for grades 2 and 3, 14 to 16 point; and for grade 4, about 12 point. For the upper grades, 5 through 8, size 10, 11, or 12 point may be used as with adult readers. Twelve point is most commonly chosen.

Other Factors

Width of line may vary considerably without important effects upon speed of reading by young children. In his report,

Gates (85) states that there is no evidence available which permits specification of optimal line lengths (widths) for materials to be read by young children. This statement also holds today. Blackhurst's (22) results appear to indicate that a 24 pica (4 inch) line width is best for the primary grades. But differences in speed for reading text in various line widths are small. Actually, when all the evidence is considered, line widths may range from about 16 to about 30 picas with little effect on the reading of young children. Practice seems to suggest a medium line width, such as 18 to 24 picas, at any age level. The tendency is to use rather short lines in grade 1 (16 to 22 picas). Children in the first four grades appear to adjust quickly to reading a specific line width. Therefore, as soon as the subject matter permits and the child has gained some proficiency in reading (about second-grade level), it is best to use the same line width for an entire book rather than to employ several widths at random on some or all pages.

Evidence of the effectiveness of leading for books in the first four grades is confusing, to say the least. According to Blackhurst (22) the amount of leading has no appreciable effect on the speed of reading in the first four grades. Buckingham (36) found that 3 or 4 point leading combined with a short line and printed in 12 or 14 point type promoted somewhat faster reading in grade 2. The current practice is to use a generous amount of leading in grade 1, somewhat less in grade 2, and still less in grades 3 and 4. Considering the maturity of level of reading performance in the early grades, it would appear that some leading is indicated, irrespective of speed of reading results. During the first three grades, regressive eye movements occur frequently (13, 39) and the return movement from the end of one line to the beginning of the next has not been perfected. Generous leading will promote greater accuracy in this and thus reduce regressions near the beginning of lines. The following will be found adequate: about 6 to 8 point leading for grade 1; 4 to 6 point for grade 2; 3 to 4 for grades 3 and 4; 2 point for grade 5 and above (same as for adults). As with type size, speed of reading cannot be considered an ideal technique to measure other factors affecting legibility of print for books to be read in the first two grades. Optimal visibility of symbols, both letters and words, is essential at these age levels, as already noted.

Legibility of styles of typeface has not been investigated for print to be read by children in the first four grades. The data cited above show that children in the fifth through the eighth grades respond to variations in typeface the same as adults. Until research shows otherwise, there is no basis for assuming that children in the early grades respond differently. Therefore, the results for adults cited in the previous chapter probably hold for children, i.e., typefaces in common use are equally legible. But, since adult readers and presumably younger ones prefer a relatively heavy or darker appearing typeface and because type of medium darkness yields optimal visibility (Luckiesh and Moss, 165), a moderately dark typeface should be used in printing books for children.

Presumably the findings for adults concerning various forms or kinds of each typeface — Roman lower case, capitals, italic, and boldface — are relevant for children. In general, as illustrated in the previous chapter, text in Roman or ordinary lower case is easiest to read and overwhelmingly preferred by adults, but boldface has no retarding effect. Italic print, on the other hand, has a significant retarding effect and is disliked by most readers. Probably italics should be used sparingly and only for brief statements and emphasis. Actually, boldface rather than italics may be better used for emphasis and for headings since then there will be no loss of legibility.

For children as for adults, all-capital print is extremely difficult to read (Chapter 11). There is good reason for this. As children learn to recognize words and make them a part of their sight vocabulary, they make maximum use of the general visual shape of the word (word form) in perception during subsequent reading. All-capital words have few clues to word form (length of word, mainly) while words in lower-case print have many. This is readily appreciated by examining the shapes of "stopped" and "STOPPED" in Figure 8 in the previous chapter. Since most words when printed in lower case have characteristic word forms due to the alternation of tall and short letters, it is easy to grasp or recognize the word as a unit, provided the reader has experienced it before so that it is somewhat familiar. But in all-capital printing the reader must, to a considerable degree, examine the separate letters to recognize the word. Consequently, text in all capitals should be avoided wherever possible. This is particularly important with young children who are still learning to employ word form as one of the important clues to word recognition.

Quality of paper and color of paper and ink will only receive brief mention here since these subjects will be dealt with in detail in a later chapter. Quality of paper refers to opacity and the nature of the surface. Book and magazine paper should be opaque enough so that the print on the back will not show through to the other side and blur appreciably the print there. In addition, the paper surface should be rough enough (mat surface) so that the glare from reflected light will be at a minimum. In order to have pictures printed in children's books look natural, some degree of compromise between a lusterless and a glossy enamel surface is necessary. A proper and adequate compromise can be achieved that will avoid specular (as from a mirror) reflection from the paper surface.

It is customary to print books on so-called white paper with black printing ink. Such papers vary considerably in "whiteness" and consequently in degree of brightness contrast between paper and ink. Pure white paper which would reflect 100 per cent of incident light is never achieved. Most book paper reflects about 75 to 85 per cent of light, and printing ink, about 5 per cent. This means a difference in reflectance (or brightness contrast) of 70 to 80 per cent. This is satisfactory. However, this value of brightness contrast should not fall below 65. Book paper tinted slightly yellow, green, or some other color may be used with little loss in brightness contrast. It is worth noting that attempts to promote colored paper for printing in order to avoid eyestrain are misleading. Color as such is unimportant. But quality of paper, paper surface, and brightness contrast between paper and printing ink are important. The experiment on the effects of varying color of print and background by Tinker and Paterson (323) led to the conclusion that greatest legibility is achieved when there is maximum brightness contrast between paper and print. This conclusion was supported by Preston, Schwankl, and Tinker (212) and Hackman and Tinker (111). If tinted paper and/or colored ink is preferred from an esthetic viewpoint, they may be used without loss of legibility provided the tint is light enough so as not to reduce appreciably the brightness contrast between paper and ink.

Coordination of Typographical Factors

In order to achieve optimal legibility of print in children's books and magazines, all the factors discussed in this chapter should be properly coordinated. This is not easy to do. Investigators have employed speed of reading to measure legibility. As noted, in the first grade or two, rate of reading is not an issue except when dawdling becomes a problem. Experimental results, therefore, must be interpreted with care. In addition, any recommendation for printing books for children should take into account the visual tasks of the young learner and to some degree the legibility findings for older readers. One may note that present practice in printing basic series of readers is fairly good. With all this in mind, certain suggestions for achieving legible print for children's books may be made.

In grade 1, adequate printing is achieved by 14 to 18 point type with generous leading, perhaps 6 to 8 point, in relatively short lines ranging up to about 20 picas. Line widths will vary considerably because of the different lengths of sentences, since customarily there is one sentence to a paragraph.

In grade 2, suitable print would have 14 to 16 point type, about 5 to 6 point leading, and a line width of approximately 20 to 22 picas.

As children reach grades 3 and 4, reading skills have attained fairly high levels so that research results are more applicable. Here 12 to 14 point type with 3 to 4 point leading in a line width of 20 to 24 picas will be found highly legible and satisfactory.

Some deviation from these specifications can be made without appreciably reducing the legibility of print in children's books. However, line widths in grades 2, 3, and 4 should not be shorter than 18 or longer than 26 picas. All-capital printing should be avoided and italics used sparingly. And there should be adequate brightness contrast between paper and print.

Beginning at the fifth-grade level, the specifications for printing adult books can be utilized. In the fifth, sixth, seventh, and eighth grades, children react as adults do to typographical changes.

13 *Color and Surfaces of Printing Paper*

Color of paper, its quality, and its surface as related to printing ink have an important bearing on legibility of reading material. As is customary, white, gray, and black as well as hues (colors of the spectrum) will be treated as colors in this discussion. The brightness contrast between print and paper is a matter of prime importance to be considered throughout this chapter. The comments here will be confined primarily to printing in ordinary reading situations although some reference to advertising practice will be made.

As noted in Pyke's 1926 summary (213) of previously published literature, many views or opinions had been expressed concerning appropriate color of paper and ink to achieve good legibility. Certain writers favored pure white paper, others preferred a tint, especially a yellow or cream tint. One considered light gray best. The consensus was that the printer should utilize paper without gloss and opaque enough to prevent print on the back from showing through. However, a few writers minimized the importance of paper quality. Apparently it was generally assumed that black ink would be used, for little attention was devoted to the selection of ink. But one writer favored deep black ink and another suggested that light blue and green ink on white paper should be avoided. Casual observation or mere opinion formed the basis for nearly all these views.

Black Print versus White Print

White print on a black background as well as black on white is employed in a variety of situations. Presumably the printer who plans to use white print will want to know whether it, or black print, is the more legible, as well as the effect of varying type size on the relative legibility of black and white print. Advertisers, editors, and commercial artists are also interested in these problems.

Let us first consider the relative legibility of white and black print in the ordinary reading situation. The investigation by Starch (250) is relevant. He discovered that, on the average, his 40 subjects read black print on white paper 42 per cent faster than white print on dark gray. This corresponded to a difference of 108 words per minute. Employing their speed of reading method, Paterson and Tinker (194) determined the relative legibility of white and black print. To maintain constant conditions, they printed both arrangements from zinc etchings on white enamel paper. White print was achieved by printing the background black. Material in black type was read 10.5 per cent faster than that in white. They also found that readers definitely prefer the black on white printing, for 77.7 per cent of 224 adults rated the black to be more legible than the white print. Taylor's study (256) of eye movements revealed 11.6 per cent more fixations in reading the white than in reading the black print. Thus, in the normal reading situation, white print has proved to be significantly less legible than black print.

The relative perceptibility of white and black print has also been investigated. In an early experiment, Kirschmann (142) measured the recognizability in peripheral vision of relatively large block letters and geometric forms by means of a campimeter (a flat chart used to map out the visual field). One to four subjects were used in various parts of the experiment. In all instances, Kirschmann found that the white symbols on a black background were recognized farther out in peripheral vision than black on white. No later investigation has been able to confirm his results. Taylor (256) duplicated the parts of Kirschmann's experiment which used letters. She found that white on black letters were 25.1 per cent less "legible" than black on white. In a supplementary experiment, Taylor showed that extensive practice only increased the difference in favor of the black on white letters. Taylor (256) next carried out an extensive series of experiments to measure the effects of type size, typeface, word form, and meaning from context on the relative legibility of white and black print. Employing the distance method (see Chapter 10), she found that the inferiority of the white print was independent of type size within the range of 6 to 14 points. Letters in Scotch Roman lower case were found to be 22.0 to 26.7 per cent less legible in white than in black print for 6, 10, and 14 point type. The picture is somewhat different for Kabel Light (a sans-serif typeface). Ten and 14 point type were equally legible in white and black type, but for the 6 point type the white letters were definitely less legible than the black.

To maintain a minimum of meaning and differential form, the li test in black and white print was read at a distance. The subject's task was to identify which combination (li or ll, or il or ii) was present. The white print was much less legible than the black: for 14 point type, 42.6 per cent; 10 point, 33.1; and 6 point, 74.8. Note that type size is not directly related to the amount of legibility differences except that 6 point shows the greatest difference. To determine the influence of word form, Taylor studied perceptibility at a distance of five-letter words and of groups of five letters in nonsense arrangement printed in black and in white lower case 10 point type. The results revealed that for words and nonsense material black was much more legible than white print, 17.2 and 22.9 per cent respectively. The words were perceived at a greater distance than the letters in a nonsense arrangement. And the white nonsense material was less legible in comparison to the black nonsense material than were white words to black words. Apparently this is due to the fact that, in the absence of word forms, clear perception of details is hindered more when the print is white than when it is black. In a final segment of the investigation Taylor found that, for text in paragraphs, white print was read 11.0 per cent slower than black print.

What is the effect of the degree of contextual meaning in the stimulus material upon legibility of black versus white print? To answer this, data from Taylor's experiments are assembled in Table 10. Examination of these data indicates that a decrease in meaningfulness in the stimulus is accompanied by an increase in the percentage advantage of black over white print. The li test involves the least amount of contextual meaning. Note that, for this test, the advantage of black over white print is three times that for reading sentences in paragraphs. And the absence of word form increases the disadvantage of white print (groups of nonsense letters versus words).

Table 10. Influence of Meaning Context on the Relative Legibility
of Black and White Print

Stimulus Material	Percentage Difference* in Legibility between Black and White Print
Words in paragraphs	−11.0
Isolated words	−17.2
Letters in nonsense arrangement	−22.9
Isolated capitals	−23.6
Letters (ll, li, il, ii)	−33.1

* Minus differences signify poorer legibility for white print.

The results of two other experiments are in harmony with the one cited above. Holmes (124) discovered a 14.7 per cent advantage of black over white print in legibility of five-letter words set in 10 point type. And Taylor (256), utilizing a short exposure technique and block letters, found that white on black was definitely less legible than black on white or dark gray on white.

It is likely, according to Taylor (256), that the universally superior legibility of black print is due to irradiation effects, i.e., the apparent enlargement of a bright (white) object when seen against a dark ground. In ordinary type with serifs, like Scotch Roman, the detrimental effects of irradiation from the white background are neutralized by the serifs which tend to preserve the distinctive forms of the letters by emphasizing their corners. But when white letters are on a black background, irradiation not only will increase the apparent size of the letters but will also tend to blur letter outlines, close their open spaces, and fuse their parts. All this hinders visual discrimination and thus reduces legibility. Such effects become most prominent when the letters are small, when their strokes are relatively wide for the size of the letter, and when there are no auxiliary clues from meaning in the context. The irradiation effects should be least noticeable or even absent with sans-serif type, especially in the larger sizes, i.e., 10 to 14 point.

Black print on tinted paper finds considerable usage in contemporary practice. Opinions are given freely but there is no consensus as to whether white or tinted paper is more appropriate for regular printing of books, magazines, pamphlets, folders, and business forms. In 1896 Griffing and Franz (109) found that, due to less brightness contrast between black ink and the tinted papers, grayish (newspaper), red, and yellow papers were inferior to white paper in promoting legibility. Luckiesh and Moss (161) studied the relative legibility (visibility) of black print on white and on tinted paper. The white paper had a reflectance (amount of incident light reflected from a surface) of 85 per cent. For eight of the tints, the reflectance varied from 70 (light blue-green) to 83 (slight cream) per cent. A fairly saturated yellowish red paper had a reflectance of 38 per cent. The only clear-cut conclusion stated by the authors was that the yellowish red paper of lowest reflectance was found to yield inferior visibility of print. Readers preferred print on white and disliked it on the yellowish red paper. The visibility measurements of black print on 16 samples of tinted paper obtained by Betts (19) revealed no significant differences between tints. And the speed of reading determinations by Stanton and Burtt (249) failed to show any significant differences in their comparisons of black print on lustro, cameo, and old style wove paper surfaces with white and ivory tints. Black print on six papers varying in tint and surface texture (antique wove versus mat) was used.

The results dealing with black print on tinted paper are easily summed up: although visibility scores vary somewhat, the variation is unimportant with respect to legibility in the ordinary reading situation for the tinted paper customarily used; when the reflectance of paper surfaces, either white or tinted, is approximately 70 per cent or greater, all materials in black print are read at about the same rate, i.e., there is no important deleterious effect on legibility; readers tend to prefer print on white or the more lightly tinted papers. Apparently the printer is free to choose a lightly tinted or an antique wove finish printing paper for esthetic values without loss of legibility.

Colored Print on Colored Paper

During recent years there has been increased use of color combinations of print and paper in a wide variety of situations. Among these are the following: magazine supplements in Sunday newspapers, books for children, books for adults (a relatively recent trend), letterheads, circulars, pamphlets, road maps, aviator maps, and also magazine and poster advertising. This practice emphasizes the need for scientific information concerning the effect on legibility of combinations of colored printing and colored backgrounds. For instance, a colored type which produces satisfactory legibility on one colored paper may turn out to be relatively illegible when combined with certain other colored backgrounds.

From 1896 to 1957 four experimental procedures were used to investigate the legibility of colored print on colored paper: perceptibility during short exposures, perceptibility at a distance, speed of reading, and analysis of eye movements (see Chapter 10).

Miyake, Dunlap, and Cureton (186), using a short exposure method, found that yellow and white print on black paper were much more legible than red and green on black. And black type on colored (tinted) paper had relatively good legibility. In a somewhat similar experiment, Griffing and Franz (109) reported that it took considerably longer exposures (legibility was lower) to perceive words on newspaper stock and on yellow and red papers than on white.

The distance method was employed by Summer (255) to determine the relative legibility of 42 combinations of colored print and background. The three most legible combinations were blue on gray, black on gray, and black on yellow; the three least legible ones were black on blue, yellow on white, and blue on black. The results suggest that legibility depended upon the brightness difference between symbol and background. Preston, Schwankl, and Tinker (212) determined the distance at which five-letter words in 11 color combinations could be perceived. They used the same color combinations as Tinker and Paterson. In general, the more easily perceived words were in color combinations with a greater brightness difference between print and paper. The rank order for perceptibility correlated +.86 with the speed of reading results obtained by Tinker and Paterson (323) who employed their speed of reading technique with 850 readers. They used Ruxton's ink to print the reading test on Rainbow cover stock. Each of 10 color combinations was compared with black on white. A summary of materials and results is given in Table 11. The texts in the first three color combinations were read only slightly slower than black on white. In fact, in the practical situation, green on white and blue on white produce print that is nearly as legible as black on white. The retarding effect of black on yellow is barely significant. But the difference for tulip red on yellow suggests that it should not be employed where speed of reading is important. The remaining col-

Table 11. Relative Legibility of Print in 11 Color Combinations
(N = 850 readers)

Trade Name	Observed Effect	Percentage of Difference* in Legibility
Black jobbing on white.....	Black on light grayish white	0.0
Grass green on white	Dark green on light grayish white	−3.0
Lustre blue on white	Dark blue on light grayish white	−3.4
Black jobbing on yellow....	Black on yellow (slight orange tinge)	−3.8
Tulip red on yellow........	Light red on yellow (slight orange tinge)	−4.8
Tulip red on white.........	Light red on light grayish white	−8.9
Grass green on red.........	Dark grayish green on red (dark tint)	−10.6
Chromium orange on black ..	Dark lemon yellow on dark grayish black	−13.5
Chromium orange on white..	Light orange on light grayish white	−20.9
Tulip red on green.........	Dark brown on dark green	−39.5
Black jobbing on purple....	Black on dark purple (violet)	−51.5

* Minus signifies less legibility than black on white.

or combinations produce print which is very illegible. The last four are so poor that it is inadvisable ever to use them. These are the same four color combinations that yielded poorest perceptibility in the experiment cited just above.

The eye-movement studies by Tinker and Paterson (331) and Hackman and Tinker (111) for reading material used in the investigation cited above confirmed the speed of reading results. The slower reading for color combinations with the lesser brightness contrasts between print and background is due to an increase in fixation frequency and pause duration.

Examination of the printed material revealed that brightness contrast between print and paper becomes progressively smaller as one goes from the black on white at the top of the table to the black on purple at the bottom, and the reading speed became slower as the brightness contrast became less. The legibility of the printed material does not depend primarily upon the color hues of the ink and paper as such. At this point it may be worthwhile to emphasize that the brightness contrast between print and background, which principally determines legibility, is not at all the same thing as color contrast, the difference between the color hues of the ink and paper. For example, dark red and blue exhibit considerable color contrast but little brightness contrast. Similarly, light orange and light grayish white are contrasting colors but have only slight brightness contrast. That is, two tints or two shades will show slight brightness contrast. When printing with colored ink on colored paper, therefore, the ink should be a shade or dark color and the paper a tint or light color, i.e., one should use a dark ink on a light background.

Another factor that is relevant and therefore should be considered by editors and printers is the change in the visual appearance of a color when printed on another color. This becomes obvious by examining the observed effect of the color combinations in Table 11. The results of the last four experiments cited (111, 212, 323, 331) hold only for colored inks (including black) printed on colored paper. When letters and background are both printed with differently colored inks on a white paper so that they do not overlap, the effect is different.

Samples of the printing used in the Tinker and Paterson study (323) were presented to 210 adult readers. They ranked the 11 samples according to apparent legibility. The ranks from most to least judged legibility follow:

1. Black on white
2. Blue on white
3. Black on yellow
4. Green on white
5. Red on yellow
6. Red on white
7. Green on red
8. Orange on black
9. Orange on white
10. Black on purple
11. Red on green

Ranks 2 and 3 were close together; similarly 5 and 6, and 10 and 11. Comparing these ranks with the speed of reading results in Table 12 reveals a close correspondence. Apparently the readers made their judgments of relative legibility in terms of *brightness contrast* between print and paper without being influenced by color preferences and color contrast. All this leads to the suggestion that publishers, printers, and editors should choose colors which produce maximum brightness contrast when combined if they are to achieve both good legibility and reader approval.

Brief references may be made to the recent trend to use in books colored print on tinted paper* which appears to have some merit. Dark colored inks coordinated with light tints of paper can be as legible as black ink on white book paper provided the reflectance of the tinted paper is 75 per cent or greater, the colored ink has a reflectance of not over 10 per cent, and the type size used is 10 point or larger. It is claimed that the use of such colors is not only pleasing to the reader but also easier on the eyes. The writer of this book doubts that it is the color as such that produces apparently easier reading. The quality and

---

* The use of colored print on tinted paper is making considerable progress under the leadership of E. A. Whiteford, president of the Whiteford Paper Company, 420 Lexington Avenue, New York 17, N.Y. His method of printing attempts to achieve better readability by adjusting the light reflectance ratio between paper and ink to approximately 8 to 1. This is alleged to reduce glare that may occur with black ink on white paper, especially under bright illumination. And pleasingness of the color combinations is claimed to be important. Two books printed according to specifications for use of colored ink and tinted paper are Robert Carse, *Blockade: The Civil War at Sea* (New York: Holt, Rinehart, and Winston, 1958) and John E. Eichenlaub, *A Minnesota Doctor's Home Remedies for Common and Uncommon Ailments* (Englewood Cliffs, N.J.: Prentice-Hall, 1960).

reflectance of the paper surface and printing ink are the important factors which control legibility and ease of seeing, other things being equal. And the argument that colored print on tinted paper prevents glare which would occur with white paper in very bright light is unimportant. One should not read in direct sunlight or even under 100 footcandles of illumination (see the later section on illumination). Furthermore, it has not been proved experimentally that colored print on tinted paper produces less visual fatigue than properly coordinated black print on so-called white paper. Nevertheless it is likely that many readers will prefer the colored print on tinted paper for esthetic reasons.

Printing Surfaces

Many and varied opinions concerning the kind of paper surface alleged to produce legible print were published prior to Pyke's monograph in 1926 (213). He has listed these views. They may be summarized briefly. Printing paper should be at least 0.075 mm. thick; be thick enough so that print will not show through; have a mat (rough) surface; have a hard surface, be unglazed, and not ribbed; be as white as possible and without gloss. One writer minimized the importance of quality and texture of printing paper provided the lighting is such that specular reflection is avoided.

Three techniques have been used to study the effect of paper surface on legibility: perceptibility at a distance, speed of reading, and visibility measurements. Roethlein (224) employed the distant method to investigate the legibility of letters in 9 typefaces printed on glazed white paper and on rough surfaced paper. She found no differences and the subjects expressed no preference for either kind of paper. Using a similar method, Webster and Tinker (344) compared perceptibility of five-letter words printed in Scotch Roman lower case on white eggshell paper stock (mat surface), on artisan enamel (moderately glossy), and on flint enamel (very glossy). Glare percentages for the three papers were as follows: eggshell, 22.9; artisan enamel, 85.8; flint enamel, 95.1. The illumination did not produce specular glare. No significant differences appeared with variation in paper surface although the score for perceiving the flint enamel was nearly 2 per cent poorer. Any eyestrain arising while reading material printed on glazed or glossy paper must be due to reading in light not uniformly dispersed so that specular reflection interferes with vision.

Two experiments dealing with the effects of varying printing surfaces were reported by Paterson and Tinker (197). They used their speed of reading method. In the first study, no significant difference was found for reading text on eggshell (mat surface) and white enamel. For the second experiment, material was printed on eggshell, artisan enamel, and flint enamel. Text on eggshell and text on artisan enamel were read equally fast. But that on flint enamel was read approximately 3 per cent slower than that on eggshell (significant between 2 and 5 per cent level). Apparently, print on paper with a moderate degree of gloss (artisan enamel) has no deleterious effect on legibility provided it is illuminated with well-diffused light. The results reported by Stanton and Burtt (249) agree with these data. Nevertheless, whenever possible mat surface paper should be employed for printing, because much reading is done under poorly distributed illumination and because readers prefer print on a mat surface. When 224 readers rated samples of the material used by Paterson and Tinker for relative legibility, 75 per cent preferred the eggshell paper; 19 per cent the artisan enamel; and 6 per cent the flint enamel. Obviously, most readers dislike reading print on glossy paper, especially that with a high degree of gloss, i.e., flint enamel. Even moderately glazed paper produces specular glare when the illumination is not well diffused and when the page of reading material is held at such an angle that the reflected light shines directly into the reader's eyes. This is uncomfortable and vision is impaired.

Luckiesh and Moss (161) obtained visibility measurements for print on several kinds of paper surface which varied from a dull to a fairly glossy finish. Little variation in visibility was found. They concluded that such papers, which may vary considerably in surface character, do not materially affect visibility of print if good black ink and type are used.

Thickness of paper used for printing must also be considered. Although no experimental data are available on the subject, there are sufficient reasons for employing paper of adequate thickness and opacity so that print on the back side does not show through. When print does show through, the resulting "shadows" blur the print on the front side. When the paper is lightweight or thin, these "shadows" become fairly prominent and reduce visibility of print, for quick discrimination of letters and words becomes difficult. While it may be more economical to print books and magazines on very thin paper, such practice is indefensible from the viewpoint of hygienic vision.

14   *Newspaper Typography*

Legibility of newspaper print is of concern to all of us who can read. Daily newspapers have appeal even to children of 10 or 11 and by age 12 about one out of every four school children can read most newspapers with satisfactory comprehension (reading grade about 8 to 10). Clear, easy-to-read print is especially helpful to both children and adults with less than normal vision. For older people, particularly those who use bifocals, print of maximum legibility and brighter illumination (see section on illumination) become increasingly important. The so-called "senior citizens" tend to have difficulty unless the visibility of print is more than adequate for the average reader. Note the number of elderly persons who use a magnifying glass to read a newspaper. Size of type, degree of contrast between print and paper, and satisfactory leading are the prime factors involved (see below). The reader of this book will discover in the following discussion that certain findings on legibility of book print reported in earlier chapters are also applicable to newspaper typography.

At any age, the legibility of print in newspapers influences the desire to read and the effort required to comprehend, and therefore the demand for the paper and the extent to which its readers are kept informed on topics of the day. Presumably any newspaper desires sales and also wants to become known as an important medium for communicating information. The well-read citizens are likely to become the well-informed citizens. They are, of course, essential both at local and national levels. Hence, legibility of our newspapers is of concern not only to the individual reader but also to all those who shape public policy.

The printing of newspapers involves a rather specialized application of typography, even the use of type faces specifically designed for this purpose. Problems concerning such matters as legibility of body type and headlines have stimulated research on newspaper typography. The results will be coordinated in the following discussion.

What typographical arrangements do newspapers employ? An up-to-date survey of printing practice is not available. Tinker and Paterson (332), however, surveyed newspaper printing practices among United States daily papers in 1935 (89 returns) and repeated the survey for the same papers in 1942 (87 returns). A look at the 1935 practice and at the changes that can be identified over the 7 year period, or the lack of them, will provide a useful point of departure for discussing research results.

The survey revealed that, although 22 different body types were employed from 1935 to 1942, only a few were used frequently. Ionic, Ideal, Excelsior, and Regal were the most popular body faces (77 papers). Changes during the seven years were mainly away from Ionic and Ideal to Excelsior, Regal, and Opticon.

The range in type sizes extended from 6½ to 8½ points but in most papers the print was 7, 7½, or 8 point. The principal shift by 1942 was from 7 to 8 point although 7 point was still employed by 31 papers.

Line width was more constant than other typographical factors. A 12 pica line was customary for most papers but a 12½ pica line appeared occasionally. No important changes occurred by 1942.

The amounts of leading most frequently employed were 1, ½, 0, and 2 point in that order. One point was most popular, with about a third using it. Very few papers changed leading during the 7 years.

At least up to 1942, many newspaper publishers did not utilize typography of the maximal legibility possible, as will become apparent in the following discussion of experimental findings. Too frequently newspaper publishers and editors have depended upon published claims based on casual inspection and opinion.

Newspaper Body Types

Apparently printers and editors are more interested in styles of typeface than in other typographical factors. Writers on typography devote far more space to description of typefaces and their uses than to all other typographical factors combined. Their discussions tend to emphasize appropriateness of specific typefaces for conveying particular messages, while legibility is rarely considered. We now turn to some experimental results.

Wiggins' experiment (352) led him to conclude that "slightly narrower letters in type fonts of shorter lower-case alphabet lengths increase speed of reading." Tinker and Paterson (330) investigated the relative legibility of 9 newspaper typefaces. The speed of reading technique was used with 900 college students as subjects. Test materials were printed in 7 point type set solid in a 12 pica line width on newspaper stock.* The 9 typefaces studied are listed in Table 12. The last eight were compared with the standard (Ionic No. 5) and a plus assigned to differences indicating greater legibility than the standard. In the table the typefaces are listed in order of legibility beginning with Opticon but these differences are all highly significant except for

Table 12. Relative Legibility of Certain Newspaper Typefaces

Typeface Compared with Ionic No. 5 (Standard)	Difference from Standard in Amount Read	
	No. of Paragraphs	Percentage of Material
Ionic No. 5 (control)	0.00	0.0
Opticon	+1.08	+7.8
Regal No. 1	+0.90	+6.4
Century Expanded	+0.83	+6.1
Paragon	+0.80	+5.6
Excelsior	+0.76	+5.3
Ideal	+0.66	+4.6
Ionic No. 2	+0.54	+3.9
Textype	+0.30	+2.2

* All studies by Tinker and Paterson reported in this chapter employed the speed of reading technique and newsprint paper stock.

Textype. The data reveal that Opticon and Regal No. 1 appear to have outstanding legibility. Ionic No. 5 and Textype possess relatively poor legibility. The others fall in between with fairly good legibility. Thus the most legible typefaces were not receiving greatest use in 1942 although a movement to Opticon was under way (5 papers). In fact the most commonly employed body types, Ionic and Ideal, are relatively low in legibility. It is possible that some of the body types used in 1942 are no longer popular with so many newspapers. If true, this may be unfortunate, particularly with respect to Opticon and Regal No. 1. It would be exceptional if a new body type were as legible or more legible than these two outstanding faces. Journalists should consider whether newness in a body type is as important as proven legibility.

Another typographical factor to evaluate is leading. Although about 16 per cent of newspapers set their body type solid in 1942, printing with some leading was rather common practice. One point appears to have been most popular as about one-third of the papers used it.

In 1947, Paterson and Tinker (205) studied the influence of 0, 1, 2, 3, 4, 5, 7, and 9 point leading on the legibility of 7 point Ionic No. 5 type in a 12½ pica line width. They found that all material with leading was read faster than text set solid. The 4 and 5 point leading promoted fastest reading. Interestingly enough, the 1 point leading improved legibility as much as larger amounts except for 4 and 5 points. Thus, the practice of newspapers, with the exception of those using no leading, is pretty much in line with experimental results.

When adult readers ranked samples of the printed materials in this study for relative legibility, that set solid was considered to be least legible by far. Text with 4 and 5 point leading was judged most legible while that with 2 point leading ranked fairly high. Thus readers definitely prefer some leading.

The fact that 1 point or more of leading improves legibility of newsprint and that readers uniformly prefer some leading over text set solid has practical implications. *One point or more of leading should be used for 7 point newspaper type with 12,*

12½, and 13 pica line widths. Small variations in line width do not affect legibility (205).

The findings cited just above do not necessarily hold for other sizes of type or for lines with marked differences in width. Tinker and Paterson (333), employing 2016 adult readers, studied the effect of line width and leading on the legibility of 8 point Excelsior newspaper type. Text in each of 6 line widths, 6 to 36 picas, each with 0, ½, 1, and 2 point leading was compared with the standard set in a 12 pica line width with 2 point leading (24 comparisons). Judgments of relative legibility and pleasingness were also obtained.

This 8 point newspaper type set in a 6 pica line width produces a marked loss of legibility irrespective of leading. While leading had no decided effect on legibility for the 8 point type in a 12 pica line width, the material set in an 18 pica line width with 1 and 2 point leading appeared to be slightly more legible than the standard (2 point leading, 12 pica). This finding does not agree with the results in a later study (see below). Text in longer lines (24, 30, 36 picas) was less legible than the standard whatever the leading, except that for 30 and 36 picas the text was about equal to the standard in legibility when 2 point leading was used. Thus satisfactory legibility is achieved for 8 point newspaper type in line widths of 12 to 18 picas and the 12 pica line width with 1 or 2 point leading appears to be best of all. Readers, in their ratings, considered that leading improved legibility and pleasingness for all widths of lines. Therefore, whether the line width is 12, 12½, or more picas, it seems best to use 1 or 2 point leading with 8 point type.

Wiggins (352), in a recently reported study, employed 8 point Regal body type, one of the faces of high legibility in the Tinker and Paterson study. He found that for the 8 point set solid speed of reading increased for text in 10 up to 19 pica line widths, and decreased for lines in 24 and 29 picas. He concluded that the optimum is between 14 and 24 picas. He stated that the tendency to reduce width of newspaper columns since about the time of World War I has decreased speed of reading significantly. Wiggins also found that text with even and uneven right margins was read at the same speed. These findings are not in conflict with those of Tinker and Paterson (333).

Investigators have paid relatively little attention to size of newspaper type as such. It is likely that some of the data on type size in relation to line width and leading discussed in earlier chapters are relevant. Apparently a reader makes a rapid adaptation to reading newsprint after reading materials in larger type sizes in magazines and books. But is newsprint less legible than book print?

To get an answer, Paterson and Tinker (204) investigated this problem. Popular type sizes and faces (7 and 8 point Opticon newspaper type; 10 point Cheltenham book type) of high legibility were used in an optimum typographical arrangement for each: the book type was set in a 20 pica line width with 2 point leading on eggshell paper stock; the newsprint in a 12 pica line width with 1 point leading on newsprint paper stock. Samples of the printing are given in Figure 10. With the book print serving as a standard of comparison for the newsprint, it was found that material in newsprint was read significantly slower than the book print: 4.27 per cent slower for 8 point and 4.79 per cent for 7 point.

Judgments of relative legibility by 117 readers ranked book type first, 8 point newsprint second, and 7 point a poor third. But the difference between the 10 point book print and the 8 point newsprint was not significant statistically. Rankings for pleasingness were in the same order as for legibility but there was a larger separation between successive average ranks. These findings suggest that at least 8 point type should be employed in newspaper printing. Factors which apparently account for poorer legibility of newsprint in comparison with book type are the smaller size of the newsprint and the lesser contrast in brightness between print and paper for the newsprint. These two factors reduce ability to discriminate quickly the printed characters in newsprint.

The deterioration in the course of time of most newspaper stock and limitations of library space have led to a serious problem for those who are concerned with preserving important

174

Cheltenham Book Type:
10 point with two point leading

26. James' fountain pen went dry when he was doing his homework for school. He was very cross because until he got some more glue he could not continue his work. 27. The boys saw coming towards them an old woman, bent with sorrow, dressed in deepest black. They thought, turning from their play to watch her pass, how happy she looked. 28. On

Opticon Newsprint:
8 point with one point leading

26. James' fountain pen went dry when he was doing his homework for school. He was very cross because until he got some more glue he could not continue his work. 27. The boys saw coming towards them an old woman, bent with sorrow, dressed in deepest black. They thought, turning from their play to watch her pass, how happy she looked. 28. On

Ionic No. 5 Newsprint:
7 point with one point leading

26. James' fountain pen went dry when he was doing his homework for school. He was very cross because until he got some more glue he could not continue his work. 27. The boys saw coming towards them an old woman, bent with sorrow, dressed in deepest black. They thought, turning from their play to watch her pass, how happy she looked. 28. On Sunday Mr.

Figure 10. Samples of book type and newsprint type compared for relative legibility. Adapted from Tinker (317).

175

newspaper accounts. Considerable use of the planographic off-set-printing process has been made in order to reduce newspaper material for easier storage. To discover how much newsprint can be reduced without undue loss of legibility, Tinker and Paterson (324) measured speed of reading when this offset-printing process was used. The original size (6¾ point on 7 point body in a 12½ pica line width) was compared with reductions to 80, 50, and 30 per cent. There was no loss in speed at 80 per cent, a 12.3 per cent loss at 50 per cent, and a 74.3 per cent loss when size was reduced to 30 per cent of the original. The last was almost impossible to read. It was concluded that, from the practical point of view, newsprint should not be reduced more than 50 per cent. Although 235 words per minute can be read at this level, it is probable that reading for an hour or more without some magnification would produce severe eyestrain.

In two studies (127, 128) Hovde attempted to measure by speed of reading the influence of type size, leading, and context (i.e., verbal meaning of printed materials) on legibility of Intertype Ideal typeface. Size of type and leading varied by small steps from 6 to 8 point and 0 to 1 point respectively. The 16 samples of printed material were estimated to be of equal difficulty. A normal rate of reading was employed. Hovde concluded that context is more important in determining legibility of type than type size or leading under his experimental conditions. The validity of these conclusions may be questioned since, in the first place, the reading samples were not objectively equated for difficulty, and second, significant legibility differences are easily obscured during reading at a "normal" rate, especially when the emphasis is entirely upon meaning as occurred here. Furthermore, he calls correlation coefficients percentages, which is erroneous. It is noteworthy that Hovde's readers preferred the larger type sizes and the print with the greatest amount of leading.

As noted in earlier chapters, typographical factors must be varied simultaneously to arrive at arrangements that are as legible as possible. With this in mind, Tinker (318) compared nine different setups with an optimum standard which consisted of text printed in 8 point Excelsior typeface with 2 point leading in a 12 pica line width. The results revealed the following:

Equally Legible Arrangements	Arrangements Significantly Less Legible Than the Standard
8 point, 12 pica, 2 point leading	9 point, 43 pica, set solid
9 point, 12 pica, 2 point leading	8 point, 18 pica, 2 point leading
7 point, 12 pica, 1 point leading	7 point, 6 pica, set solid
7 point, 12 pica, 2 point leading	6 point, 6 pica, set solid
	6 point, 12 pica, 2 point leading

In addition, reader preferences were obtained in this investigation. The judgments of relative legibility and pleasingness agreed with each other and very well with measured legibility except that readers do not like 7 point type even with leading. Apparently readers made their choices in terms of type size, leading, and line width. They like the larger type sizes, generous leading (2 point), and moderate line widths.

These data on legibility and readers' opinions furnish the newspaper publisher with valuable and practical information. *If he desires to cater to reader preferences and at the same time maintain maximal legibility, he will employ in his printing 8 or 9 point type in a line width of 12 or 12½ picas with 2 point leading.* Since readers do not like newsprint in 7 point type, it should be avoided.

Newspaper Headlines

Newspaper publishers, editors, psychologists, and journalists have not agreed on whether newspaper headlines printed in all-capital letters or those in lower case with only the initial letters of the important words capitalized produce the greater legibility. In 1928, Tinker and Paterson (321) had demonstrated that adults read continuous text printed in all capitals about 12 per cent slower than text in lower case. But printers and editors argued that this finding could not apply to newspaper headlines. Experimentation must resolve the problem.

In an initial experiment, Breland and Breland (29) compared the legibility of single-column newspaper headlines printed in all capitals and in lower case with only initial letters

177

of the important words capitalized. They selected 120 five-word single-column headlines of uniform length from the *New York Times*. These headlines were printed in 24 point Cheltenham boldface extra-condensed type in two lines on newspaper stock. Each of the 120 headlines was printed in all capitals and in lower case. Then the investigators mounted the headlines on cardboard of proper size to be exposed singly for a short controlled period of 1/20 second. The exposed material was 15 inches from the subject's eyes. Practice effects were controlled by presenting the two kinds of headlines in a counterbalanced order. There were 22 subjects. The results revealed an 18.9 per cent loss in legibility in reading the all-capital headlines in comparison with the lower case. Thus lower-case single-column headlines, viewed at the normal reading distance, were significantly more legible than the all-capital headlines.

Are these single-column headlines in the lower case also more legible than in all capitals when viewed at a distance? Paterson and Tinker (203) cite an unpublished study (Warren's thesis) of single-column headlines viewed for ⅓ second at a distance of 5½ feet, i.e., about the distance for reading a headline across a table or over another person's shoulder. The same headlines and short exposure apparatus employed by Breland and Breland were used. Forty college students were subjects. Under the conditions of the experiment, no difference was found between the two kinds of print. From the viewpoint of the headline writer, therefore, neither all capitals nor lower case has an advantage in legibility for single column headlines when they are viewed at a distance of 5½ feet.

Multi-column or banner newspaper headlines are intended to be read at some distance. In the second part of the Warren study cited above, the relative legibility of all-capital versus lower-case printing in banner headlines was determined. In a carefully controlled experiment, 5 word headlines printed in 60 point Memphis Bold were viewed by 46 subjects in a group testing situation. At 6 to 8 feet distance, lower-case headlines were significantly more legible. In everyday life situations, as in walking past a newstand on the street or in a store, this is approximately the distance at which one would catch momentary sight of a banner headline. It is doubtful if publishers expect people to read their multi-column headlines from much more than 7 feet away. At about 11 and 14 feet the all capitals were slightly but not significantly more legible. There was a significant difference in favor of the all capitals at 17 feet. However, at 17 feet, the headlines had become quite difficult to read and only an occasional word was identified. Because the capital letters are larger and hence easier to identify, this facilitated correct reading of a few more all-capital words at the greater viewing distances.

The data in these studies are not in conflict when customary reading situations are considered. In single-column headlines, lower-case printing is markedly superior to all capitals in legibility at the normal reading distance of 15 inches. Although the same headlines are equally legible in the two kinds of printing at 5½ feet, single-column headlines are not intended to be read that far away. And banner headlines, designed to be read at not more than 6 to 7 feet away, are more legible printed in lower case. It seems clear, therefore, that *in the situations where single-column and banner headlines are normally expected to be read*, the headlines printed in lower case are distinctly more legible than those in all capitals.

Similar results were reported for single-column headlines by English (69). He found lower-case printing to be far superior to all capitals in legibility when read at 14 inches from the eyes. English also found that Bodoni and Tempo type faces were equally legible and both were significantly more legible than Karnack when used in headlines.

All experimental results reported in the literature are consistent since they reveal that newspaper headlines, single column or multiple column, read at customary distances from the eyes, are markedly and significantly more legible in lower case than in all capitals. This superior legibility of the lower-case print depends upon at least three factors:

Whenever words possess characteristic word form or shape, they tend to be read as units rather than by parts or letter by letter. Such word form is far more striking in lower-case print than in all capitals. See Figure 8 and the accompanying discussion of word form as a factor in legibility of print in Chapter 11.

All-capital printing requires much more printing surface than lower case in the same point size. Thus a 60 point banner headline is about 38 per cent longer in the upper case printing. This alone requires more fixation pauses and consequently a longer reading time than for the same headline in lower case.

Nearly all material one reads is printed in lower case. Reading habits, therefore, should favor the more familiar kind of print.

It should be perfectly clear from the discussion above that, if the printer is concerned with maintaining good headline legibility, he should abandon all-capital printing except for an occasional use to attract attention through novelty. This is relevant not only for headlines but also for the practice of interspersing all-capital printing of words, phrases, and sentences within paragraphs (see Chapter 11).

Two points of prime importance to newspaper publishers emerge from the experimental results surveyed in this chapter: From the practical viewpoint, newsprint set in 8 or 9 point body type in a 12 to 12½ pica line width with 2 point leading and with any one of several typefaces will maintain a high level of legibility and satisfy reader preferences. And since both single-column headlines and banner or multi-column headlines are more legible in lower-case than in upper-case letters, all headlines should be printed in lower case.

15 *Spatial Arrangement and Position of the Printed Page*

Reports of experimental work on spatial arrangement of the printed page began to appear in 1940. Before this time there was a general absence of consensus in advice based on casual observation and inference as shown by Pyke's summary (213) published in 1926. Conflicting suggestions were offered on such problems as whether lines should be indented at the right side of the page, how wide margins should be, and how much inter-column space should be used.

Page Size and Margins

Paterson and Tinker (197) reported a survey of printing practice with regard to size of the full page of publications to discover whether or not there was agreement among publishers and printers. If practice is based upon some uniform set of principles that have proved to be of lasting value in terms of esthetics, convenience, or economics, there should be general agreement in usage. In the survey, published in 1940, the page sizes of 1500 journals and college textbooks were measured. Although there was some concentration in rather broad groupings for each kind of journal and for the textbooks, the range for height and width of pages was relatively large (for details, see Tinker, 317). This diversity of practice suggests that it might be desirable for publishers, printers, and paper manufacturers to arrive at an agreement on page sizes that would minimize waste of paper stock.

In this same survey, it was discovered that there was as great diversity of practice in the size of the printed page as in the size of the full page. Obviously, the area of the printed page is co-ordinated with that of the full page.

Widths of the four margins on a page were also measured in the survey. Pyke notes in his summary that Jacobi in 1912 argued that the inside or gutter margin should be narrow, the top margin should be next in width, the outer margin next, and the bottom margin the widest. Although somewhat vague about total page size, style manuals tend to assert that the area occupied by the type should cover 50 per cent of the total page.

Measurements of printed area and page size in 400 college textbooks revealed the following proportional range: from 29 per cent print and 71 per cent margins to 76 per cent print and 24 per cent margins. In the average book, the printed area occupied about 52.8 per cent of the page and the margins 47.2. Thus, on the average, printers follow closely the principle that 50 per cent of a page be reserved for margins.

Readers overestimate the area of print on a page. When 928 college students made this judgment, over 90 per cent believed that 60 per cent or more of the total page is devoted to printed matter. The modal (most frequent) estimate was about 75 per cent. Thus there is about 25 per cent overestimation of the actual amount of print customarily found on a page. With a carefully controlled psychophysical design, Paterson and Tinker (196) tested experimentally the existence of an illusion effect to explain this overestimation. The stimulus material consisted of cards: one series had black centers on white backgrounds; the other had white centers on black backgrounds. The centers represented printed areas and the backgrounds, the margins. The 300 subjects, on the average, overestimated the center areas (analogous to the printed area on a page) in relation to total page areas by 18 per cent. It made no difference whether the central area of the page was black on white or white on black. This demonstrates the "illusion" effect that undoubtedly influences a reader's judgment as to what portion of a book page is devoted to print. After being informed that the general practice of publishers is to use 50 per cent of a page for margins, about two-thirds of the readers believed the practice was justified because it was necessary to promote legibility, while 27 per cent approved on esthetic grounds, and 2 per cent because of tradition. Only 9 per cent stated that the practice was not justified because the extra paper for margins increases the cost of books. The strong belief that generous margins will increase legibility agrees with the opinions of most "experts" expressed between 1883 and 1911 (213). Only one of these authors insisted that margins are superfluous.

While there is an "average" consensus, printing practice in use of margins in individual books varies greatly (197). Whether this is motivated by an attempt to produce a more pleasing page or by an unconscious departure from the 50 per cent rule, or both, is uncertain. However, some trends in usage are evident. In general, printers and publishers showed an inclination to make the bottom margin widest, the top margin next widest, and the inside and outside margins narrowest with the inside one slightly the wider of the two.

As noted above, certain authors insist that margins at the right and left are necessary to promote legibility of the printed material. Paterson and Tinker (197) put this view to experimental test by comparing results on speed of reading material with no side margins and those on material with ⅞ inch margins at right and left of the printed lines. No significant difference appeared. They concluded that margins as such do not promote legibility. Obviously, margins on a flat page must be justified, if at all, solely in terms of esthetics.

Another experiment by Tinker (311) has a bearing on appropriate width of gutter margins. Two reading stands were employed: a flat surface maintained at 45 degrees to the table top and an 8 inch cylinder which was set in three positions, slanted 45 degrees down from the vertical, at 90 degrees down or horizontal, and at the vertical or upright. Speed of reading and visibility of words were recorded for material on the flat surface held constant at 45 degrees in comparison with the three positions on the curved surface. The results were consistent. There was significantly reduced legibility for the curved text in all three positions in comparison with the flat material. Likewise, visibility of curved print was markedly poorer. In all comparisons, the deleterious effects of the curved surface were large. Apparently the reduction in reading speed for the curved text was due chiefly to reduced visibility of the print.

These results have a practical application. Curvature of the text as used in this experiment was a close approximation to that found on the pages of large books and bound journals when they are open. The marked curvature of lines of print near the inner or gutter margin of such volumes without doubt adversely affects legibility. The situation would be greatly improved by the use of much wider gutter margins. Therefore, the practice of employing narrow gutter margins in printing large books and journals should be modified.

Arrangement of Columns

Any survey will reveal that nonscientific magazines, scientific journals, and even some books are using multiple-column printing, especially a double-column arrangement. In multiple-column printing, legibility depends upon the same factors as single-column printing. These have been discussed in earlier chapters. However, reader preferences are also involved.

Paterson and Tinker (197) submitted samples of single- and double-column printing to 241 college students. The samples were taken from a psychological journal, one page from an issue with single-column printing, and one page from a later issue with double-column composition. Each subject examined the samples placed side by side and decided which printing arrangement he would prefer to read. The results showed that 60.5 per cent of the group preferred the double-column arrangement. Interestingly enough, a group of typography experts and printers gave precisely the same judgment, i.e., 60.5 per cent preferred the double arrangement. These results from general readers and from typography experts seem to justify the increasing trend toward double-column printing in both journals and books. Furthermore, there are important practical reasons for using double-column printing in scientific journals and textbooks.

These include economy in use of paper and in the arrangement of tables and formulas (317).

When multiple-column printing is used, the printer or publisher must decide whether to employ a space, a rule, or both between columns. Newspapers ordinarily use intercolumnar rules, while magazines and scientific journals generally use space (1 pica usually) without rules. Does the intercolumnar arrangement affect legibility of the print on a page? How wide should the space between columns be? If a rule is used, should there be some space on each side of the rule?

The report by Paterson and Tinker (197) answers these questions. Text was set with the following intercolumnar arrangements: ½ pica space, 1 pica, 2 pica, rule with ½ pica space on each side, rule with ¼ pica on each side, rule without space. No significant differences in speed of reading were discovered. In other words, all the intercolumnar arrangements of text are equally legible. But readers do have decided preferences. Samples of the arrangements used here were ranked by 224 subjects according to judgments of relative legibility. The results are given in Table 13. A rule with ½ pica space on each side is judged to yield the best legibility. But a 2 pica and a 1 pica space follow closely in preference and probably the differences are not significant. It is clear that readers do not like a narrow space (½ pica) either with or without a rule. A rule with no space is distinctly disliked. Newspapers which employ this last arrangement to save a bit of paper should take note. For instance, the ordinary paper which now employs a rule with no space could improve its apparent legibility greatly with no increase in page

Table 13. Reader Preferences for Intercolumnar Arrangements

Space and Rules between Columns	Average Rank	Rank Order
½ pica space	4.5	5
1 pica space	2.7	3
2 pica space	2.5	2
Rule with ½ pica space on each side	2.1	1
Rule with ¼ pica space on each side	3.8	4
Rule with no space	5.4	6

width by using a rule with ¼ pica on each side. The ⅝ inch used for this could be taken from the side margins, part from each side.

Other Factors

Printed material is organized mechanically into separate "thought units" by indenting the beginning of the first line of every paragraph, i.e., regular indentation. Other lines in the paragraph are flush. Does this practice affect speed of reading? Paterson and Tinker (197) were able to check this. In some of their studies each form of the test material consisted of 30 short paragraphs of 30 words each. In others, it was necessary to rearrange the page composition so as to approximate the usual appearance of paragraphing of a printed page. This was done by combining 5 of the short 30 word paragraphs into a given "paragraph composition unit." This produced a 6 unit printing arrangement for each test form that looked like 6 paragraphs although the same 30 "thought units" were retained. In this new arrangement, the equivalence of the test forms was maintained and the reliability remained high. The speed of reading material in the 6 unit printing arrangement was 7.3 per cent slower than for the 30 paragraph arrangement. This finding indicates that indentation at the beginning of a paragraph in good writing improves legibility by a significant amount.

In his 1906 report, Dearborn (58) suggested that legibility might be improved by indenting every other line at the left. He considered that such an indentation of a few millimeters would increase the accuracy with which the eyes would fixate the beginning of each succeeding line on the return sweep from the end of the preceding line. Huey (131) considered the suggestion to be sound.

Paterson and Tinker (197) reported a study to ascertain what effect indenting alternate lines within paragraphs by 1 pica has on legibility. All material was set solid in a 19 pica line. In comparison with regular paragraphing, the indented material was read 3.4 per cent slower. This is a statistically significant (2 per cent level) retardation. The wisdom of the current practice, in which all lines at the left of a paragraph, except the first, are printed flush is confirmed by these results. But, as noted in Chapter 14, Wiggins (352) found that text printed with uneven right margins was read at the same rate as that with even right margins.

Is it possible that a vertical arrangement of words printed in columns might produce a more efficient typographical arrangement than the traditional horizontal arrangement in lines? Hucy (129) argued that a vertical arrangement should prove more efficient owing to elimination of practically all horizontal eye movements during reading. He also pointed out that use of the vertical as well as the horizontal span (extent) of vision should make it possible to have more words in clear vision during any fixation pause. Some support for his view was obtained by Huey in preliminary experimenting. He suggested that with practice the vertical arrangement might eventually be read faster.

Tinker (308) investigated the effect of a limited period of systematic, controlled practice in reading vertical materials upon speed of reading and patterns of eye movements. After practice extending over six weeks, there was a marked improvement in eye movements and speed of reading the vertical material, but no change for the horizontal. At the end of practice, on the average, the vertical reading was significantly less efficient than the horizontal. However, one of the 10 subjects was reading the vertical arrangement faster and two others were only slightly slower than for the horizontal.

Even if practice could develop faster reading of printed material when words are arranged in vertical columns, there are important obstacles to such a typography: traditional practice; the marked variation in length of English words; lack of knowledge concerning optimal typographical arrangements for words in columns; and the possibly greater difficulty and cost of linotype printing of words in columns. Thus the efficiency of vertically arranged printing is apt to remain a matter of theoretical interest.

A compromise between the vertical and horizontal arrangements is to print material in double-line blocks, such as the following:

Sue	the children	to come	cake and
asked	she knew	and eat	ice cream.

With such an arrangement, the reader should be able to utilize both the vertical and horizontal vision and in this way improve speed and comprehension. Only one fixation should be needed for reading each block of words. If such an assumed advantage were due to grouping the words into thought units, which is necessary for efficient and quick comprehension, the same results might be obtained by spacing regular printing into thought units in the following manner:

Sue asked　　the children she knew　　to come and eat

In an unpublished investigation by the writer, speed of reading material was organized in three ways: regular printing; double-line blocks; separated into thought units by insertion of additional space in regular printing. Comprehension was checked and was close to 100 per cent. Sixty college students (i.e., mature readers) were subjects. Practice effects were controlled by having the material read in a counterbalanced order. The results revealed no significant difference in legibility between regular printing and the material separated into thought units by additional spacing. But the material printed in double-line blocks was read 12 per cent slower than the regular printing arrangement. Apparently the square block printing is much less legible than ordinary printing, at least for readers not experienced in reading print organized in this manner. Using a different experimental design, North and Jenkins (191) discovered no difference in speed of reading text in the double-line block arrangement and regular printing but a slight advantage for material separated into thought units.

Position of the Printed Page

There is marked variation in the way people hold a book, magazine, or newspaper while reading. When a page is flat and is at a right angle or perpendicular to the line of sight, letters are seen in their exact form. As the page is tipped downward and away from this perpendicular alignment, visual perception of letter forms and words becomes distorted more and more. For the reader who is sitting up straight, the normal and comfortable line of vision is perpendicular to the plane of the copy when the latter is sloped about 45 degrees up from the table top or down from the vertical. Consequently there is considerable distortion of letter forms when the material is lying flat on a table or desk, i.e., 90 degrees from the vertical. This probably reduces the legibility of the printed material.

Tinker (309) measured the influence of sloped text on legibility in terms of speed of reading and visibility of words for both 10 and 8 point type. It was determined that both speed of reading and visibility of printed words were most efficient when the copy was at a right angle to the line of vision, i.e., when the reading material was at 45 degrees down from the vertical. As the text was placed flat on the table (90 degrees) and then slightly below this horizontal position, speed and visibility became progressively worse by large and significant amounts. The conclusion follows that when material is lying flat on a table top or other horizontal plane and the reader is sitting approximately upright, there is a significant loss of legibility in comparison with reading print slanted at about a 45 degree angle from the vertical.

Since many readers, children and adults, tend to read printed material held somewhere between a flat position of 90 degrees and that of 45 degrees from the vertical, it would be useful to know how far the copy can depart from the 45 degree position without significant loss of legibility. Tinker in an unpublished report had his subjects read material at 45, 60, 75, and 90 degrees from the vertical. The data show a definite trend. As the copy was sloped downward by successive steps of 15 degrees each from the 45 degree position, the deleterious effects became greater and greater by significant amounts. Visibility scores showed the same trend.

The results of these two experiments have important implications for schools, libraries, the home, and other situations where reading is done. Reading copy should be maintained at about 45 degrees down from the vertical (the same as 45 degrees up from the horizontal). A few schools have sloping desk tops but the slope is not nearly as much as 45 degrees. A deviation of as little as 15 degrees below this reduces legibility somewhat. In any case, students and other readers should be encouraged to sit fairly straight and to hold their books up from the horizontal at an angle of about 45 degrees. Inexpensive book racks are now available that support books at this angle and are being used in some schools and homes.

When material is held so that the printed lines are perpendicular to the median plane of the body, eye movements in reading are relatively uncomplicated. But when the copy is rotated (like a wheel on its axis) to the right or the left so that the printed lines run obliquely downward or upward, the oculomotor adjustments in reading become more complex, for the eyes have to move obliquely from one fixation pause to another. Such adjustments are intricate and relatively difficult to make in comparison with simple right and left horizontal movements. Furthermore, as the printed material is rotated, word forms are in an unfamiliar orientation.

The alignment of printed lines departs from the horizontal position in many reading situations, as when a book is lying flat on a table or desk and the reader is taking notes. Practical considerations of title length and type size require that many backbone titles of books and magazines be printed in vertical alignment. Some are printed upward, some downward. Any complication that interferes with smooth eye movements or visibility and hence with rapid perception may reduce legibility. Tinker (310) measured speed of reading and visibility of words in various angular alignments: horizontal (standard), 45 degrees clockwise, 90 degrees read down, 45 degrees counterclockwise, 90 degrees read up. Speed of reading was retarded approximately 40 per cent at a 45 degree rotation in either direction and by about 160 per cent for reading upward or downward. Visibility was also less efficient by significant amounts on rotation of the text: about 11 per cent in the 45 degree positions and 20 per cent in the up or down orientation. Any considerable deviation from the horizontal alignment, therefore, reduces legibility by large amounts. Reading obliquely from lower left to upper right and from upper left to lower right is equally difficult. And reading vertically up or down is also equally difficult. Probably, slower speed of reading when the alignment deviates from the horizontal is produced not only by the reduced visability but also by unfamiliar orientation of word shapes and inability to make effective use of clues in peripheral vision, as well as the increased complexity of the eye movements required. These findings are sufficiently impressive so that it is advisable for all readers to maintain the lines of print approximately horizontal left to right and perpendicular to the median plane of the body. Further research is needed to determine just how much deviation from this horizontal alignment can take place without loss of legibility.

Those who attempt to read while riding on a train or bus are fully aware of the annoying vibration of their reading material. Subjectively it seems to be the blurring due to the vibration that makes reading difficult. In his first experiment on this problem, Tinker (296) investigated the effect of vibration approximately like that on a fast moving train upon the reading of 10 point type. The vibration retarded speed of reading about 5 per cent. In another study, Tinker (302) compared speed of reading 6 point Roman and 6 point italic type with and without vibration to speed of reading 10 point type without vibration. Each type size was printed in an optimal typographical arrangement for that size of type. With no vibration, the 6 point Roman type was read 8.49 per cent slower than the 10 point. When the 6 point Roman text was vibrating, retardation in speed was 10.99 per cent. And when the 6 point italic print was vibrating, the loss in speed was 14.21 per cent. Thus the effect of combining nonoptimal conditions, i.e., small type, italics, and vibration, appears to be cumulative in reducing speed of reading. In general, vibrating printed material is difficult to read and this difficulty is greatly increased when reading nonoptimal typographical arrangements.

16 *Special Typographical Arrangements*

In addition to the typographical arrangements considered in earlier chapters, there are numerous special printing situations. Some of this special printing is read like books, some quite differently. A host of research reports have dealt with print or writing used in these situations.

Numerals, Formulas, and Mathematical Tables

The legibility of numerals requires consideration of several related problems: relative legibility of the digits; Modern versus Old Style digits; reading of numbers grouped in mathematical tables; numbers and other symbols in formulas; Roman versus Arabic numerals; and others.

Tinker (303) notes that Babbage, writing in 1827, considered that numerals of uniform height (Modern) rather than those with ascenders and descenders (Old Style) are more legible. After collecting opinions, the Committee on Type Faces (221) recommended in 1922 that Modern, or modernized Old Style, numerals (without ascenders and descenders) be used in mathematical tables, that type size should be up to 8 point (presumably 6 or 8 point), and that there should be adequate space inserted after every fifth row. But Milne (185), in 1915, stated that Old Style numerical symbols, in which many of the digits have heads or tails, are more legible than those of uniform height (Modern).

Employing the distance method, Tinker (273) determined the perceptibility of 10 point digits in Modern and in Old Style type. The order of perceptibility from most to least legible follows:

Modern (isolation) 7	4	1	6	9	0	3	2	8	5
Old Style (isolation) 7	4	6	0	1	9	3	5	2	8
Modern (groups) 7	1	4	0	2	9	8	5	6	3
Old Style (groups) 8	7	6	1	9	4	0	5	3	2

The rankings of Modern and Old Style digits for relative legibility are more nearly alike when viewed in isolation than when in groups. Although there was little advantage in perceptibility for Old Style numbers in isolation, the advantage was marked when they appeared in groups. However, there was no appreciable difference between Modern and Old Style typefaces in the speed and accuracy of reading numbers in groups. In a normal reading situation, therefore, differences in legibility between these two typefaces are unimportant. This is confirmed in a later study of mathematical tables (see below). Apparently it is universal practice to employ Modern numerals in mathematical formulas. This is fortunate, especially in the case of exponents and subscripts which are printed in small type size. The Old Style digits 0, 1, and 2 are quite small and the 1 is relatively illegible. In studying the effect of form in the legibility of digits of a size employed in much printing, Soar (246) found that the numbers most readily perceived have a height-width ratio of 10 to 7.5 and a stroke width to height ratio of 1 to 10. Actually, as noted by Tinker (270) most of the digits fall within the group of lower-case letters having fair legibility.

Presumably Roman numerals are more difficult to read rapidly than Arabic. Apparently this is due to interpretation rather than to visibility of the symbols. The ordinary reader has little experience with Roman numerals and such numerals are relatively cumbersome and complex, as XXXVII versus 37. In his report, Perry (206) shows that the Arabic numerals are read significantly faster and more accurately than the Roman. And the differences increased greatly as the numerals became larger. Obviously, Arabic rather than Roman numerals, because of their greater "legibility," should be employed for most purposes, such as volume and table numbers in magazines and journals; chapter numbers in books and in the indexes; dates of historical events in certain books and documents; and dates on the title pages of books.

As pointed out by Terry (262), numerals are more difficult to read than words. This is so because words are read as familiar wholes while numerals are perceived pretty much digit by digit. He found that as many as 5 fixation pauses were employed to read a 7 digit numeral. The straightforward progress in reading breaks down when a numeral of more than one or two digits is encountered in context. Nevertheless, Tinker (267) found that arithmetical problems with Arabic numerals were read faster and with fewer fixations than when the numbers were printed as words. Apparently the compactness achieved by employing numbers as numerals rather than words produced the faster reading. For instance, note 36,864 versus thirty-six thousand eight hundred and sixty-four.

Symbols employed in formulas and equations involve letters, numerals, and mathematical signs. Employing a short exposure method, Tinker (268) found that there is a tendency toward configuration in reading formulas. That is, there occurs some subjective grouping so that combinations of symbols and mathematical signs are frequently grouped as units rather than read as separate items. Nearly twice as many items in formulas as in letter series were perceived correctly at a glance. In another experiment, Tinker (266) discovered that the principal factors affecting legibility of characters in formulas were size of symbol, alignment of characters (fractions, exponents, and subscripts), and the relative legibility of letters selected for symbols. Confirmation of these results was obtained by Tinker (271) in a further experiment. In addition, he discovered that reading algebra and chemical formulas in context increased perceptual difficulties in comparison with the rest of the text.

Inspection of mathematical tables as they appear in numerous publications will reveal marked variation in type size, typefaces, grouping of numerals down columns, space and rules between columns, and arrangement of column headings. Some of these factors may well affect legibility of the tables. Too frequently, economy of space seems to be the sole consideration in the typographical arrangements used.

Two investigations of legibility of mathematical tables are now available. In the first study by Tinker (303), the time taken to find squares, square roots, and cube roots in 5 different printed tables was recorded. The results indicated that in these tables Old Style and Modern typefaces are equally legible; numerals in 8 point are more legible than those in 6 point; separation of entries down a column in groups of 5 or 10 items promotes legibility; a 1 pica space between columns seems better than a rule; paper of low reflectance and so thin that print on the reverse side shows through reduces legibility. In a more carefully controlled experiment, Tinker (316) had tabular material printed according to specifications. The findings indicated that grouping numerals in columns by fives or by tens promotes quick finding of powers and roots; in general, the grouping by fives tends to be more effective than grouping by tens for both 6 and 8 point type; when numerals were grouped by fives in columns, the advantage in locating a numeral was always with the 8 point, but the differences were not statistically significant; apparently it makes little difference whether 1 pica space or 1 pica space plus a rule between columns is used in tables of powers and roots.

Other suggestions which should promote legibility of mathematical tables include the following: use of boldface printing in the first column in which the base numbers are listed; choice of opaque, mat white paper; avoidance of an excessive number of columns in a single table, i.e., avoid including reciprocals, areas, etc., in addition to squares, square roots, cubes, and cube roots. (For details of methodology and results, see Tinker, 317.)

Other Special Typographical Arrangements

In addition to the special situations considered above, legibility research has dealt with such materials as typewritten text, stencil-duplicated copy, dictionaries, telephone directories, and timetables.

In investigating the legibility of typewritten material by a speed of reading technique, Greene (108) found that texts in 7, 10, 12, and 14 point type printed in a 41.5 pica line width were equally legible. His leading experiment used only 10 and 7 point type, each in 41.5 and 21 pica lines. The leaded print (3 point for 10 point type and 1.2 point for 7 point type) was considerably more legible, especially that in the long lines. And although the 21 pica line width was rather consistently read faster than the text in a 41.5 pica line width, the differences were not significant. All of Greene's findings cannot be applied to typewriter print in general because the line widths used are not typical of typewriter material.

In Bell's investigation (15), typewriting was found to be more legible than manuscript or cursive script, and manuscript was more legible than cursive script in the meaningful prose specimens. But typewritten letters and nonsense syllables were found to be less legible than cursive script. These results, as noted in an earlier chapter, emphasize the need for caution in inferring legibility of print in connected material, such as sentences and paragraphs, from the legibility of single letters or letters in nonsense arrangement. In his second study, Bell (16) obtained conflicting results. He suggests that the earlier investigation, in which easy prose was employed, yielded a truer picture of the relative legibility of typewriting, manuscript, and cursive script.

It is important that stencil-duplicated materials be of good quality. Luckiesh and Moss (163) measured visibility and speed of reading average (the printed sample appears to be of poor quality) and superior grades of stencil-duplicated materials. The average quality of duplication was only about 70 per cent as visible as the superior quality, and it was read 6 per cent slower than the superior.

Even casual observation reveals that reading printed material in the ordinary comic book is a severe visual task. Luckiesh and Moss (168) have compared the visibility of 12 point Bodoni type with print (lettering) used in comic books of average and superior quality. When the visibility of the 12 point Bodoni type is set at 100 per cent, that for the print in the average run-of-the-mill comics was 36 per cent and for the superior comics 74 per cent. Tinker (288) has evaluated the factors which determine legibility of print in comic books. He calls attention to the unfortunate practice of using all-capital printing (lettering) in the large majority of comics. As noted in an earlier chapter, material in all capitals reduces legibility by a large amount. When all-capital lettering is combined with small size of print and small brightness contrast between print and paper, as frequently happens, the visual task of the reader is severe indeed. A marked improvement in the legibility of comic books could be achieved by employing well-drawn lower-case lettering of adequate size on white paper of good quality. This lower case lettering is like engineering lettering or manuscript writing, or like serifless type such as Kabel Light.

The visual task in reading projected material depends upon the nature of the projection. When microfilm was enlarged and projected onto a white surface so that the print was about book size or the size of the original print, Carmichael and Dearborn (45) found no significant decrement in six hours of reading the projected microfilm material in comparison to reading book print. But when the microfilm is projected onto the ceiling for bed patients to read, the situation is different, for then the projected material is rather large. Anderson and Meredith (7) had 20 subjects read from a book for two hours and at another session read the microfilm material from the same book projected onto the ceiling. The projected material was read 12.8 per cent slower than the book print. They concluded that, although projected materials are read more slowly than materials in good book print, they may be used for bedridden patients without undue visual fatigue. The reading of such projected text is facilitated if there is no surrounding light in the room.

Practice in printing dictionary materials varies. Glanville, Kreezer, and Dallenbach (98) investigated the relative legibility of two of the typographical arrangements commonly employed in printing dictionaries. In one, the dictionary vocabulary words were printed in 6 point boldface lower-case type and the accompanying text in ordinary 6 point Roman lower case.

Vocabulary words in the other were set in 12 point boldface lower case and the text in 6 point ordinary Roman lower case. Materials were taken directly from published dictionaries. They found that the perceptibility (short exposure method) of the 12 point words was 43 to 47 per cent better than the 6 point. But when the exposure time was increased from 60 to 210 milliseconds, the advantage for the 12 point type was only about 7 to 10 per cent. Although the times taken to locate the words in 6 point boldface were not markedly greater than for the words in 12 point, the differences were statistically significant for both children and adult subjects. And a large majority of both the adults and children chose the larger type as easier to use, as the preferred one to use, and as having a more pleasing appearance. Thus the results indicate that the dictionary words in 12 point boldface type can be perceived more accurately, located faster, and are strongly preferred. Publishers of dictionaries should take account of these findings in their publications.

The identifying key to items in bibliographies tends to vary in print; the following are common forms: 1904a; 1904 a; 1904ᵃ; 1904 ᵃ; 1904.1. Pratt (209) investigated the relative legibility of these arrangements and found that items printed like 1904 ᵃ were most legible, i.e., with the letter suffix above the line and separated from the date by a space. The other four arrangements were considerably poorer.

The enormous number of listings in the telephone directory of a large city presents serious legibility problems of a practical nature. The degree to which such a directory can be condensed and at the same time be legible enough to ensure the greatest possible accuracy of reading is of considerable importance. Baird's experiment (12) tackled this problem for the New York City Telephone Company in 1917. He compared four arrangements of the printed page. All printing was 6 point, names were capitalized, and the exchange name and telephone number were in boldface. He found that arrangements of 3 and 4 columns set solid were equally poor. Slight indentation of alternate lines at the left increased legibility about 5 per cent, and use of 1 point leading between entries in the 4 column page improved legibility about 13 per cent. This last arrangement was adopted by the telephone company. The new arrangement was not only more legible but, because of the increase from 3 to 4 column printing, the bulk of the directory was about 20 per cent less, a decrease of approximately 200 pages. In a later report, Lyon (171) claimed that 1 point leading produced no appreciable gain in legibility of telephone directories printed in 6 or 7 point type. Information on the experimental design is lacking in Lyon's study. It seems strange that 1 point leading has no effect on legibility of a telephone directory (on paper similar to that used in newspapers) since it does improve the legibility of 7 point newsprint significantly. In any case, the reader or user of telephone directories and other printed materials prefers some leading because the printing then looks more legible. The general practice in most contemporary telephone directories is to use some leading, such as ¾ to 1 point.

Library workers using the *Library of Congress Catalog of Printed Cards* reproduced in book form by the photolithoprint process judged the reproduced material to have unsatisfactory legibility. The main sources of difficulty in reading the reproduced cards appeared to be the marked reduction in type size, blurring of the print, and reduced brightness contrast between print and background. Bryan (35) investigated the relative legibility of the printing on the original cards and that on the offset reproductions. She found that, in transcribing from the two types of material, the number of errors and the net output per minute was in most comparisons significantly in favor of the Library of Congress printed cards. The output was 15 per cent less and the errors 900 per cent greater for the reproduced materials. A majority of the catalogers were convinced that it would be a mistake to substitute reproductions for the Library of Congress cards. In light of these results, it would probably be unwise for libraries to employ the book reproductions rather than the cards themselves until more legible reproduction of the material becomes possible.

In studying the relative legibility of railroad timetables, Scott

(235) discovered that a difference of about 1 point in type size produced a loss of 13.3 per cent in reading time and 45 per cent more errors for the smaller size. This held for both regular and boldface type. And all the subjects in this study preferred the larger type.

In many instances, backbone titles on books and magazines are printed to be read upward or downward. The data of Gould, Raines, and Ruckmick (100a) showed that, when viewed at eye level, there was no difference between the two directions in legibility of the printing. When the shelf holding the books was above eye level, the bottom to the top direction was the more favorable, and when below eye level the top to bottom direction was just slightly better. A large majority of the 92 subjects preferred the bottom to top direction. In general, the evidence was not decisive that one arrangement was more legible than the other. Burtt, Beck, and Campbell (37a) found backbone titles that were read downward were more efficient. But since single word titles were used, the results can have little application to general legibility of backbone titles, which usually run to several words. Tinker's investigation (310), reported earlier, revealed that there were no important differences in either speed of reading or visibility of print for reading material vertically upward and downward. When all experimental evidence is considered, the implication is that backbone titles on books and magazines are equally legible whether they are printed upward or downward.

On thicker books, the backbone title is frequently printed with words horizontal, one word below another. This arrangement is the most legible of all. As noted above, Tinker (310) has shown that reading material in horizontal alignment yields about a 20 per cent advantage in visibility and a 160 per cent advantage in speed of reading over any vertical arrangement. Unfortunately, many publishers continue to employ all-capital printing for book titles on both the backbone and front cover of their books. In addition many such titles are printed with a minimum of brightness contrast between the color of book cover and type. Either one of these conditions reduces legibility greatly. And when all-capital printing and small brightness contrast occur together, the result is a book title that is extremely difficult to read. Such occurrences are not rare. Highly legible titles on book covers are important from many standpoints, including that of advertising, especially when books are displayed at educational and scientific meetings as is done frequently every year.

Part Four: Visual Functions and Illumination
for Reading

17   *Physiological Factors Influencing the Hygiene of Vision*

An adequate discussion of the hygiene of vision in reading should include consideration of all factors that may influence comfortable, healthful, and efficient functioning of the eyes in the reading situation. In this connection, certain characteristics of eye movements and the legibility of print that have already been discussed in earlier sections should be kept in mind. Still other factors are relevant.

Obviously, illumination is one of the more important of these factors. Various aspects of illumination related to reading include color of light, intensity of illumination, the role of brightness, the distribution of light, and glare. These will be discussed in succeeding chapters. The factor to be considered in this chapter is the condition of the reader's eyes.

Visual Efficiency of Young Children

With the young child one of the first things to consider is visual efficiency in relation to maturation. At the time a child begins to read print, he should be able to focus his eyes for clear vision at the reading distance of 12 to 18 inches (near vision) and also at 20 feet (far vision), i.e., see clearly at all working distances. And for visual efficiency, the eyes must be able to adapt for effective seeing when the illumination intensity varies, and they must coordinate properly (good muscle balance) so as to maintain single vision (as contrasted with double images) during visual work.

There is a decided lack of consensus concerning the time when a child's visual processes are sufficiently mature for learning to read, as revealed by the wide range of views that have been expressed on the subject. Thus Schubert (234) reports Dr. Jacques' statement that the eyes of children generally are not mature enough to cope with the printed page before the age of 8. And Cole (51) says that, if a child's "eyes are developing at a perfectly normal rate, at the age of six they are still too far-sighted to see clearly so small an object as a word. It is not until a normal child is eight years old that one can be certain his eyes are mature." (Page 282.) Children are alleged to be farsighted at birth. According to Gray (102), while "infantile farsightedness decreases gradually with the growth and lengthening of the eyeball, some children do not develop the ability to focus on objects at close range until they are seven or eight years old" (pages 106–107).

The incidence of myopia or nearsightedness increases during the school years, as does the severity or degree of myopia. Some eye specialists, such as May and Perera (173), consider that excessive study or close work, indistinct print, poor illumination, and faulty posture are exciting causes favoring development and progress of myopia. These views are based upon the fact that myopia is progressive during the school years, not upon experimental findings. The idea that progressive myopia is a result of the demands placed upon young children to do much reading under poor hygienic conditions (small print, poor illumination, etc.) is far from being universally accepted. For instance, Davidson's experiment (57) has demonstrated that children four years old or younger are able to learn to read without harm to their eyes. Also, some children learn to read before entering school and various authorities are now recommending that systematic reading instruction be given in the kindergarten. In fact, children are taught reading at 5 years of age in Great Britain without demonstrated harm to vision. Obviously, children do not have to wait until they are 8 years old to see well enough to learn to read. It would seem that progressive myopia is developmental and occurs irrespective of the visual activities of children.

Do visual defects hinder progress in reading or cause reading disability? As pointed out by Bond and Tinker (26), the evidence concerning the relation between specific eye defects and reading disability is not unequivocal. Some investigations reveal greater incidence of ocular defects among reading disability cases than among good readers, while other studies fail to show such a difference. Many pupils learn to read well in spite of ocular defects that might have been supposed to be handicaps. But there is sufficient positive evidence to indicate that such defects as farsightedness, binocular incoordination, fusion difficulties, and aniseikonia (unequal ocular images in the two eyes) may contribute to reading difficulties in certain cases.

What view should one take? Everyone should recognize that eye defects may be a handicap to good, as well as to poor, readers. Optimum conditions for reading require efficient and comfortable vision. All eye defects should be corrected where that is possible. Furthermore, the print read should have good legibility, and illumination where the reading is done should be satisfactory.

Visual Efficiency after Forty

It is well established that there is considerable reduction in the normal functioning of the eyes as a person grows old. Changes in eyesight which take place after 40 fall into two categories: normal developments that are related to changes in tissue and muscle tone; and changes related to certain diseases to which the aged are more prone.

Komzweig (143) has outlined the important physiological effects of age on the visual process. In the eye, the most important of the transparent media through which light must pass in seeing is the crystalline lens. Its curvature can be altered so that images of objects at different distances from the eye can be brought to a focus on the retina for clear seeing. This automatic adjustment or accommodation of the lens is achieved by the elasticity of the lens itself and by the operation of the ciliary muscle located within the eyeball. The lens develops opacities as it ages. In time, a cataract may form which partly or completely obscures vision. Although a cataract may develop by age 20, most cases occur around age 60 and later. Only about 5 per cent of a group of 100 elderly patients in Komzweig's study had surgery for removal of a cataract. It seems that many persons with cataract in one eye and fair vision in the other eye are able to get along satisfactorily in their environment with the use of the better eye and so do not have surgery. Cataracts may be removed and good vision for reading restored to a large segment of the aged population. The surgery is successful in nearly all instances. With modern procedures, a cataract operation is seldom serious.

The retina, the innermost coat of the eyeball, is the organ of vision. It shows the least amount of change due to aging. But, according to Komzweig, some older patients show degeneration in the macular region of the retina. This is the area that mediates clearest vision. The impairment of vision due to this degeneration cannot be aided by medical or surgical means. Among Komzweig's 1000 aged patients, one of the major causes of visual impairment was degeneration of the retina.

The normal eye has a remarkable ability to adapt for clear vision to a wide range of light intensities from relatively dim to very bright. Research indicates that this function resides in the retina. In this discussion, primary interest is in adaptation of the cones, sensory end organs in the retina that are concerned with seeing the finer details, as in printed words. It takes 7 to 8 minutes for the cones to adapt to dim light, and 60 to 90 seconds to adapt to bright light (Geldard, 90). The effect of adaptation upon visual efficiency is illustrated in an experiment by Tinker (283). He determined speed of reading under various intensities of light with 2 minutes of adaptation to each illumination used and also with 15 minutes of adaptation to the light levels. The illumination intensities employed were 0.1, 0.7, 3.1, 10.3, 17.4, and 53.3 footcandles (fc). With only 2 minutes of adaptation, light intensities below 10.3 fc significantly retarded speed of reading. The rate of reading was the same for 10.3, 17.4, and 53.3 fc. In contrast, with 15 minutes of adaptation, only the light intensities below 3.1 fc significantly retarded speed of reading, while the reading rate was the same for 3.1 fc and above. Thus, with ample time for adaptation (15 minutes), the speed and accuracy of vision in reading was just as good at 3.1 fc as at brighter levels of illumination. Adequate adaptation to the dimmer light produced greater visual efficiency than when no adaptation was provided for. In the same investigation, visual fatigue was measured by the li test of Ferree and Rand (72). Clearness of seeing measured by this test confirmed the results of adaptation obtained by the speed of reading measurements. Another study by Tinker (286), described in Chapter 18, provided supplementary evidence of the influence of visual adaptation. He found that people tended to prefer for reading the intensity to which they were adapted, whether relatively low or high. The results of these two studies indicate the important role of adaptation in visual efficiency. Komzweig (143) reports two studies that show a significant age decline in sensitivity of the dark-adapted eye. This was most marked in subjects beyond the age of 60 years. This decline in sensitivity seems to be associated with vitamin A deficiency which is a significant component of visual purple in the retina. Hecht and Mandelbaum (116) have demonstrated that deprivation of vitamin A causes less increase in sensitivity (lesser degree of adaptation) in both the cone and rod (light sensitive end organs) portions of the adaptation curve at all points from 1 to 30 minutes of adaptation. Presumably elderly persons possess a decreased ability to metabolize vitamin A. The decrease in ability to see clearly in dim illumination with increased age prevents the elderly person from seeing well enough to read in relatively low intensities of light, which he could readily do at a younger age. As will be described in Chapter 19, these older people need relatively bright light for good visual discrimination.

There are suggestions that ability to discriminate colors decreases in old age. The data cited by Tiffin (265) seem to indicate that there is a deterioration of color vision starting at about age 40. These data are suspect, for Foster's study (79) indicated that a four-plate color discrimination test such as that used to obtain the Tiffin data is not a valid test of color vision. Boice, Tinker, and Paterson (25) employed the Ishihara (32 plates) and the American Optical Company (42 plates) tests for color blindness. Both tests are reliable and valid tests of color vision. A group of 236 faculty men of all academic ranks at the University of Minnesota were tested. This highly selected group was relatively homogeneous with respect to intelligence, education, occupational level, and socioeconomic status. For the group as a whole, the percentage of color blindness was 7.5. This corresponds to what is ordinarily reported when these tests are used. There was no evidence of deterioration of color vision efficiency from age 20 to 59 years. But one fourth of a small sample of 21 faculty men aged 60 years and over were found to be color-blind. In an additional sample of 19 men age 60 or above, 16 per cent were color-blind. Of the total of 40 men age 60 and above, 20 per cent were color-blind. It seems possible, therefore, that for those men of age 60 years or over there may be a higher than normal expectancy of color blindness.

According to Komzweig (143), there is some evidence of a positive relation between visual acuity and color vision test scores. He also found that the color vision of his patients was good after cataract operations, with perhaps an excess of bluishness in the environment. Possibly, therefore, color vision diminishes in some aged persons for the same reason that visual efficiency diminishes. The possible loss of effective color vision in the aged is important for a person to be aware of when viewing colored pictures in relation to the descriptions in the accompanying text.

The lessening in accommodation power with age is known as presbyopia. As persons with normal distance vision reach middle age (40 to 50 years), they ordinarily need to wear glasses for reading. This is the so-called bifocal age. Presbyopia is caused mainly by the lens of the eye losing its elasticity so that it cannot change its curvature sufficiently at a close distance to read without the aid of glasses. Those who wear glasses for presbyopia get bifocals or a separate pair of glasses for effective near vision. Ferree and Rand (76, 77), in two experimental reports, show that proper conditions of lighting are of great service to presbyopic eyes. They also point out that adjustment of illumination aids vision for eyes with other refractive difficulties. For details see Chapter 19.

It is well established that visual acuity gradually decreases with age after about age 30. There are, according to Weston (348), other factors involved besides presbyopia or the diminution of the power of accommodation. They include reduction in the size of the pupil which reduces the amount of light entering the eye and absorption of light owing to yellowing of the lens and changes in the ocular media. Possibly there is some loss in retinal transmission and sensitivity. "In any case, there is experimental evidence that speed and accuracy in discriminating small details decline with advancing age and that this decline may be noticeable from the twenties onward" (pages 178–179). It will be shown in Chapter 19 that increased intensity of light is helpful for such cases.

18   *Basic Considerations in Illumination and Vision*

To provide a basis for discussing illumination for reading in the two succeeding chapters, certain explanations are in order. They include definition of terms, evaluation of techniques of measurement, and an appraisal of illuminants.

Terminology

Technical terms are defined here so that each one will not need to be explained when it is used in Chapters 19 and 20. Some of the definitions in this section are based upon materials in the *IES Lighting Handbook* (132) and in Luckiesh and Moss (167).

Accommodation is a change in the focus of the eyes. It is achieved by a change in the curvature of the eye lens as a person shifts his gaze from one object to another located at a different distance from the eyes. It occurs automatically and becomes less effective by middle age.

Brightness is the amount of light emitted from a luminous body (surface of a light fixture) or a reflecting surface such as a sheet of paper. It is measured in footlamberts (fL).

Brightness contrast refers to the difference in brightness between an object and its background, such as print and paper, or between two areas within the visual field.

Candlepower refers to light intensity expressed in candles. An ordinary candle used in the home produces about the same light intensity as the standard candle used in research, or one candlepower.

Critical illumination level for reading refers to the light intensity at and above which there is no increase in speed of reading, or change in visual fatigue or clearness of seeing as measured by the li test, and below which there are deleterious effects in both speed and fatigue.

Diffuse reflection factor is the ratio (percentage) of the diffusely reflected light to the incident light, e.g., ordinary "white" paper has a diffuse reflection factor of around 75 to 85 per cent. *Reflectance* means the same as *reflection factor*.

Direct lighting is a system in which 90 to 100 per cent of the light is sent directly to the working surface, usually from an open-faced reflector. This results in a concentration of light on the working plane, usually with a marked sacrifice of evenly distributed illumination because of brightness extremes in the visual field. Illustration of the 5 types of lighting is given in the *IES Lighting Handbook* (132, pages 10–16).

Indirect lighting is a system in which the source of illumination is entirely or almost concealed from the eyes and in which 90 to 100 per cent of the light is first directed against the ceiling, upper sections of the walls, or perhaps some other surface from which it is diffusely reflected throughout the reading area.

The semi-indirect system represents a compromise between general diffuse lighting and indirect systems. A large part, 60 to 90 per cent, of light shines against the ceiling and is then reflected downward to the working plane. A smaller part, 40 to 10 per cent, is transmitted through underhanging translucent reflectors of varying density directly to the reading surface.

In *general diffuse lighting*, the light is emitted through a diffusing enclosure about equally in all directions for spherical globes; or for the direct-indirect enclosure, about 50 per cent shines upward and the same amount downward.

Semi-direct lighting is a system in which 60 to 90 per cent of the light is directed downward and 40 to 10 per cent upward to the ceiling where it is reflected diffusely about the room. Some distribution of light is achieved by the diffusing enclosure.

Equivalent footcandle (efc) is the same as footlambert (fL).

Footcandle (fc) is a unit of measured intensity of light. It is the light intensity upon a surface perpendicular to the light rays from a standard candle at the distance of one foot, i.e., from a light source of one candlepower. Thus a footcandle is about the light intensity on a small area of surface held vertically one foot from an ordinary candle.

Footlambert (fL) is a unit of brightness which is equal to the uniform brightness of a perfectly (100 per cent) diffusing and reflecting surface illuminated by one footcandle. Thus, the brightness in footlamberts on a sheet of paper is equal to the incident footcandles multiplied by the reflectance of the paper surface. If the diffuse reflectance of the paper is 80 per cent and the footcandles of light shining on it are 30, the footlamberts equal 24.0.

Glare refers to a brightness condition which produces a severely unequal distribution of light. This may reduce ability to discriminate details and also result in visual discomfort and eyestrain. Direct glare is usually from insufficiently shielded light sources in the visual field, or from areas of severely contrasting brightness within the working environment. Indirect glare is due to specular reflection (as from a mirror) from a polished or highly glazed surface.

Margin of safety refers to the light intensity in footcandles that should be added to the critical illumination level to assure effective and comfortable vision in reading. Thus, if the critical level of illumination for reading material set in 10 point type is 4 footcandles, 10 to 12 footcandles should be added to assure good conditions for reading by persons with normal vision.

Millilambert is a unit of brightness equivalent to 0.929 footlambert.

Normal reading distance varies from person to person. It centers around 14 inches but may be anywhere from 10 to 18 inches. A person holds the printed material he is reading at a distance which allows clear and comfortable vision. He is apt to change the distance to adjust to the size of type; for example he probably will hold it nearer for relatively small type.

Line of vision is the line along the optical axis of the eye to the center of the fixated area where accurate seeing of fine details occurs.

Photopic vision is mediated by the cones in the retina. It is active in illumination sufficiently intense to distingush colors and fine details. Reading is done with photopic vision. In contrast, very dim light seeing, mediated by the rods in the retina, is called scotopic vision.

Reflection factor is the percentage of incident light reflected from an object. It is also called reflectance.

Surroundings of the visual task are the areas outside the central field in which is located the page of reading material or other items to be discriminated. In studies of visual functioning, the surroundings which are crucial cover an area extending about 30 degrees from the optical axis (line of sight to center of visual task) in all directions. Beyond this are the peripheral areas where visual acuity is very slight. At a distance of 14 inches from the eyes, the surroundings cover a circular area about 16 inches in diameter.

Visibility of a detail, such as a letter or word, indicates the threshold of discrimination, i.e., the conditions which barely permit perception of the item.

Visibility meter is an instrument employed for precise measurement of visibility.

Visual acuity is the capacity to distinguish fine details. It is ordinarily measured by determining the ability to discriminate the position of the break in the Landolt ring. The breaks are of different sizes. Visual acuity varies inversely with the angle subtended by the break that is just large enough to be seen. The normal eye is able to recognize breaks in the Landolt ring that subtend a visual angle of one minute or less, i.e., designated ordinarily as 20/20 vision.

Techniques of Measurement

Results obtained from studies of the relation between illumination and reading depend to a considerable extent upon the method of measurement used. This is also true for the conclusions based upon the results. For instance, the results derived from threshold visibility measurements lead to conclusions which differ from those based upon speed of reading where the stimuli are supra-threshold. It seems desirable, therefore, to describe and evaluate the principal methods used in this field of research.

Visual acuity measurements have been used widely as a basis for prescribing illumination for reading. Luckiesh (153) and Luckiesh and Moss (156) list visual acuity as a basic factor in seeing and by implication in specific visual tasks such as reading. They state that, for black test objects on a white background, visual acuity improves up to 100 fc. As a matter of fact, Lythgoe (172) has demonstrated that, under certain conditions of measurement, visual acuity improves up to and beyond 1000 fc. But inspection of his data reveals that gains in acuity, when illumination intensity is doubled, are very slight for levels above about 20 fc. It is questionable whether the almost microscopic gains in visual acuity obtained under the relatively high fc of light justify their application to visual tasks such as reading where supra-threshold visibility is involved. Visual acuity measurements yield threshold values of seeing. Evaluation of all the data on increase of visual acuity with increase of light intensity indicates that they have little value as a basis for prescribing illumination for reading.

Lythgoe's method (172) is typical of the better procedures of measuring visual acuity. He presented the test object, the Landolt ring or broken circle, to a subject for 1.6 seconds. The Landolt broken ring is shaped like the letter C with the breadth of the line and the width of the gap equal to one-fifth of the diameter of the ring. Nine sizes of ring were used. The subject had to identify the direction in which the gap in the ring pointed. The gap could appear in any one of 8 positions: up, right-up, right, right-down, down, left-down, left, left-up. Eleven brightnesses of illumination on the test object were used, ranging from 0.0073 to 1275 efc or fL. Many measurements were made at each brightness for each size of test object. The number of mistakes was recorded. The purpose was to determine the smallest size of test object which the subjects could discriminate at different illuminations. Two criteria for being able to discriminate the object were employed: 4.5 correct responses out of a possible 8; and 7 correct out of 8. Results for 4 subjects revealed that visual acuity continued to improve up to 1275 fL, but the increase in acuity by doubling the brightness was extremely small beyond 38.8 fL.

Certain other techniques are virtual measures of threshold visual discrimination and therefore of visual acuity. Thus speed of vision (least time taken to discriminate a test object) decreases with increase of light intensity. Again, since this is threshold seeing, it has little application to the normal reading situation. Another technique is measurement of visibility with the Luckiesh-Moss Visibility Meter. This also involves threshold vision and thus visual acuity. The method has been evaluated in Chapter 10.

Various attempts have been made to use preferences of the reader as criteria for the intensity of light needed for reading. These have been appraised by Tinker (304). In all the studies reported, the authors neglected the role of visual adaptation. This led to erroneous specifications of high intensities for reading. In an intensive investigation with 144 university students as subjects, Tinker (285) determined the effect of visual adaptation upon intensity of diffused light preferred for reading. At one laboratory session, each subject was adapted for 15 minutes to 8 fc of light; at another session, to 52 fc. Then by the method of paired comparisons, a subject chose which light intensity he considered most comfortable for reading. The light intensities ranged from 1 to 100 fc. When adapted to 8 fc, the subjects tended to choose 8 fc as most comfortable for reading; when adapted to 52 fc, they chose 52 fc most often. The data indicate that status of visual adaptation at the moment determines to a large degree the intensity preferred for reading. It would seem, therefore, that preference for illumination intensity is not a satisfactory method for determining the intensity of light needed for efficient visual work. Apparently, by picking an intensity and adapting the reader to it, one can obtain preference for that intensity. If the investigator is interested in promoting use of lights of high intensity, the method of preferences will support it. Furthermore, with strictly local illumination, which is an undesirable visual situation, subjects choose relatively high intensities (291, 292). Also, as pointed out by Tinker in these reports, a small spot of light surrounded by dimly illuminated areas and shadows in the visual field provides a situation that rapidly produces visual fatigue. In a situation of this kind, the greater the intensity of light in the limited area of the reading material, the worse it becomes for visual work since the demarcation between the small lighted space and the dimly illuminated surroundings becomes more pronounced (see the discussion of glare in Chapter 19).

The rate of involuntary blinking has been used extensively to study the influence of changes in illumination intensity on ease of seeing with special reference to the reading situation. The method was devised and promoted by Luckiesh (153). It is assumed that the more severe visual tasks produce significantly more blinks than an easier task during a given period of reading or other visual work. Luckiesh cites data which indicate that during one hour of reading under 100 fc the blink rate increased 8 per cent; under 10 fc, 31 per cent; and under 1 fc, 72 per cent. These results are typical findings in all the relevant researches of Luckiesh.

Tinker (298) evaluated the use of this technique in the reading situation. The specifications of Luckiesh, Guth, and Eastman (169) and of Luckiesh and Moss (162) for use of the blink technique were followed in detail. Forty-two university students, tested individually, read material for 55 minutes under 2 fc of light and at another sitting under 100 fc. Visual adaptation to the light used and order of illumination used were controlled. Blinking was recorded for the first and for the last 5 minutes of reading. The data, adapted from the original report, are shown in Table 14. Examination of the trends in the table reveals an appreciable increase in blink rate from the first to the last 5 minutes of reading but the gain is the same for the 100 fc as for the 2 fc: 32.0 versus 31.6 per cent. It is obvious, as shown by literature on the subject, that reading under 2 fc of light is a

Table 14. Influence of Illumination Intensity upon Rate
of Blinking during 55 Minutes of Reading

Foot-candles	Blinks in First 5 minutes		Blinks in Last 5 Minutes		Percentage of Difference
	Mean	SD	Mean	SD	
2	25.8	23.2	33.9	27.9	31.6
100	26.8	19.4	35.4	24.5	32.0

more severe visual task than reading under 100 fc. As a matter
of fact, all researchers except Luckiesh and his co-workers have
failed to confirm the claims of Luckiesh for the blink technique
as a measure of ease of seeing (see Chapter 10). In view of these
results, it is hazardous to prescribe illumination for reading on
the basis of blink-rate results.

Luckiesh (153) has also promoted nervous muscular tension
and heart rate as measures of ease of seeing. Tinker's analysis
(278) of the data on nervous muscular tension demonstrates
that this technique is not a valid measure of ease of seeing. And
Bitterman (21) presents convincing experimental evidence that
changes in heart rate cannot be employed as a true measure of
visual efficiency.

To a large degree, the illumination intensities specified by illuminating engineers for reading have been based on visual acuity measurements of one kind or another (Tinker, 294). Weston, in two experiments (349, 350) and in a discussion (347),
has presented basic data and formulated a method for deriving
the illumination intensity necessary for 90, 95, 98, or any other
desired percentage of visual efficiency, taking into consideration
the size of detail to be discriminated and the brightness contrast
between object and background. Crouch (56) has given the
technique more definite formulation and has devised a nomo-
gram to facilitate the computation.

Tinker (300) has evaluated this Crouch-Weston method of
computing illumination intensities. He determined the illumination intensities required for maximum speed of reading material
in 7 point newsprint and 10 point book type with 100 per cent
accuracy. The Crouch-Weston method was then used to com-

pute the light intensity needed for 100 per cent visual efficiency in reading the same material. Maximum speed of reading was achieved at 7 and 3.1 fc for the 7 and 10 point arrangements respectively. The computed values were approximately 250 and 100 fc for the same tasks. It seems that this computational technique of deriving levels of illumination intensity needed for effective visual discrimination is not valid for reading material in 7 point newsprint and 10 point book type. The reason for this is probably twofold: First, the Crouch-Weston computations are based upon data that are essentially measures of visual acuity and involve, therefore, threshold discrimination. The validity of prescribing illumination intensities for effective seeing in suprathreshold tasks (as reading) on the basis of visual acuity data is questionable, as already demonstrated. Secondly, it is also possible that it is not valid to make a direct transfer from visual acuity data to a seeing situation where integrated visual patterns are involved. In reading print, one is dealing with a complex, structured situation in which fine visual discrimination is neither required nor even used most of the time. To a large degree, the reader reacts to word forms rather than to the minute details of individual letters. Only occasionally, when the word form is not individually characteristic, and when the verbal context does not clearly suggest the meaning, does the reader exercise discrimination of letter details — as when "horse" must be distinguished from "house," or "then" from "than."

It seems probable that many more illumination specifications, other than for reading, derived from computational techniques are also in error. Certainly one may justifiably question such practices and urge that experimental checks be made. The light needed for most effective seeing in reading or for any other practical task requiring visual discrimination should be arrived at experimentally, i.e., by determining the illumination that permits most efficient results.

Another fallacious technique is to base specifications for proper illumination upon graphs plotted on a logarithmic scale. Data for visual discrimination plotted in this manner show what look like large and consistent gains with increase in light intensity up to and beyond 1000 fc. Examination of the data from which the curves are constructed reveals that the gains in acuity and similar discrimination tasks are relatively very small for increments above 20 to 30 fc. Tinker (278) has pointed out the hazards of using logarithmic curves for this purpose.

Performance tests have been widely used to determine illumination levels required for most effective visual work. Speed of reading has become one of the most efficient performance techniques for determining light intensities suitable for reading. Details of this method are given in Chapter 10. Tinker and Paterson (326) have shown that the method has satisfactory reliability and validity. And as also noted in Chapter 10, relatively short work or reading periods are satisfactory in visual research of this kind.

Color of Illumination and Vision

Certain colors and tints and shades of colors are preferred over other colors, tints, and shades. Psychologically, colors carry meanings. There are warm and cool colors, and exciting and subduing colors. Some color combinations are pleasing, others not. Attention to these factors can make our environment more pleasing and interesting. The relation of color to seeing is not well understood by many. Owing to high-pressure promotion, many unsupported claims concerning the aid to vision of tinted paper for printing and writing, and the use of colored lights and special illuminants, are accepted by the uninformed.

Color or wave lengths of light have a bearing upon seeing. The visible spectrum is composed of a continuous series of colors as seen in a rainbow. At one end are the violet and blue colors, in the middle are yellow and green, and at the other end is red. Light rays derived from a limited range of the spectrum are relatively uniform in wave length and produce an approximately pure spectral color. Deviation from purity of light affects clearness of the visual image of an object, such as a word, through chromatic aberration. This is due to the fact that the lens of the eye has a slightly different focal length for each color or wave length. Thus, for very near vision, it is possible to focus exactly

221

for violet rays, but very difficult to focus for red rays. In far vision the reverse is true. For intermediate distances it is easiest to focus for yellow rays. Next to the yellow is the orange on one side and the green-yellow on the other. When the object is illuminated by mixed wave lengths, as in daylight or ordinary artificial lighting, there is chromatic aberration in which the violet rays come to a focus farther in front of the eye than the red rays, and the yellow rays occupy an intermediate position (17). These intermediate rays are automatically focused upon the fovea of the retina for clear seeing, while the focal point of the violet rays lies in front and that of the red rays behind it. This results in aberration circles for the red and violet which produce a slight blurring of the optical image, and consequently a reduction in visual acuity. This blurring is not noticeable in ordinary circumstances because the brightness of the yellow rays in the illumination is very much greater than that of the violet and the red. The aberration effects of the intermediate colors, such as orange and green-yellow, are even less. Consequently the effects of the yellow predominate. One might expect, however, that vision would be clearer if all light rays but those from one region of the spectrum were eliminated. That is, the more nearly monochromatic a light, the sharper the image on the retina.

Early experimental evidence reported by Luckiesh (150), 151, 152) in 1911–1913 indicated that the closer we get to monochromatic light the greater is visual acuity. For instance, mercury arc light, which has relatively homogeneous wave lengths, produced greater visual acuity than tungsten light which has a rather wide spectrum. For discrimination of fine detail, therefore, it seems that monochromatic illumination is superior to light composed of mixed wave lengths.

Visual acuity varies from one monochromatic (colored) light to another. In a careful determination, Ferree and Rand (74, 75) found the order yielding greatest to least acuity to be as follows: yellow, yellow-green, orange, green, red, blue-green, and blue. It is well established that the eye is more sensitive to yellow and yellow-green light than to other colors. White light (sunlight) composed of rays from all parts of the spectrum was superior to the yellow when the test object was black on a white background.

What are the applications of the above to ordinary reading and other tasks requiring visual discrimination? With the exception of yellow, it is practically impossible to obtain pure spectral lights of sufficiently high intensities for everyday use. And pure yellow light (sodium vapor light) is not desirable for general use since all color but yellow in the illuminated area is absent. Only yellow and tints and shades of yellow remain.

Various illuminants have been compared for effects on ease of seeing. Luckiesh and Moss (155) measured visual acuity under sodium vapor and under tungsten filament incandescent light. The sodium light was virtually monochromatic. The acuity of 9 subjects was determined by means of the Ives-Cobb acuity apparatus through a light range of 0.018 to 20 millilamberts. Visual acuity was somewhat greater at all levels of brightness for the sodium light. In the same study, they found that speed of visual reaction was quicker under the sodium than under the tungsten light when the test object was small, the contrast between the test object and background was small, and illumination was at 1 millilambert. But no difference in speed was discovered with a dim light of 0.1 millilambert when a large test object was used which had small contrast with its background. It is clear that sodium vapor light produces greater visual acuity, i.e., threshold vision, than tungsten light. However, Luckiesh (153, page 246) has pointed out that this advantage for sodium or any monochromatic light disappears for supra-threshold discrimination. For instance, the visibility of words printed in 8 to 10 point type is approximately the same under tungsten as under sodium light.

For some time it was generally held that mercury arc light, which has relatively homogeneous wave lengths, should yield greater visual acuity than tungsten light. In another experiment, Luckiesh and Moss (158) measured the visual acuity of 10 subjects under 5, 25, and 125 fc of illumination from a low-pressure mercury arc lamp and from incandescent light of a tungsten filament lamp. No significant differences appeared at any level of light intensity. Under the conditions of the experiment, the mercury arc light with less chromatic aberration produced no greater visual acuity. In another experiment, Luckiesh and Moss (159, page 418) showed that the visibility of print in 8 point type is the same under mercury arc and tungsten light. All data, therefore, indicate mercury light is no better and no worse than tungsten for threshold or supra-threshold visual work.

According to the findings of Luckiesh and Moss (166), fluorescent and tungsten filament light are equally effective in promoting ease of seeing. Questions have arisen concerning the possible harmful effects on the organism of radiation from fluorescent lighting. In evaluating these criticisms, Luckiesh and Taylor (170) present evidence which led them to conclude that ultraviolet, infrared, and the visible radiant energy emitted from these lamps is not injurious to the human organism. Nevertheless, there seem to be certain psychological factors which are objectionable to at least some persons. Holway and Jameson (126) found in 1947 that the quality of light from fluorescent lamps of any kind was considered by readers and other clerical workers to be unpleasant and distracting. It was described as harsh, thin, and cold — undesirable qualities not present in daylight or tungsten incandescent illumination. The authors considered this psychologically undesirable quality of fluorescent illumination to be detrimental to ease and comfort in reading and recommended that incandescent lighting be used in reading rooms and offices. It is likely that illumination from some of the newer fluorescent tubes or from a combination of fluorescent and incandescent light sources would be less psychologically objectionable to readers.

Results of numerous research studies point to the following conclusions: In situations where discrimination is supraliminal, as in reading printed material, no illuminant that is suitable in spectral character for general use in lighting is better for adequate seeing than any other such illuminant. As stated by Luckiesh (153), at brightness levels above 0.1 fL, there is no basic difference in visibility or ability to read ordinary print. This holds for diffuse daylight, incandescent light from tungsten filaments, light from mercury arcs, and fluorescent lamps.

19   *Illumination for Reading*

To achieve comfortable, healthful, and efficient functioning of the eyes in reading, it is necessary to know the relation between light and vision. To accomplish this, one must evaluate the effects on vision of variation in color and light, of intensity or brightness, and of distribution of illumination. The last includes various forms of glare and brightness contrast. Lighting practice, although much improved during the past 30 years, is still far from ideal. Eyestrain, with resulting functional disturbance of other organs, is held to be directly traceable at times to faulty illumination. Economy and artistic effects are of purely secondary importance in comparison with maintaining healthful working conditions for the eyes in reading or in any other situation that requires visual discrimination.

Although much of the work of illuminating engineers deals with improving the sources of light, emphasis must also be placed upon efficient and comfortable functioning of the eyes in relation to lighting arrangements. As in any field of science, additional research on the relation of illumination to seeing is desirable. However, there are now sufficient data from investigations by psychologists, physiologists, and engineers to provide a fairly adequate basis for hygienic illumination in the reading situation. Since a large amount of a person's reading is done under artificial illumination, much of the following discussion will be concerned with this aspect of lighting. Color or wave lengths of light has been dealt with in Chapter 18.

Intensity of Light

In any situation where reading is done, it is necessary to decide how much light, i.e., what intensity, is required for easy and effective visual discrimination, taking into account the typographical arrangement involved (see Chapters 10 to 16). Various approaches, as described in Chapter 18, have been employed to arrive at proper light intensities for effective seeing. The results obtained by use of these techniques, which need to be coordinated in the following discussion, deal with the relation of illumination intensity to visual acuity, size of the object discriminated, speed of vision, brightness contrast, and efficiency of performance. An attempt will now be made to show the usefulness of the results in determining the light intensity proper for reading.

When considering the relation between illumination intensity and visual acuity, keep in mind that such measurements are concerned with discrimination of fine details, or threshold vision (Chapter 18). Intensity is ordinarily measured in footcandles (fc). In all experiments, visual acuity increased as intensity of illumination was raised. A few citations will be sufficient to show the consistent trend. Ferree, Rand, and Lewis (77) employed illumination intensities ranging from 0.5 to 100 fc. With the subjects who had normal vision, acuity increased rapidly from 0.5 to 10 fc and slowly from 10 to 25 fc. From 25 to 100 fc, the increase in acuity was very small. In a major study, Lythgoe (172) used illumination steps ranging from 0.0029 to 1275 equivalent footcandles (efc, i.e., footlamberts, fL). Increase in visual acuity was rapid up to 5 efc; then slower to 38, and only slight from 38 to 1275 efc. The measurements of Luckiesh and Moss (159) showed a marked increase in visual acuity from 5 to 25 fc of light intensity, but the slight change in acuity from 25 to 125 fc was not significant.

These data on the relation of visual acuity to intensity of light reveal the following trends: visual acuity increases rapidly as light intensity is increased from a fraction of a fc to 5 fc and then gradually in acuity up to between 25 and 40 fc. As the illumination intensity is further increased up to 100 or even above 1000 fc, the improvements in acuity are slight. Although the gains in acuity with intensities above 50 fc may have theoretical implications, they have no practical significance for reading. Since the relation between visual acuity and light intensity is logarithmic, the results of these studies are usually plotted on a logarithmic curve. This magnifies the appearance of the tiny acuity gains at the higher illumination levels so that inspection of the curve gives a false impression that the gains are large and significant. To argue from these data that high intensities are best for ordinary reading is not valid.

Size of the object to be discriminated is a factor in seeing. And intensity of light affects ability to see objects of any size. Weston (349) determined the ability to discriminate the break in Landolt rings with gap sizes of 1 to 10 minutes of visual angle under illumination intensities ranging from 0.16 to 500 fc. Marked improvement of seeing occurred for all sizes of test objects as intensity was increased up to 4 fc. With the larger objects, 4 to 10 minute gaps, there was no appreciable improvement in seeing beyond 20 fc. And for the smaller objects, there was no significant increase for intensities above 50 fc. The author noted that increasing the illumination greatly will not make the 1 minute gap as readily discriminated as a gap of 6 minutes. Actually these and other analogous data (153, page 98) represent another way of measuring visual acuity. Hence, the small improvements in visual discrimination at relatively high intensities cannot be the basis for specifying light intensities for ordinary reading.

Obviously it takes time to see clearly. And the quickness of the seeing is affected by both light intensity and the size of the object to be discriminated. Experiments which determine the smallest fraction of a second that can be used for discriminating a test object of a given size again are virtually measures of visual acuity. The data reported by Luckiesh (153, page 131), Cobb (50), and Ferree and Rand (73) show the same trends as the visual acuity studies. That is, the relation between light intensity and speed of vision is logarithmic. Thus the plotted curves are deceptive (minute gains for the higher intensities look big) and should not be employed to specify illumination for reading.

The brightness contrast between print and paper must always be considered in specifying light for reading. Seeing tends to improve with the increase of brightness contrast at all intensity levels. In most newspapers, the brightness contrast between paper reflectance and print (ink) reflectance is about 62 to 68; in books, it is 75 to 80 (except for most paperbacks where the difference tends to be like that in newspapers). Weston (350) used three degrees of brightness contrast: 36.5, 68.3, and 91.6 per cent. His subjects had to discriminate and cancel all Landolt rings of a given gap orientation. Illumination levels ranged from 0.8 to 500 fc. With the 6 minute size of test object there was little change in performance with illumination above 4 fc for the two higher brightness contrasts. For the smaller contrast, performance improved up to 20 fc but not beyond. With the 3 minute size of detail (about the size of detail in 10 point type), performance did not improve significantly at intensities above 20 fc with the two higher contrasts, but for the lowest contrast the performance increased through 20 but not beyond 100 fc. (There was no intensity used between 20 and 100 fc.) All performance was on a lower level for discriminating the 1 minute detail. This performance slackened off at intensities above 20 fc and seemed unimportant beyond 100 fc. It is noteworthy that increasing the illumination level becomes less effective in improving performance as the brightness contrast becomes smaller.

Tinker (315) employed speed of reading and visibility measurements with 367 subjects in his experiment on brightness contrast, illumination intensity, and visual efficiency. The test materials were printed on paper of various reflectances so that the brightness contrasts were 0.756 (white paper), 0.581, 0.348, and 0.217 (dark gray paper). The illumination intensities used were 5, 25, 50, 100, 200, and 400 fc. Increasing the light intensity above 5 fc had no important effect on speed of reading when the brightness contrast between print and paper was large, i.e., 0.756. But, with contrasts of 0.581 and 0.348, speed of reading increased from 5 to 25 fc but not for greater intensities. And with the poor contrast of 0.217, light intensity had to be raised to somewhere between 50 and 100 fc to obtain a significant increase in speed of reading. No further improvement occurred with 200 and 400 fc. Except for the very low contrast, therefore, there was no significant increase in speed of reading for intensities of 25 to 400 fc. And this low contrast (0.217) does not occur in ordinary reading situations. Thus, excessively high intensities of light are not necessary for quick perception in reading connected material printed in 10 point type in everyday situations.

With each degree of brightness contrast, the visibility scores increased consistently with each increase in illumination used (5 to 400 fc). These increases were directly proportional to the brightness contrast of the printed materials. Since visibility scores involve threshold discrimination, they should not be used as a basis for specifying illumination levels satisfactory for reading. Because of the nature of visibility measurement and other techniques which involve threshold discrimination, they provide no way to determine the difference between adequate and surplus light in situations which involve the supra-threshold vision in reading. Speed of perception in reading, with comprehension constant at virtually 100 per cent, appears to be a more satisfactory method for specifying what light intensity is adequate for efficient vision in a particular reading situation.

The critical intensity of light for reading is the level beyond which there is no further increase in efficiency of performance as the footcandles become greater. Reading or other visual work should not be done at critical levels of illumination. There should be a satisfactory margin of safety to provide for individual variation. In the reading situation, addition of 10 to 15 fc to the critical level will ordinarily provide an adequate margin of safety. Tinker found that the critical level of intensity for reading material in 10 point book type was between 3 and 4 fc (283) and for reading 7 point newsprint was 7 fc (289). And Tinker (301) also found that the critical intensity for reading 6 point italic print was about 25 fc.

Do persons with subnormal vision, i.e., less than 20/20 as measured by eye charts, profit more than those with normal vision from a higher light intensity? Luckiesh (153, page 151) cites data which show that those with subnormal vision have a marked increase in visual acuity when illumination is increased from 1 to 10 to 100 fc. This improvement was present whether or not they were wearing their corrective glasses. The increased intensity is not a substitute for glasses, since glasses plus higher intensities produce better results than higher intensities without glasses.

It is well established that visual efficiency tends to decrease with age. This becomes pronounced at the bifocal age, usually between 40 and 50 years. In two studies, Ferree and Rand (76) and Ferree, Rand, and Lewis (77) obtained convincing evidence that increased intensity of light improves seeing for persons with presbyopic vision before they obtain bifocal glasses as well as when they are wearing the bifocals. The improvement was much greater than for persons with normal vision. As pointed out by Luckiesh (153, page 150), high intensity of light is a marked aid to those with mild cataracts. A more recent investigation by Weston (346) provides additional evidence that considerable increase in level of illumination improves the visual efficiency of elderly people.

The results of Kunz and Sleight (144) are relevant to the problem of eye disability and illumination. They determined the effect of target (test object) brightness on subjects with normal and subnormal visual acuity. One group of 12 normal subjects possessed visual acuity above 1.0 (normal); another group of 12, below 1.0. The test object brightness values used were 3.16, 10, 31.6, 100, 316, and 1000 fL. Those with subnormal vision showed no significant improvement in acuity scores for brightness values above 31.6 fL. But for the group with normal vision, there was no significant improvement beyond 10 fL. Nevertheless, there were minor but statistically insignificant gains in seeing up to the 1000 fL for both groups. The authors conclude that adequate illumination for discriminating details is between 10 and 30 fL for those with normal vision and somewhere between 30 and 40 fL for those with subnormal vision. This is a valid interpretation and in contrast with the conclusions of those investigators who base their inferences on logarithmic curves for visual acuity data. Note that Kunz and Sleight's suggestions are for discriminating details in the test object. The 10 fL would be about 12.5 fc, the 30 fL about 38 fc, and the 40 fL about 50 fc if shining on ordinary white book paper. For reading ordinary book print, the fL levels would be lower, probably equivalent to 15 to 25 fc for those with normal vision and about 35 to 40 fc for those whose vision is subnormal. It is noteworthy that no suggestion was made that more than 50 fc (40 fL) would be needed for those with subnormal vision to achieve efficient visual acuity.

Recently, Blackwell has attempted to devise a method for determining desirable levels of illumination for practical seeing tasks. His original data (23) involved threshold discriminations, i.e., the ability to identify the presence of a faint spot of light. Then his device, the Visual Task Evaluator, was employed to equate the obtained data to practical tasks ranging from reading 10 point type to discriminating brown thread on brown cloth (greater than 10,000 fc). He apparently derived his conclusions from logarithmic plots with no attempt to evaluate the significance of obtained differences. For instance, in his 1963 publication (24), he plots Tinker's data (315) on a logarithmic curve so that the insignificant gains in speed of reading from 5 to 400 fc look large and significant. He states that the performance index increases up to the 400 fc level. At the same time he ignores the fact that no statistically significant increase in speed was discovered for any intensity above 5 fc. In the 1963 report, Blackwell (24) states that the Illuminating Engineering Society in 1959 adopted his method for determining desirable intensity levels, and the result was that "without exception, the levels of illumination recommended" for the home, schools, offices, and industrial areas were "higher than those previously recommended by the IES" (page 581).

Examination of the experimental literature in the field indicates that illumination for effective seeing in such a task as reading cannot be determined validly by the Blackwell method. From the viewpoint of theory, perhaps Blackwell's contribution is worthwhile, but it has little or no application to practical seeing tasks. Furthermore, Taylor's analysis (258) of Blackwell's data and procedures revealed that the determinations and conclusions of Blackwell were erroneous and that the most effective visual discrimination does not require the high intensities arrived at by Blackwell. In any case, it is hazardous to attempt to specify light for seeing in supra-threshold situations by reference to threshold discrimination data, whether such specification is done by computation or adjusted by a device like the Visual Task Evaluator.

During the last 30 years or so a knowledge of illumination has been forced upon most of those who perform visual tasks and upon those who control the environment in which visual work is performed. Although this interest in lighting has been stimulated by frequently appearing popular articles, and by reports written by educators and medical men, the more fundamental information has appeared in the experimental literature. Most of this experimental material is not readily available to or easily interpreted by most people. The tendency, therefore, is to consult pamphlets on recommended levels of illumination.

In 1915, the Illuminating Engineering Society began issuing codes in which standards for practice in lighting were recommended. These, appearing in pamphlet form, have been revised periodically and new ones have been added. At present there are separate pamphlets on school, library, office, residence, and supplementary lighting as well as separate ones on one aspect or another of industrial lighting. The data on intensity in these publications have been combined in tabular form in the *IES Lighting Handbook*, 9–76 to 9–90 (132). Also, the British Illuminating Engineering Code of recommended intensities is reprinted by Weston (348). In the latter, the recommended intensities for visual tasks are moderate and considerably lower than in the American code. A comparison between the two codes for intensities recommended in various reading situations is presented in Table 15.

As noted above, illumination for reading should be somewhat above the critical levels determined by research. The values suggested below should be maintained, i.e., they are minimum values. It should be emphasized that, when dealing with illumination for effective and easy seeing in situations which involve

Table 15. Suggested Footcandle Levels of Illumination for Reading

Reading Situation	American Code	British Code
Home		
Prolonged reading	30*	15*
Study desks	70	15
Office		
Regular work	100	20
Ordinary reading	30	15
Library		
Reading tables	30	15
Study area	70	15
School		
Reading area	30	15
Drawing	100	20
Printing machine composition	100	20

* Minimum fc on the task at any time.

supra-threshold visual discrimination as in reading, the findings based upon visual acuity, visibility, and other threshold discrimination should be discounted to a considerable degree. The same is true for values computed by some formula or other device used to transmute threshold scores into illumination levels suitable for effective reading. The following light intensities should be adequate for reading:

For sustained reading of material in books and magazines printed in 10 to 12 point type with satisfactory leading, use 15 to 25 fc. This agrees with Holway and Jameson's finding (126) that 20 fc was the best average intensity for reading rooms and offices.

For sustained reading of small print, such as 7 to 8 point type found in most newspapers, use 25 to 35 fc.

In ordinary schoolrooms, use 20 to 30 fc; for mechanical drawing, use about 40 fc.

For casual (short) periods of reading good book-sized print, use 10 to 15 fc; for smaller print, use 15 to 20 fc.

When the brightness contrast between print and paper is 40 to 55 (medium low contrast), use 35 to 50 fc; with very low contrasts of 20 to 30, use 75 to 100 fc. This latter condition is seldom found in practical reading situations. In fact, it would be difficult to find in homes, schools, offices, and libraries any reading situation that would require more than 50 fc for adequate visual discrimination.

For eyes with less than normal visual acuity, use 25 to 30 fc for casual reading; 40 to 50 fc for sustained reading.

Illumination in sight-saving classes should be maintained at 50 to 60 fc.

The illumination intensities suggested above tend to be less than those in the American code but higher than those in the British code. There is nothing final or absolutely exact in any list of recommended practices for adequate light intensities. It is helpful, nevertheless, to have some suggestions for light intensities which will provide illumination adequate for efficient and easy reading for the majority of people. If one wishes to pay for it, higher intensity of light may be employed with safety, provided diffusion of the light is properly controlled, but it is not necessary.

In the United States the trend seems to be to specify as high intensities as the traffic will bear and at the same time to advise the consumer that, if he uses a still higher intensity, he will improve his ease of seeing. All will agree that there should be sufficient light for adequate seeing. It is important, nevertheless, that one should know what is adequate and what is surplus.

Distribution of Illumination

The control of light distribution or diffusion of illumination throughout the working or reading area is exceedingly important. Healthful visual functioning is possible only when the intensity and distribution of light are properly coordinated. To increase the intensity of light without ensuring satisfactory distribution only makes a bad situation worse. The result of unsatisfactory diffusion of light where visual work is performed is to reduce visual efficiency and produce eyestrain. Poor distribution of light results from glare due to poor arrangement and type of fixtures, from specular surface reflection, and from alternation of bright areas and dark areas or shadows in the visual field. Luckiesh (153), Tinker (284, 317), the *IES Lighting Handbook* (132), and pamphlets issued by the Illuminating Engineering Society, such as the one on *School Lighting* (3), summarize the literature in this area.

The disturbing effect of bright spots of light above or off to the side of the line of vision (i.e., the line from the eye to the fixation on the immediate working surface, such as the page of a book) while reading, doing other visual work, or even when no close visual discrimination is involved, is a common experience. If the light sources are made brighter, or are moved closer to the line of direct vision, the disturbing effects become greater. Visual discrimination is less efficient, speed of reading becomes slower, and discomfort increases. And if the number of peripheral light sources is increased, the detrimental effect upon vision becomes greater. To eliminate this disturbing side illumination, it is necessary to reorganize the lighting arrangement and to employ more satisfactory fixtures. Fortunately, modern lamps, lighting fixtures, and installation practices make it possible to eliminate or control glare in this kind of situation.

Uncomfortable glare and loss of visual efficiency result also from highly polished or glazed objects within the visual field. These surfaces reflect light, as from a mirror, and thus produce specular glare. Striking examples are reflections from glossy, hard-surface printing paper, polished chrome or nickel parts of equipment, desk and table tops with a high polish, and perhaps worst of all a glass-covered desk top. Specular glare can be reduced by maintaining well-diffused illumination throughout the work area. When the light is poorly diffused, the specularly reflected images tend to reduce ease of seeing and visibility of essential details. Such illumination shining on a printed page where the paper has an enamel or glazed surface can produce a situation in which it is almost impossible to distinguish enough details to perceive the words correctly. It appears like a haze spread over the surface of the printed material.

Visual fatigue and lessened efficiency are produced by brightness contrast within that portion of the visual field where critical visual discrimination is required (printed page) and also within the immediate surroundings, i.e., within 30 degrees in all directions from the visual fixation on the printed page. When the eyes need to shift back and forth from bright to dark areas, or when there is a sharp division between dark and bright portions of the immediate working area, the eyes must continuously re-adapt to the different degrees of brightness. Experimental results show that these conditions produce eyestrain, visual discomfort, and a reduction in efficiency of visual discrimination. Examples of situations which result in unfortunate brightness contrast are the following: use of a desk lamp which provides bright illumination of a small portion of the working surface, leaving the rest dimly lighted or in a shadow; sheets of white paper on a dark desk top; and the dark under-surface of an opaque eye shade used in a brightly illuminated room.

How severe must the brightness contrast be to produce these harmful effects? The term "brightness ratio" is ordinarily employed to denote the relation of brightness in adjoining areas, such as on a book and in the surroundings. The surrounding may be the same brightness, or greater, or less bright than the task. When the surrounding is brighter than the task, which occurs only infrequently, visual sensitivity is markedly reduced. Ordinarily, the surrounding is less bright than the task. A ratio of 1 to 3 or less is highly satisfactory, for there is then no noticeable visual discomfort or loss of efficiency during continuous reading or other visual work. In any case, brightness ratios smaller than 1 to 5 are desirable, and any ratio greater than 1 to 10 should be avoided wherever visual discrimination is sought. According to data cited by Luckiesh (153), a ratio as great as 1 to 5 reduces visual sensitivity to a considerable degree, i.e., to 77 per cent as great as when the ratio is 1 to 1. In general, in the reading situation the ratio should be no greater than necessary. A ratio of 1 to 1, the theoretical ideal, is practically impossible to maintain. If the ratio is no greater than 1 to 3, the visual situation may be considered ideal. Thus, if the brightness on the page of a book is 30 fL and that on the surrounding area 10 fL, the ratio is 1 to 3. If the brightness ratio approaches 1 to 100, visual discrimination becomes practically impossible and the fatigue intolerable.

Coordination of decoration with lighting is discussed by Tinker (317), in the *IES Lighting Handbook* (132), and in such pamphlets as those on school (3, 233), home (148, 219), color (52), and office lighting (220). Discussion in this section assumes that intensity and diffusion are satisfactory. Both the color and reflectances of painted or papered walls and ceilings, of furnishings, and of floors should be coordinated with lighting in specifying the illumination in an office, or schoolroom, or home, or other area where visual work is to be done. With adequate planning, a sizable portion of the well-diffused illumination in a room should come from light reflected off the ceiling, walls, and furnishings. In addition, to assure proper brightness ratios within the field of vision, the reflectances of adjoining areas in the room must be properly balanced. The pamphlet on *School Lighting Application Data* (233) and the *IES Lighting Handbook* (132) suggest reflectances that are suitable for schools, offices, and libraries: ceilings, 70 to 90 per cent; walls, 50 to 70 per cent; walls around windows, 75 to 85 per cent; trim around doors, 30 to 60 per cent; desk and table tops, 35 to 50 per cent (also appropriate for file cabinets and business machines); tackboards, 30 to 60 per cent; floors, about 30 per cent. The reflectance of chalkboards ranges from 5 to 20 per cent. The reflectance of walls adjoining chalkboards should be intermediate between that of the chalkboard and the remaining walls. This provides a shading off by steps of the reflectances and thus avoids a sharp demarcation in brightness between adjoining areas.

Brightness contrast is perhaps the most important factor in the hygiene of vision. For satisfactory visibility in reading there must be a high brightness contrast between print and paper. In addition, efficient and comfortable seeing depends upon maintaining proper brightness ratios between adjoining areas in the field of vision. The same principles are applicable to the coordination of light and decoration in the home (132, 219).

The use of color in living and working areas is very important. Certain color combinations are pleasing and should be the ones chosen for decorating. Tints (the soft subdued colors which are lightened by adding white) tend to be the most preferred, the shades (colors darkened by adding black) next, and the saturated colors (highest intensity of a pure color) last. Color harmony implies preferred color combinations. Colors also carry meaning. Thus red and orange are considered warm colors; white and blue-green, cool colors. The "warm" hues of colors are considered exciting, and the "cool" hues, tranquilizing. These psychological aspects of preferences and harmonizing of colors are important and should be considered if pleasing living and working environments are to be achieved. Fortunately, preferred colors and harmonizing color combinations can be obtained and used while at the same time maintaining proper brightness ratios.

To achieve the more pleasing environments there should be some contrast in decoration, both of color hues and reflectances. Color contrast is entirely different from brightness contrast. It is possible, therefore, to introduce color contrast without upsetting proper brightness ratios.

The kind of illumination used affects the perceived color of the decoration. Thus, most objects and surfaces do not have the same color appearance under incandescent or fluorescent lights as in daylight. Incandescent illumination tends to enhance soft, warm appearances. But the light from many fluorescent tubes is described as cold and harsh owing to the abundance of blue and/or green wave lengths and tends to take the warmth and softness out of the color in decorations (and human complexion). Illumination from some of the recently manufactured fluorescent tubes, such as the soft white, is less objectionable. Additional information on color and illumination uses may be found in the IES pamphlet on color (52), Cox (54), and Commery and Stephenson (53).

Tinker (317) has outlined certain aids which will help to maintain well-distributed illumination and eliminate glare effects:

Certain light fixtures, such as wall brackets and low-hanging fixtures which reach down into the field of vision and are not adequately shielded, should be avoided, i.e., employ only lighting fixtures which are properly shielded and which diffuse the emitted light as much as possible.

Strictly local lighting like that produced by most desk lamps with opaque shades should not be tolerated. To obtain illumination of satisfactory brightness upon the work surface, use a general illumination of moderate intensity, about 10 fc, plus local lighting on the working area. This is both more practical, more economical, and in most instances more satisfactory than trying to maintain a general illumination of high intensity throughout a room. Single lighting units which yield both general and diffused local illumination are now available (see Chapter 20).

Avoid as far as possible the use of highly polished desk and table tops, glass-topped desks, glazed paper, and highly polished metal objects.

As far as possible, maintain within the field of vision brightness ratios that are not larger than 1 to 5, preferably not over 1 to 3. Coordinate the use of color and illumination so that proper brightness ratios are preserved. In general, achieve as equal a distribution of illumination as possible at the location where visual discrimination takes place and within the immediately surrounding area.

20   *The Reading Situation*

In providing a hygienic reading situation it is necessary to deal with a number of factors. Attention has been given to various aspects of the essential conditions by Tinker (317), the *IES Lighting Handbook* (132), and several pamphlets issued by the Illuminating Engineering Society (3, 148, 217, 218, 219, 220, 233).

To maintain good conditions for reading, the typographical arrangement must be legible and both intensity and distribution of light must be satisfactory. These prerequisites have been discussed in earlier chapters. The present discussion will deal with kinds and locations of light source, and arrangement of copy in relation to the eyes.

The Lighting Arrangement

Whether in the school, office, library, or home, the goal should be to produce a visual environment where seeing may be achieved efficiently and comfortably. This is accomplished by lighting fixtures that provide an adequate quantity or intensity of light and at the same time eliminate all preventable glare. The particular lighting arrangement to be used in a living room, at a study table or desk, in one section or another of a business office, or in some other location depends upon the nature of the visual activity carried out there. Perhaps the illumination is primarily to provide a cheerful environment in a living room, kindergarten, or reception room. But if critical seeing is to take place, as at a home study table, or in a library or office, there must be illumination of proper intensity and, of course, control of possible glare sources. Cox (54) gives suggestions for laying out lighting in several situations where reading takes place. And highly useful information on specifying lighting for specific situations is found in the *IES Lighting Handbook* (132) and in the several pamphlets mentioned above. Before choosing a lighting arrangement for a particular environment, those interested should consult these sources or subsequent editions which appear from time to time. The main caution is to note that the intensities of illumination recommended tend to be higher than needed.

Electric lighting systems are classified as indirect, direct, semi-indirect, semi-direct, and general diffuse lighting (220). Although the particular fixtures may vary for incandescent and fluorescent light sources, one or another of these five systems or modifications of them are used. The systems are described briefly in Chapter 18. Which system is best for illuminating a reading area? Each system has distinctive features which may or may not provide the best light in a given situation. It is impossible, therefore, to recommend one system to the exclusion of all others. The system chosen for a particular situation should provide illumination that permits efficient, easy, and comfortable seeing. In addition, the installation of the system chosen should be in harmony with the architectural and decorative design of the room. In general, any ceiling lighting fixture should be hung as high as possible. Glare from a given light fixture becomes less the farther it is from the normal line of vision, as occurs in reading or desk work. According to Ferree and Rand (71), 3 to 4 hours of reading produced greatest loss of efficiency (fatigue) with direct lighting, next greatest with semi-indirect, and least of all with the indirect system which was nearly as good as diffuse daylight where there was practically no loss. In relatively small interiors such as homes, schools, and offices, most light sources should be screened from view. It is noteworthy that Ferree and Rand (71) found practically no difference in efficiency between the systems tested when no lighting fixtures were in view. All this points to the conclusion that any light source, even though enclosed in a diffusing translucent bowl, should be outside the visual field when the posture for visual work is assumed, as in looking at a desk or a book. When this is not possible, the surface brightness of the light fixture should be reduced greatly, by diffusing media, perhaps to 3 to 6 candles per square inch. In any case, to get the best conditions for seeing where critical vision is required, the light fixture should be out of the field of vision when the eyes are directed at the work surface. Cox (54) says, "*I state flatly that no modern electric light bulb or tube should ever go unshaded in any interior*, regardless of what the scientists who have devised these lamps may say, and regardless of the bright ideas of some 'modern architects' " (page 58).

In many situations where extensive reading or other visual discrimination is carried out, adequate illumination is best achieved by general plus supplementary lighting. Supplementary lighting, as the name implies, is local lighting used in addition to a general lighting system. It is employed to provide a specific intensity of illumination that is needed for effective seeing while performing a specific visual task. As discussed earlier, visual discrimination in reading depends upon size of details and contrast between the detail and its background, as well as upon other typographical factors. For instance, take reading of material printed in 6 point type on a poor quality of paper that provides a brightness contrast between paper and print of only 0.48. Presumably about 50 fc of light are needed for greatest possible ease and proficiency of reading in this situation. Such an intensity is best achieved by a general illumination of the room by ceiling or other fixtures plus supplementary lighting at the location where the reading is done. The fixture which provides the supplementary illumination should be of such a nature and so located that direct glare, shadows within the surrounding, and reflected glare are absent (217).

Attention should be directed to the relation of the light source to the reader. It is still a common belief that the light from a floor or table lamp should come over the left shoulder while reading. This notion probably originated because most people are right-handed. Their writing hand does not cast an annoying shadow on the working surface if the light comes from the left. But when reading, it is immaterial whether the light is at the right or the left. However, the light should be so placed that it does not shine into the reader's eyes or produce shadows on the reading material. Some light sources located behind a person with spectacles cause a disturbing reflection in one or the other lens of his glasses. The reflection may be avoided by shielding the light source and by moving the lamp more to one side.

Well-designed portable lamps that yield direct-indirect light are now available (54, 148, 219). Some light goes directly to the ceiling and is then reflected diffusely about the room, and part of the light shines directly onto the working surface, diffused usually by a frosted-glass, plastic, or porcelain bowl in the lamp. The lamp shades provide suitable shielding of the eyes from any glare from the light. This type of lamp is made in desk models and in floor models.

When reading or writing at a table or desk, the illumination should be distributed evenly over the working surface which includes the surroundings, i.e., 30 degrees in every direction from the line of vision when the eyes are directed at the visual task (page of a book). If the diffuse illumination extends over an area the size of a large blotter pad, about 18 by 24 inches, it should be adequate for reading a book placed at the center of the area. But if a person is taking notes from material in a book, which means that he is looking back and forth, the right-to-left evenly illuminated area should be increased, perhaps to 36 or 40 inches. When local lighting is used, there should also be general illumination of 5 to 10 fc. The desk lamp for the local lighting should be placed at the side, and should be without flicker such as is present with some of the single tube fluorescent lamps. The lower edge of the shielding shade should not be less than 15 inches from the desk top. And, if the supplementary lighting is from a floor lamp set beside the desk, similarly the lower edge of the shade should be at least 15 inches above the top of the desk. These floor lamps tend to have the lower edge of the shade 47 to 49 inches from the floor (148). Illumination over the surface of the desk may also be obtained from a pin-to-the-wall lamp with a proper shade and a plastic, porcelain, or frosted glass bowl below the bulb or tube to diffuse the light shining through it onto the desk. The lower edge of its shade should be

15 inches above the desk top, i.e., 45 inches above the floor. Any desk lamp, such as the gooseneck type or fluorescent tube lamps with opaque shades that are dark colored on their outside, used as strictly local lighting is decidedly undesirable. The lower edge of their shades is ordinarily less than 15 inches above the table top. Therefore, the dark shade is within the field of vision and produces a marked brightness contrast with the emitted light. In fact, these types of light fixtures are bad even when there is also general illumination unless the lower edge of the shade is at least 15 inches above the desk top. Few if any are that high.

When a person is seated in an easy chair while reading, a table or a floor lamp like those mentioned just above may be used to good advantage. If such a table lamp has the lower edge of its shade level with the reader's eyes, the lamp base or shaft should be in line with one's shoulders and about 20 inches to right or left from the center of an open book or other reading material. But, if a floor lamp is used for such reading and when the bottom of the shade is above eye level as it usually is (about 47 to 49 inches from the floor), the shaft of the lamp should be approximately in line with the shoulder front to back, and about 10 inches behind the shoulder (148). It is worth emphasizing that all portable lamps, table or floor, that are used for reading should have a diffusing element of porcelain, frosted glass, or plastic under the shade. The diffusing unit may be either a bowl type or a disc. In any case, it should be located within the shade and slightly above the lower edge so that the reader's eyes are prevented from seeing the brightness of the disc or bowl.

As noted in the IES pamphlet (219), the recommended posture for reading in bed locates the eyes at 20 inches above the mattress. This permits the desirable 45 degree tilt (see below) of the reading material. With wall-mounted fixtures of either fluorescent or incandescent type, the lower edge of the shielding should be about 30 inches above the mattress. With table lamps of the recommended types (see above), the lower edge of the shade should be at eye level, that is, 20 inches above the mattress. The shaft or axis of the lamp should be about 22 inches out from the center of the printed page and slightly back from the plane of the reader's eyes. Additional approved arrangements for interior lighting are given in two pamphlets published by the Illuminating Engineering Society and the *IES Lighting Handbook* (132, 148, 219). The spotlight or bull's-eye lamp used alone for illumination while reading in bed is considered decidedly unsatisfactory. The background surrounding the reader's book or magazine is too dark for comfortable reading.

With the marked improvement of lighting fixtures that permits satisfactory control of brightness contrast and other glare factors while providing adequate light intensity, the illumination of large and small offices and of reading rooms in libraries has changed. Recently constructed or remodeled business offices and reading rooms in libraries have abandoned low-level general illumination supplemented by local lighting at desks or reading tables. The trend is to use general illumination suitable for reading or other work requiring visual discrimination. Ordinarily, the installations are fluorescent luminaires (hanging fixtures), troffers (fixtures flush with the ceiling), or a plastic Louverall ceiling (the whole ceiling illuminated by recessed fixtures so arranged that the ceiling surface has a low brightness). However, in many instances, incandescent filament lamps in hanging fixtures are still used, particularly in old libraries where the ceilings are very high.

When the lighting arrangements are specified, other factors affecting comfortable seeing must not be neglected. In addition to providing satisfactory illumination for the particular reading task, one must control unfortunate brightness contrast and other sources of glare. That is, as explained in Chapter 19, there should be sufficient brightness on walls, floors, files, desks, and other furnishings to avoid high brightness-ratios with the work, reading or other visual tasks. With present knowledge of requirements for comfortable vision, there is no excuse for using dark-paneled walls, darkly shaded desks, files, tables, and floors. A striking example may be cited. An illuminating engineer asked the writer to inspect a new lighting arrangement which he had installed in the accounting room of a new bank building. He was proud of the job. On entering the bank, the writer asked the guard for permission to inspect the lighting in the accounting room, stating that the engineer had requested the inspection. The guard said, "Yes, you may look at it but no one who works in the room likes the lighting." The trouble was easily diagnosed. Troffer units delivered 75 fc of light about the room. But the desk tops were very dark; the numerous files were a dark shade of green; and many other parts of the visual environment were also dark. The workers complained of visual fatigue and discomfort. The trouble was the marked brightness contrast between their work and the visual surroundings as well as most of the room. At the present time there is little justification for such a working environment. Building materials and furnishings of sufficiently high reflectances and of equal or more preferred decorative character that can provide attractive working space and satisfy visual requirements are now available. Larson (146) presents information on illumination that is fundamentally sound and of high importance. Many pictures illustrate the text.

Position and Shape of the Reading Page*

The position of a printed page in relation to the visual axis, and also the shape of the page, affect visibility of the printed symbols and the speed with which the print can be read. Experiments concerned with some of these problems have been discussed in considerable detail in Chapter 15. At this place a brief statement of results will show the relation to the reading situation. For ease and quickness of seeing, the best position of a printed page is on a plane perpendicular to the line of sight or the visual axis, i.e., about 45 degrees up from the table top or down from the vertical. The visual shape of letters is distorted markedly when copy is lying flat on a horizontal table or desk top. In fact, a deviation from the 45 degree plane of only 15 degrees interferes with easy and fast reading.

Another factor here is the angular alignment of the lines of print. Experimental results indicate that for best seeing it is advisable for all readers to maintain the lines of print approxi-

* This section is partly based upon the summary of Tinker (317, Chapter 16).

mately horizontal left to right and perpendicular to the median plane of the body.

Other relevant factors were not dealt with in Chapter 15. With printed copy lying flat, the accommodation changes in the lenses of the eyes, required for clear seeing as the eyes shift from fixation to fixation along a line of print, are relatively slight and do not appear to interfere with the mechanics of reading. Furthermore, on flat copy the word forms or shapes are clearly visible. In some books, such as thick texts, dictionaries, and bound journals, the printed material does not lie flat. There tends to be considerable curvature of the page near the inner or gutter margin where the pages are bound. It seems possible that this marked curvature might well interfere with visual discrimination in reading. For instance, the lenses of the eyes must accommodate in order to see clearly with each change in focal distance that occurs with each eye movement to a new fixation along the line of print on the curved surface of the page. Since accommodation changes are relatively slow, speed of reading under such conditions may be retarded. In addition, when part of a curved line of print is farther from the eyes than other parts, letter and word shapes along the line are distorted. Although this distortion probably does not become important when the printed page is nearly flat, it may seriously interfere with visibility of words and therefore with clear and rapid perception when there is considerable curvature.

In an initial experiment, Tinker (305) determined the effect upon speed of reading and visibility when the printed text is slanted so that parts of each line are at varying distances from the eyes. Performance while reading material slanted at 45 and at 60 degrees was compared with that for flat copy. The deleterious effect of the slanted copy was highly significant. Speed of reading was retarded 5.7 per cent by the 45 degree slant, and 16.4 per cent by the 60 degree slant. Visibility of words was reduced 31.3 per cent by the 45 degree slant, and 48.4 per cent by the 60 degree slant. It was suggested that the major portion of the retardation in reading speed was due to the reduced visibility of the words.

Before these results can be applied to the effects of curvature of print in books, one must devise an experiment that more closely approximates the book-reading situation. Tinker (311) did this in his next experiment. Again speed of reading and visibility of words were measured. Printed material was mounted on a cylindrical reading stand 8 inches in diameter so constructed that it could be set at any position from the vertical to the horizontal. The standard situation was a flat copy sloped 45 degrees above the table top. All scores were compared with the standard, as shown in Table 16. With the curved material tipped to 45 degrees up from the table, the loss in speed was 7.2 per cent; in visibility of words, 9.7 per cent. And when the cylinder holding the print was either horizontal or vertical, the losses were much greater. Although accommodation changes were required in moving from one fixation pause to another in reading the curved print, the losses in visibility were so great that they would seem to be dominant in reducing the speed of reading.

The curved text employed in this experiment was a close approximation of the practical situation found in many large books and bound journals. The results obtained indicate that the marked curvature of lines of print near the inner margin of such volumes without doubt adversely affects efficiency and ease of seeing during reading. If much wider inner or gutter margins were used, the situation would be greatly improved because most of each printed line would then be relatively flat.

In the printing industry it is traditional, of course, to make the gutter margin narrowest or nearly narrowest of all. This is espe-

Table 16. Effect of Curved Text upon Speed of Reading and Visibility of Print

Position of Copy Compared with Flat 45° (standard)	Percentage of Difference* from Standard in Speed	Percentage of Difference* from Standard in Visibility
Flat 45° (standard).......	0.0	0.0
Curved 45°	−7.2	−9.7
Curved vertical	−11.4	−39.1
Curved horizontal	−36.5	−20.0

* Minus indicates slower reading and poorer visibility. All differences are significant at the 1 per cent level.

cially prominent in the larger volumes where it does the most damage to seeing. Since, as shown in Chapter 15, margins have nothing to do with readability of print, they must be justified, if at all, in terms of esthetics. And admittedly esthetics demands the use of some marginal space. Nevertheless, it would seem that an attractive printed page could be worked out with a rearrangement of marginal space so that the inner margin would be considerably wider than it normally is now. In any case, the reader should try to maintain the page he is reading as flat as possible and at right angles to the line of vision, as well as at a slope of about 45 degrees above the horizontal.

Certain other factors relevant to a consideration of the reading situation were considered in Chapter 15. Vibration of the reading copy, such as occurs while riding on a train, is not only annoying but also a hindrance to easy and fast reading. And when a nonoptimal typographical arrangement is present, such as 6 point italic print, the combined effect of the poor typography and vibration produces a severe visual task. In the study cited in Chapter 15, reading speed was retarded more than 14 per cent (302). Finally, as noted in Chapter 7, long periods of reading, even as much as six hours at a stretch, do not injure the eyes or produce measurable fatigue. This assumes, of course, that such factors in the reading situation as condition of eyesight, typography, and illumination are favorable.

Part Five: Appraisal of Reading Proficiency

21 *Nature of Reading Appraisal*

Appraisal of reading ability is concerned with two related aspects of a pupil's progress in learning: one deals with growth in reading of the normal child and the other with strengths and weaknesses of the child who has reading difficulty. It will be noted in the following discussion that there is considerable overlapping of the two aspects. To adjust reading instruction to the specific needs of pupils, it is necessary to evaluate their reading abilities at rather frequent intervals, as at the beginning of a grade and then subsequently from time to time in support of the instructional program. Such evaluation should be inclusive, detailed, and related to the objective toward which the teaching is directed. In such an appraisal, as noted by Tinker and McCullough (320), consideration must be given to reading attitudes, interests, tastes, and study skills in addition to the basic and special reading abilities. "In other words, if one is to know how well the reading objectives have been achieved, and how well the teaching program is planned to meet individual needs, there must be periodic measurements of reading ability in addition to the day-by-day observation and checking by the teacher" (page 307). The methods used at any given time will be determined by what is to be appraised. For example, one technique may be more serviceable for ascertaining how well pupils use phonics, another for speed of reading, another for vocabulary knowledge of specific terms employed in a unit of reading just completed, and still another to determine how well the pupils read for the general idea. Any appraisal should be made in situations that

Author's note: The discussion in this section is designed to present a general statement of the factors involved in appraisal rather than specific programs of appraisal.

closely approximate actual reading conditions. The alert teacher will discover that good instruction requires a thoroughgoing program of appraisal of progress in reading.

Consistent and balanced growth in reading proficiency is fostered by appraisal. It must be a continuing program, not a one-time event. If the data obtained in the appraisals are evaluated and used, "the teacher will be able to select appropriate materials and shape her instructional program to take care of the individual needs that are disclosed by the initial appraisal, the subsequent appraisals, and day-by-day or week-by-week testing and observation" (320, page 307). Unfortunately, as noted by Austin and Morrison (11), too frequently the test results are stored in a file rather than used efficiently by principals and teachers. However, when a teacher does use the data collected, she will soon discover that appraisal of reading and adjustment of instruction to the discovered individual needs are complicated operations because the reading process itself is a highly complex skill.

Tinker and McCullough (320) have emphasized that appraisal is necessary for best progress in the development of reading proficiency. The appraisal has two aspects: that concerned with achieving reading goals; and that which deals with guidance or adjustment of teaching in the classroom or clinic to individual needs.

These aspects have been outlined by Tinker and McCullough (320). Any adequate reading program has clearly stated aims or goals to be achieved at each successive stage of development. Appraisal is largely concerned with progress in learning and this is, at least partly, the outcome of teaching. That is, appraisal of growth in reading is carried out to discover the degree to which the goals designated for successive levels have been reached. If instruction to promote steady progress toward the next level in the developmental program is to be effectively planned and executed, this periodic appraisal is essential.

Of high importance is appraisal to promote guidance in individual instruction, i.e., to promote the best adjustment of teaching to individual needs. These differ from pupil to pupil and in the same pupil from time to time. Successful guidance can be achieved only when the teacher determines the proficiency level of the pupil in each specific reading skill. Then, and only then, can she adjust instruction so that the pupil may progress naturally in achieving the skills which experience indicates are necessary to forge ahead to the successive levels in the developmental program.

Every systematic treatise on reading emphasizes the necessity of adjusting the teaching program to the needs of individual pupils in a class (320, pp. 255–272). And, as pointed out by Bond and Tinker (26), the range of individual differences in reading proficiency in any class is large and increases from grade to grade. It is shown on their page 37 that the normal range of reading ability found in typical classrooms at the beginning of the school year is 2.5 grades in grade 2; 3.6 in grade 3; 4.8 in grade 4; 6.1 in grade 5; and 7.0 in grade 6. At the beginning of the second grade, the reading ability extended from grade 1.3 to 3.8; and in the sixth grade, from grade 2.5 to 9.5. These data are typical. When a teacher has knowledge of the range of reading ability in her class and knows just where each pupil is located in that range, she will possess much of the information needed for guidance in organizing her instructional program. This information also furnishes much data for grouping her class for instruction, providing individualized teaching, selecting proper teaching materials, and maintaining a satisfactory balance in instructional emphasis (320, page 308). After these findings are secured, the individual needs of pupils must be taken care of. Appraisal will show which ones need remedial help with such skills as some aspect of phonetic analysis, reading by thought units or phrasing, or sight vocabulary.

Factors Affecting Reading Proficiency

Austin, Bush, and Huebner (10) present an up-to-date statement of the factors involved in reading achievement. Some of the factors reside in the child and what has affected him in the past. Others originate in the school organization of the reading program, efficiency of the teaching, and teaching materials.

Mental ability plays an important role in reading proficiency. An abundance of research reveals the positive relation between mental ability and success in reading. Bond and Wagner (27) cite evidence that the relationship between intelligence and reading success becomes more pronounced at successively higher grade levels: the correlations increase from about .35 at the end of the first grade to about .60 at the end of the fifth grade, and to about .80 in the high school years. However, factors other than mental age influence the child's success in reading. Bond and Wagner state: "The mere fact that the child has high intellectual capability does not in and of itself guarantee that he will be successful in reading, especially in the early years" (page 130). Evidence cited by Tinker and McCullough (320) suggests that a child must have reached a mental age of at least 6 years before it is probable that he will be successful in learning to read, and that the chances for success are much more certain if the mental age is 6 years and 6 months. Nevertheless, it is hazardous to set a specific mental age for success in beginning reading. Evidence from several studies shows that children with mental ages less than six years can be taught to read. Gates (86) states that, when modern methods of instruction well adjusted to individual differences are employed, reasonable progress in learning to read can be achieved by most first-grade pupils. But this does not mean that the best time to teach reading is before a pupil reaches a mental age of 6 years or somewhat more. In fact the evidence is against it. Teaching reading to children with lower mental ages is more difficult, requires greater individual help, and progress is slower. In fact there is no valid argument for teaching reading to mentally immature children.

The lower correlation between intelligence and reading achievement in the lower grades seems reasonable when the reading activity there is examined. Success in the early stages of progress, as noted by Bond and Wagner (27), tends to rest heavily upon the more mechanical aspects of learning to read. For instance, skill in word recognition depends to a marked degree upon skill in auditory and visual discrimination. Only in the higher grades, where increased emphasis on the more complex aspects of comprehension occurs, is there a greater demand on mental ability. So the higher relationship between reading ability and intelligence there is not surprising. Quality and type of teaching, of course, play an important role at any grade level.

It is necessary to relate the reading program for a given pupil to his abilities. And it follows from the discussion above that a pupil's mental level should determine in part what is expected of him. To find out whether a child is reading up to expectancy, the teacher must have two items of information: a measure of his reading ability from a satisfactory standardized test and a measure of his mental age based upon a valid standardized test (see Chapter 22). A group test of intelligence is satisfactory only if the child is reading at the grade level where he is located. If he is retarded enough to be reading below his grade location, the only satisfactory measure is an individual test such as the Binet or the Wechsler (i.e., W.I.C.S.) given by a trained examiner. If this is not possible, the next best recourse is a carefully standardized nonverbal or performance test such as the *California Test of Mental Maturity, Non-Language Section.* For other performance tests, see Austin, Bush, and Huebner (10, page 37). If a performance test is used, it should be understood that the resulting mental age is not as dependable as that obtained by the Binet or W.I.C.S. Although a given mental age may not guarantee success in reading, it can be employed to indicate a general expectancy level when converted to mental grade by use of a table prepared by Gates (88, Table II, Appendix 2). Thus a mental age of 10 years and 8 months is equivalent to mental grade 4.9. Comparison of reading achievement grade with mental grade will reveal whether the child is retarded in reading or is reading up to expectancy. Note the three examples shown below. According to John's M.A., he should be reading at grade 6.7 (6 years, 7 months) although he is in grade 4.5 and his reading achievement is at grade 2.8. He is retarded 3.9 grades in reading, i.e., John is 3.9 grades below the expected grade level, a very serious retardation. Peter is in the seventh month of grade 4 and his mental grade is 4.6. Since his reading grade is 4.6, he is reading at the expected grade level and approximately at the

257

Item	Age (Years and Months*)	Grade Placement (Years and Months)
	John	
Actual age and grade	10-2	4.5
Binet M.A.	12-5	6.7
Average reading test	8-3	2.8
	Peter	
Actual age and grade	10-5	4.7
Binet M.A.	10-4	4.6
Average reading test	10-4	4.6
	Edward	
Actual age and grade . . .	9-8	4.2
Binet M.A.	11-1	5.2
Average reading test	9-10	4.1

* Chronological age in years and months is ordinarily indicated in the form 10-2, and mental grade, actual grade, and reading grade with the month expressed as a decimal, such as 4.5, because there are 10 months in the school year.

level of his grade placement. Edward is a different type of case. Since his reading grade is about the same as his grade placement, his teacher might infer that he is reading at a satisfactory level of proficiency. But his M.A. of 11-1 and mental grade of 5.2 indicate that he is a relatively bright boy and actually is retarded 1.1 grades in reading. These are typical cases that may be found in any classroom. For additional diagnosis, see Chapter 22. Occasionally one will find overachievers, those who read at a level above expectancy (10, page 31).

Estimating reading expectancy is usually done in terms of M.A. or mental age, as described above. Mental age does yield a rough estimate of expectancy. But what about the bright child with 140 I.Q. or M.A. of 9 years who enters school at the chronological age of 6-5? He cannot be expected to start reading at 3.5 grade level even though that would be about his mental grade. Ordinarily such a child would be able to read little if any on entering grade 1. Since he has not yet been taught, he has had no real opportunity to learn to read.

G. L. Bond and T. Clymer, cited by Bond and Tinker (26, pages 76–81), devised a method of estimating reading expectancy that takes into account the brightness of a child and the number of years he has been exposed to teaching in school. For instance, the average child with 100 I.Q. is expected to gain about one grade during one year in school; the child with 150 I.Q. can be expected to progress about one and a half times as fast as the average child; and the child with a 75 I.Q. can be expected to learn only about three-fourths as fast as the average child. If it is assumed that the I.Q. is an index of rate of learning, a child at the end of the first grade will have learned to read according to this formula: I.Q. times years in school plus 1.0 equals reading grade. The 1.0 is added since the child starts school at grade 1.0. After a year in school, an average child is at grade 2.0 or just entering second grade. Similarly, a child with 80 I.Q. will be expected to read at grade 3.4 at the end of three years in school; a child with 130 I.Q. should read at grade 3.6 at the end of two years in school. An unpublished study by Bond and Clymer, cited by Bond and Tinker (26), indicates that the relation between intelligence and reading achievement as computed by their formula is valid. Their data (Table 4, page 78) on 379 randomly selected pupils halfway through the fifth grade supports this conclusion. It would seem that reading expectancy computed by use of the Bond-Clymer formula is more realistic than the mental grade based upon M.A. alone.

When the teacher has secured a measure of reading proficiency and of reading expectancy, she can readily note whether a pupil is reading below expectancy, close to expectancy, or above expectancy, i.e., is an overachiever. If the pupil reads enough below expectancy to be classed as a retarded reader (see Chapter 22), a profile of his reading skills is needed to provide information for adjusting corrective teaching to his needs. That is, a picture of his strengths and weaknesses is necessary.

A disabled reader is made, not born that way. Similarly, as noted by Austin, Bush, and Huebner (10), the successful reader is made, not born. He is a mature reader who has attained the goals specified for satisfactory reading achievement discussed in Chapter 1.

It bears repeating that reading is a complex process and the instructional program is developmental in nature. That is, the program is sequential in which each new skill taught follows naturally what has been learned previously. As the child advances in school, he acquires skill in word recognition, expands his knowledge of words and concepts, learns to read by thought units, and, perhaps most important of all, learns that reading is thinking. With progress in reading efficiency, the child's store of sight words increases and word-recognition techniques operate with facility and speed. And, as he encounters more and more work-type reading, the reading material becomes more complicated in terms of vocabulary and concepts, length and structure of sentences, and intricacy of language. All this brings a growing demand upon the child's interpretation of meanings, his appreciation of style in writing, of vividness of description, and of humor.

From the very beginning the teacher, if the instructional program is to be successful, must keep informed about the progress of the individual pupils, discover difficulties encountered, and correct them. In addition to day-by-day observation, periodic measurement of reading achievement by means of standardized and teacher-made tests is recommended (see Chapter 22).

Other Factors Affecting Progress

In addition to those considered above, certain other factors are likely to influence progress in reading. Obviously a child must see to read. Certain children are subject to visual difficulties that may interfere with the clear seeing needed for reading (see Chapter 17). Both parents and the school are responsible for assuring as good vision as possible for each child. Visual correction by glasses should be provided through the school if parents are unable to do so. For screening tests to be used by the school nurse and symptoms to be observed by the teacher, see Bond and Tinker (26). In a similar manner, hearing deficiency should be detected by periodic audiometer tests and speech disorders noted by the teacher. Referrals for expert diagnosis and correction should be made when needed (10). In addition, the general health of a child may affect his progress in learning to read. Illness or undernourishment or glandular disturbance may interrupt learning so that certain instruction is missed or may so reduce stamina that sustained effort in the learning situation becomes impossible. Evaluation of personal needs must always include consideration of physical status.

Appraisal of personal and social adjustment, which is intimately linked with the pupil's emotional adjustment, should also receive attention. Most children who are having difficulty with their reading are laboring under some disturbing emotional stress. Ordinarily this is manifested by shyness or retiring behavior, lack of sustained attention, habitual nailbiting, a tendency to stutter, lack of self-confidence, irritability, or aggressive compensatory attention-getting behavior. For techniques of rating personal and social adjustment and use of personality inventories, see Austin, Bush, and Huebner (10).

How well a child learns what is taught and how much he will read on his own depend largely upon his interests. Interests provide the motivation that induces him to respond eagerly to various activities, including reading. With good motivation, a child will improve his reading under almost any well-recognized method of instruction. "Interest breeds motivation, the will to do something, including the drive needed for learning. This is true in learning to read — the interested child becomes the well-motivated child, the habitual reader." (26, page 395.) Without motivation a child will learn little or nothing. For appraisal of motivation, see Chapter 23.

The environment in which the child lives, especially the home, affects a child's reading progress. Emotional turmoil caused by broken homes, marital troubles of the parents, constant arguments among family members, unsatisfactory parent-child relationships, and other unfortunate conditions tend to interfere with effective learning. On the other hand, good home conditions which encourage interest and progress in reading include family conversation that improves vocabulary, verbal facility, and thought concepts, an abundance of reading material of proper difficulty, and opportunity for leisure-time activities including reading. Austin, Bush, and Huebner (10) give a sample questionnaire for gathering information on the home environment. In their Chapter 2, they discuss in detail the various factors that may affect progress in reading. The modern approach to reading appraisal as outlined in this section of their book has proven its worth in all school systems where it has been well developed and its adoption throughout public and private elementary schools is increasing year by year.

22   *Techniques of Appraisal*

In addition to the use of teacher observation and the teacher-made tests, questionnaires, and rating scales mentioned in Chapter 21, an up-to-date reading program requires that results be obtained from standardized tests and informal tests for other aspects of appraisal. A technique of appraisal in reading is a method employed to discover the grade level at which a child, with skillful teacher guidance, can progress at a normal rate in learning to read. In addition, methods of appraisal provide knowledge of a pupil's reading status in a number of areas to be discussed in Chapter 23, such as vocabulary knowledge, word recognition, rate of reading, and comprehension.

Nature of Standardized Tests

Standardized reading tests are measuring devices designed to give help to the teacher, the clinician, and the administrator. They may be used to determine the current status of the whole class and how it compares with national norms; the reading status of each pupil in a class; types of classroom instruction possible and desirable; strengths and weaknesses of retarded pupils as well as of those who are superior or average in their performance. In addition, they show the need for further testing and the degree to which the objectives of the reading program have been achieved (10).

There are many standardized tests available. Comprehensive descriptions and evaluations of all reading tests are given by Buros (37). Annotated lists of reading tests are provided by Tinker and McCullough (320), Bond and Tinker (26), and

Harris (114).* The statement of technical recommendations for tests and diagnostic techniques issued by the *Psychological Bulletin* (260) furnishes helpful information on reliability, validity, norms, and what should be included in the manual of instructions. Also see Stanley's revision of Ross (248a).

The better standardized reading tests furnish norms (standards of achievement) for a stated series of school grades. Austin, Bush, and Huebner (10) list items to check in choosing reading tests for one or another purpose. Any test, to be of maximum use, should possess satisfactory reliability and validity. A reliable measuring instrument is one that yields comparable scores on successive administrations to the same subjects; that is, if a pupil takes a test a second time a few days after the first testing, he will, if the test is reliable, achieve about the same score as on the first testing, except for some small gain due to a practice effect. "No absolute level of requirement can be set up for the reliability coefficients of those tests which are to be employed in individual diagnosis. . . . However, if the reliability coefficient is .90 or above, the reliability is excellent; in the high 80's, it is satisfactory; if in the low 80's, possibly satisfactory, though the results should be interpreted with reservations." (320, page 79.) When the reliability coefficient is below .80 for the total score, the test is considered unsatisfactory for individual diagnosis. But when reliability is .60 or above, the test may be safely used for group comparisons. Reliabilities of tests are (or should be) given in the manual of instructions for a given test. The prospective user of a test should examine the reliabilities of part scores as well as total score. Some part scores on certain tests do not have reliabilities that justify making individual diagnosis with confidence.

The validity of a test indicates the degree to which the test measures what it has been devised to measure. For instance, does a vocabulary test measure vocabulary knowledge, a comprehension test measure comprehension, and a speed of reading score measure speed? Methods of computing reliability and va-

* Standardized tests mentioned in the following discussion will be found in the lists of tests in these books.

lidity of test scores are given in most books on statistics, such as Johnson and Jackson (137).

Several other items of information are available and should be checked before purchase of tests in quantity. The publisher will send a specimen copy with the manual of instructions at a small cost. Harris (114), Bond and Tinker (26), and Tinker and McCullough (320) in the annotated lists of tests in their appendixes furnish title of test; type, group or individual; grade or age levels for use; number of forms; subtitles of parts; and time taken to administer the test. The reviews in Buros (37) give opinions of the test, methods of scoring, information in the manual, and some of the other items mentioned above.

Standardized reading tests may be roughly grouped as readiness tests, survey tests, group diagnostic tests, and individual diagnostic tests. The two main objectives in using reading tests are surveying the students' levels of achievement and diagnosing their strengths and weaknesses. Furthermore, there is no clear-cut separation between the survey type of test and the diagnostic tests designed to be given to groups. Almost any survey test also provides information useful in individual diagnosis and almost any diagnostic test provides survey information. In addition, reading readiness tests are used to diagnose weaknesses of retarded readers as well as to predict readiness for beginning reading.

Reading Readiness Tests

Numerous tests are available to appraise readiness for learning to read. Tinker and McCullough (320, page 581), Bond and Tinker (26, page 463), and Austin, Bush, and Huebner (10, page 46) list a number of them. Such tests attempt to measure the more important abilities involved in beginning reading. Ordinarily there are scores for each part of a test as well as a total test score. Teachers find that the part scores tend to be more meaningful than a total score. Gates (87), Bremer (30), Karlin (141), and others state that a total readiness score, although useful, provides less essential information than that derived from the part scores which deal with strengths and weaknesses of the pupil in each of the important skills, abilities, techniques, and interests that may affect progress in beginning reading. In fact, these part scores can be very useful for directing the teacher's attention to individual needs of pupils during the primary grades and for diagnosis of specific difficulties of retarded readers during these first three years of school. The classroom teacher should not misuse the knowledge derived from these tests. When a child measures low on a subtest, he should not be drilled on the kind of items in that subtest or similar ones found in certain reading readiness workbooks. Such exercises tend to become artificial and meaningless to the pupil. If a child is found especially deficient in such areas as language facility or visual and auditory discrimination, it is more profitable to teach these skills in the context of his immediate concrete experiences in which facility in talking and precision in seeing and hearing can be increased in a natural and interesting manner. That is, he should receive training by means of experiences selected to overcome these deficiencies.

The content of reading readiness tests varies considerably. In one or another test the following subtests appear: picture directions; word matching; letter matching; rhyming; reading letters and numbers; word meanings; information; memory span for sentences; speed of learning words; motor control; using symbols; and using context. Most prominent are tests of visual and auditory discrimination and vocabulary knowledge. As noted by Robinson and Hall (223), reading readiness tests tend to yield highly reliable measures which fairly well predict success in reading. None of the tests examined was found to be consistently better than the others. In many of the published results, the validity coefficients between reading readiness total scores and achievement in reading range from .45 to .60 and coefficients for the part scores range from .30 to .50. In this situation, any validity of .40 or above is satisfactory. If a validity coefficient above .60 is found, it is considered exceptionally high. Although reading readiness tests are useful, as suggested by Bremer (30) and Karlin (141), they should not be employed alone to predict reading achievement in grade 1. Tinker and McCullough (320) point out that, where possible, the results of mental tests should supplement the readiness scores, as each makes a unique contribution. They also note that no particular test of reading readiness measures everything pertinent to predicting success in reading. Moreover, certain relevant factors such as attitudes, interests, and the kinds of behavior that aid a pupil in adjustment must be appraised by other means. With certain pupils, it is advisable to use more than one readiness test to secure a more comprehensive diagnosis. Also, appraisals derived from systematic teacher observations and ratings are important; in fact they are an essential complement to readiness test scores. Skill in specific rating develops, of course, only with practice. Such estimates or ratings are best made by comparing a pupil with other pupils in the same class with respect to behavior traits, performance, and other sorts of adjustment. For example, the teacher, in estimating the degree to which each child cooperates with other children in group activities, might make the rating on a 5 point scale: quarrelsome, causes some friction, exhibits indifference, usually cooperates, and exceptionally cooperative. Rating of other traits may be made in like manner. Actually, as stated by Henig (117), many first-grade teachers after having children under their guidance for a few weeks can predict rather well their ability to learn to read. However, such teacher judgments should complement standardized tests results rather than replace them. Tinker and McCullough (320) have outlined procedures for constructing teacher-made tests for checking ability to understand and follow directions in marking pictures, making visual and auditory discriminations, and identifying letters and digits, etc. (pages 88–89). Such tests are particularly useful for checking the progress of pupils engaged in reading-readiness activities in the absence of equivalent forms of standardized tests. They also present on pages 92 and 93 a check list for reading readiness reproduced from Russell and Ousley (229, pages 55–57). The list has sections devoted to physical readiness, social readiness, emotional readiness, and psychological readiness. This check list, or one similarly constructed, can be very useful for summing up the various measurements and ratings on each child.

It is the obligation of the school to appraise both visual and auditory efficiency of every child before he begins reading. Screening tests should be used. To check far vision only with the Snellen Chart, as too frequently happens, is not adequate. Appraisal of near (12 to 14 inches) vision as well as distance (20 feet) should always be done. The farsighted child, rated normal by the distance test, will be unable to see clearly at the close distance required for reading.

Two satisfactory screening tests are the *Keystone Visual Survey Test* (Meadville, Pennsylvania), and the *Eames Eye Test* (Harcourt, Brace, and World, New York). The latter is inexpensive. Certain symptoms of visual disability may be noted by the teacher: blinking and watering of the eyes; squirming about; inflamed eyelids; complaints of headache after visual discrimination work or reading a short time; contortions of the face and tilting of the head while reading or attempting other visual discriminations. A child should be referred to a specialist for diagnosis when there is presumed evidence of visual difficulty obtained either in screening tests or from observation of behavior of the child.

Appraisal of auditory efficiency is best made by means of an audiometer (Graybar Electric Company, N.Y., or Maico Electronics, Inc., Minneapolis). Whisper or watch-tick tests reveal only major hearing disabilities. The teacher may note signs of hearing deficiencies: inattentiveness; requests for repetition of statements; misunderstanding of simple directions; tilting of the head with one ear directed toward the speaker; and reports of ringing and buzzing in the head. Referral to a specialist is indicated if a hearing difficulty is suspected.

Appraisal of a few other factors is needed to complete the evaluation of reading readiness. Speech disorders can contribute to reading disability. Every classroom teacher should have at least one course in speech in which there is emphasis upon identification of speech defects and the teacher's role in their correction. And in every school a speech therapist should be available whenever needed. Her role is to help the classroom teacher identify speech problems and to organize a program of improvement for individuals or groups of children with such difficulties. All speech problems should be identified as soon as possible after the child begins school and corrected to a considerable extent before much reading is attempted, i.e., in the kindergarten or early in the first grade. Successful early therapy will prevent speech defects from unduly interfering with learning to read.

Techniques for obtaining data on general health, personal and social adjustment, interests, and environmental factors are described by Austin, Bush, and Huebner (10).

Survey Tests

An important aspect of appraisal is discovering the level of proficiency attained by a given class or individual pupil in vocabulary, comprehension, speed, and sometimes accuracy as related to reading. Progress in proficiency is determined by appraisal of growth from initial to subsequent measurements made at periodic intervals.

Reading proficiency is measured by the use of standardized survey tests. Such tests are designed to give fairly accurate measures of the grade level at which a pupil can read in a competent manner. The norms of survey tests ordinarily cite grade equivalents for the score obtained. For instance, in the *Gates Primary Reading Tests*, a raw (obtained) score of 23 for paragraph reading corresponds to a reading grade of 3.2. This indicates that the score is equivalent to that made by the average pupil who has finished 2 months in the third grade. Some survey tests also give percentiles corresponding to raw scores, listed for a specific series of grades. In the *Gates Primary Reading Tests*, percentiles are given for grades 1B, 2.2, 2.5, 2.8. Sometimes, reading age equivalents are given. However, use of the reading grade scores is more common and is preferred by most teachers.

Contents of survey tests vary greatly. The following are examples: comprehension (*Los Angeles Elementary Reading Test*); speed (*Chapman-Cook Speed of Reading Test*); vocabulary and comprehension (*Nelson Silent Reading Test*); vocabulary (*Wide Range Vocabulary Test*); vocabulary, comprehension, rate, alphabetizing, and indexing (*Iowa Silent Reading Test*). Ordinarily, however, one expects a survey test to measure at least vocabulary knowledge and comprehension. In any case, the school should choose the test or tests that best take care of its needs.

The results of survey tests may be used for various purposes. The average score is employed to obtain the proficiency level of a class as a whole. Thus, if the average grade status at the time of testing is 4.3, that is, three-tenths of the way through grade 4, and the average of the reading scores obtained from the testing turns out to be 4.8, this class is on the whole superior in achievement to the average class by about one-half a grade. In a similar manner, the teacher can determine whether her class is reading at grade or below grade in comparison with the norms of the test.

The grade norms published for specific reading tests have certain limitations in their use. For instance, they tend to imply a degree of mathematical exactness which may not be warranted in some cases. Again, two different tests, say of comprehension, may not be comparable. Furthermore, it is easy to overemphasize the use of published norms which are usually derived from nation-wide testing. Local norms have a certain value. To establish local norms for a specific school or a specific school system, test all pupils in the same grade and at the same time in the school year, as at the beginning of the year. Then compute the median or average score. Similarly, average scores can be obtained for any tenth of the way through a grade, i.e., at grade 4.2, 4.5, etc.

The proficiency level of each pupil in the class is obtained by survey tests. The grade scores reveal whether a pupil is at, above, or below the grade level in which he is located. This information is a help to the teacher in organizing her instructional program to take care of individual differences in reading proficiency. It also helps to identify pupils who need a more thorough diagnosis to ascertain their degrees of retardation in reading.

The teacher should exercise caution in the use and interpretation of norms. The grade equivalents of obtained scores are based upon the average achievement of children at a certain grade status. There is always a wide range of individual scores below and above the average. An average is not necessarily a goal to aim at. Probably excellent instruction can raise a class average above the published norms. And a pupil who measures at grade may not be reading up to his capability (see Chapter 21).

Diagnostic Tests

In general, diagnostic tests are designed to ascertain the strengths and weaknesses in a child's reading performance, especially in the case of retarded readers. Pupils who may be retarded are identified by survey tests like those described above. Actual retardation of a child is checked by ascertaining his reading expectancy by means of the mental grade or by the Bond-Clymer formula presented in Chapter 21. If a child is not reading up to, or nearly up to, expectancy, he is retarded in reading and needs diagnosis and remedial instruction. It is for these cases that diagnostic tests are used.

There are available both group and individual diagnostic tests. It has been found that the group diagnostic tests are more effective when given to relatively small groups. They can, of course, be given to one child at a time. The only excuse for group testing is to save time for the teacher or the clinician. The group diagnostic, i.e., analytical, tests are superior to survey tests for use with retarded readers because they provide a profile of silent reading abilities. Such a profile shows strong and weak areas in a pupil's series of abilities measured in the subtests. Typical examples of these analytical tests are *Ingraham-Clark Diagnostic Reading Tests, Silent Reading Diagnostic Tests, Diagnostic Examination of Silent Reading Abilities*, and *Diagnostic Reading Tests*. For a comprehensive list of reading tests, see Tinker and McCullough (320).

The information derived from analytical tests is useful to both the remedial teacher and the classroom teacher. A first step in the analytical diagnosis of reading disabilities is usually to give

271

a group diagnostic test and to study the obtained scores. These scores show, within the limits of the subtests included, those reading areas in which a pupil is deficient. In those cases where a pupil's retardation in a certain skill is not great, such as trouble with initial consonants and consonant blends in word recognition, or a tendency to lapse into word-by-word reading, a moderate amount of individual instruction will correct the difficulty in most instances. Occasionally a teacher may discover that her class as a whole is deficient in reading for the general idea, or in some other skill. To remedy this, the teacher probably should modify her instructional emphasis to achieve a better balance among basic reading skills.

When a serious deficiency in reading skills is discovered, the child is ordinarily referred to a remedial teacher for a detailed diagnosis and intensive instruction (see below). What indicates a serious deficiency in reading? When a child is enough below expectancy to prevent him from achieving satisfactorily in the grade in which he is located, he is in serious trouble. There is no rigid standard for designating serious retardation. The following may be used as a rough guide: one-half to three-fourths of a grade at the primary level; one grade in the intermediate grades; and one and one-half grades in high school. The degree of retardation that is serious depends somewhat upon the nature of the disability. In any case, a retardation of one-half grade at the primary school level and of one grade at higher levels warrants an individual diagnosis (see below). If the more intensive diagnosis shows that the deficiency is confined to a single area such as sentence or paragraph comprehension, the difficulty can usually be cleared up by remedial instruction in the classroom. Sometimes a group test will reveal extensive disability which involves all, or nearly all, of the abilities measured. Such cases should be referred to an expert.

The main uses, therefore, of the group diagnostic tests are to identify specific needs of pupils with moderate reading deficiencies in grade 4 and above; to help the classroom teacher appraise the relative proficiency in various reading skills; to discover the specific needs of those pupils who are retarded seriously enough

272

to require additional diagnosis and remedial instruction by an expert. In addition, the group diagnostic tests are useful in severe disability cases for locating the area or areas that need additional intensive diagnosis.

Preliminary diagnosis of reading ability and deficiencies do not have to be made by use of standardized diagnostic tests. It is possible and sometimes desirable to employ an informal procedure, although this requires individual testing. First, a carefully graded series of basic readers is picked which the child has not used before. Then selections of 100 to 150 words are made from each successive book in the series. For each grade level, e.g., grade 2.0, take material about 25 pages from the beginning of the first page at that grade. Likewise, for halfway through a grade (grade 2.5, etc.) pick material near the beginning of the second book for that grade. A series of questions concerned with ideas and facts are made up for each selection. The child, starting at a level that is easy for him, reads each selection orally to the teacher or other examiner. After each selection is finished, the pupil attempts to answer the comprehension questions. After reading the easy selection where no difficulties are met, the pupil continues with successively more difficult selections (26) until his reading levels are determined. Betts (20) has outlined the reading levels as follows:

The *independent reading level* is decided upon from the book in which the child is able to read with only one error in pronunciation, or word recognition, in 100 running words. His comprehension must be at least 90 per cent. The oral reading must be in a natural, conversational tone, rhythmical and well phrased. The child's silent reading is faster than his oral reading and without obvious vocalization. At this level, the child should do extensive supplementary reading for pleasure or for information in line with his interests. Also, he has complete control of concepts, vocabulary, construction, and organization. Hence he has maximum opportunity to accomplish the thinking that is necessary for the understanding of what he is reading.

The *instructional reading level* is obtained from that book in which the child can read with not more than one word recognition error for each 20 words (5 per cent). Comprehension should not be less than 75 per cent. Here, the child reads orally, after silent reading, in a conversational tone, without noticeable tension, with satisfactory rhythm, and with suitable phrasing. He makes proper use of word-recognition clues and techniques. His silent reading is faster than oral. At this instructional level, a pupil can make appropriate progress in reading when provided with teacher guidance and adequate materials.

The *frustration reading level* is identified when a book is reached in which the child labors in vain when he attempts to read. His oral reading is without rhythm or phrasing and in an unnatural voice. He commits many errors and refuses to attempt numerous words. Tension is obvious. Comprehension is less than 50 per cent. When it is clear that his frustration level has been reached, the testing should stop. All teachers should realize that a frustration level exists and all should know how to recognize it. Too frequently, when instruction is not properly adjusted to individual differences, some children are working at their frustration level. No child in any classroom should be required to continue reading at the frustration level in any situation, instructional or otherwise.

The *probable capacity reading level* is revealed by the most advanced book in the basal series in which a pupil is able to comprehend as much as 75 per cent of the material when it is read aloud by the examiner. In answering questions and during discussion of what has been read, the child can pronounce and use properly a large number of the words in the selection. In addition, he should be able to use in his oral discourse some language structures comparable to those in the material read to him.

Determination of these reading levels is useful both to the classroom teacher and to the remedial teacher. The classroom teacher, seeking to identify the instructional needs of particular pupils, employs the information to adjust her instruction to meet those needs. The remedial teacher, to be successful, must know these levels for each case (see below).

The analytical diagnostic tests employed by the clinician and remedial teacher and reading specialists are ordinarily designed to be given individually. The following are representative: *Durrell Analysis of Reading Difficulty, Monroe Diagnostic Reading Examination, The Gates-McKillop Reading Diagnostic Tests,* and *Diagnostic Reading Scales* by George D. Spache. These, and other individual programs, provide a thorough analysis of the pupil's grasp of the skills involved in learning to read. All include an oral reading test which provides a wealth of information, as discussed below.

Other skills and types of errors examined in one or another individual diagnostic test include word recognition; vocabulary knowledge; reversal errors; phrase perception; visual perception skills, such as giving letter names, giving letter sounds (vowels and consonants); recognition of syllables and phonograms; auditory skills, such as blending letter sounds, giving consonant blends, blending word elements, giving words with specific initial sounds, and specified ending sounds; visual memory for words; and learning rate. Some diagnostic tests provide a test of listening comprehension. And all tests provide for an individual mental test.

Use of the oral reading test as a diagnostic instrument deserves special mention. Proper use of such a test yields a large amount of information. In fact, analysis of responses on a standardized oral reading test often provides enough information upon which to base remedial instruction. As with any individual diagnostic test, the examiner must be well trained in administering an oral reading test. All errors made by the child must be accurately recorded. Specific directions for so doing are given in the test manual. In addition, the examiner uses a check list to record his observations of the child's behavior and performance while reading. It is probably best to pause at the end of each paragraph to complete this checking. A set of comprehension questions accompany each paragraph. A grade equivalent for the child's score is readily computed.

Analysis of the errors made by the child provides information on aid given by the examiner, gross mispronunciation, partial mispronunciations, omissions, additions or insertions, substi-

275

tutions, repetitions, reversals or inversions, wrong beginnings, wrong middles, wrong endings, wrong several parts.

Additional valuable information is obtained from examining the recorded check list of observations. The following are examples: word-by-word reading; inadequate phrasing; incorrect phrasing; nervousness; tenseness; insecurity; reading in a monotone; poor enunciation of difficult words, or of all words; inadequate use of context; ignoring of punctuation; inadequate word analysis abilities; too much guessing from context without checking accuracy of word by use of phonics; depending mainly on letter sounds; giving up very easily or being too quick and superficial.

If the teacher has learned how to record errors and make observations of behavior, the informal oral reading test described above can be used with considerable success. Of the standardized oral reading tests besides those which are a part of individual diagnostic tests, the 1963 edition (four forms) of the *Gray Oral Reading Test* edited by Helen M. Robinson is perhaps the most useful for diagnosis of reading difficulties.

In addition to the comprehensive diagnostic tests, there are certain specialized tests available. The *McCullough Word Analysis Tests* diagnose 7 types of word analysis skills, grade 4 through college. Another type is the *Dolch Basic Sight Word Test* which measures the degree of recognition of the 220 words in the *Dolch Basic Word List*. The *Doren Diagnostic Reading Test of Word Recognition Skills* measures those skills which should have been learned by the end of the third grade if progress has been normal.

Bond and Tinker (26) have pointed out advantages and limitations of certain diagnostic tests. The *Durrell Analysis of Reading Difficulty* has a number of distinct advantages. The instructions for administering the tests are clear and thorough. The type of disability for which each subtest is suited is indicated. Administration of the various parts of the test is not difficult. For instance, tests for the moderately retarded reader can be given by an experienced, competent teacher who is familiar with the methods and objectives of teaching reading. Durrell states in the manual of directions that "The check-lists of errors are more important than the norms." These check lists are extensive, detailed, and complete. Their appropriate use furnishes sufficient information for diagnosing the strengths and weaknesses of a majority of disability cases although occasionally the grade norms will also be found useful. This test is most helpful for diagnosing pupils with not more than moderately severe deficiencies.

The Durrell test has certain limitations. Even though the revised edition provides also for diagnosis of markedly retarded readers, it is still generally more appropriate for use with the less severe cases. In all likelihood, the recording of eye movements by direct observation will provide little useful information. And certain tests for the more seriously retarded cases require considerable clinical experience for correct interpretation. Few classroom teachers are qualified to do this.

The Monroe diagnostic program is characterized by certain favorable features. The directions to the examiner are noteworthy for clearness and completeness. This technique is especially useful for diagnosis of the more complicated and difficult cases. It has been found to be readily modified for use with slow-learning children who are disability cases. The remedial instruction based upon the diagnosis is remarkably successful for correcting the disability of both moderately and severely retarded readers.

The Monroe program of diagnosis has limitations that should be kept in mind by the prospective user. Its procedures are time-consuming, exacting, and laborious. Apparently it is not the most appropriate technique to use with moderately retarded readers. And the program of remedial instruction based upon the diagnosis is ordinarily very detailed and takes an excessive amount of time. Furthermore, there is a strong emphasis upon phonics and other drill. Users of this program must be expertly trained clinical workers.

Several favorable features characterize the Gates-McKillop program of diagnosis and remediation. It appears to be the most complete program of diagnosis available. The tests are designed to identify any and all types of reading difficulties. A wise selection of appropriate tests makes the technique readily adaptable to reading cases of any degree of severity. The transforming of obtained scores into grade scores is especially helpful in identifying and evaluating a child's reading difficulties. The subtests are carefully standardized.

There are a few limitations for users of the *Gates-McKillop Reading Diagnostic Tests* to keep in mind. The tests should be given only by an examiner who has had thorough clinical training in administering them. This prevents use of the test in many school systems. It is a relatively long and complex task to complete a diagnosis. Scoring and rating of results on some of the subtests are complicated. In certain instances, the directions to the examiner are involved and not easy to follow. The evaluation of performance on a particular test tends to be confusing when the examiner is directed to compare this test score or rating with those on a large number of other subtests without stating which comparisons are more significant. Finally, the clinician is not sufficiently informed as to which tests to select for use with pupils who are less severely retarded in reading.

Any well-trained remedial teacher or clinician working with reading disability cases should become familiar with all of the more important individual diagnostic tests, in addition to receiving a thorough training in administration and use of individual mental tests. The worker in diagnostic and remedial reading should be able to select the test most appropriate for a particular case. There is little to be gained by administering the complete series of the Gates-McKillop tests or any of the Monroe program to children with only slight or moderate degrees of retardation. In other words, the examiner should be able to choose a program of diagnosis which will be economical of testing time, yet will provide adequate information concerning the child's reading deficiency. It is neither wise nor feasible to specify rigid rules about how to choose a diagnostic technique. The reading expert, through experience, will acquire the ability to select the best series of tests for a particular case.

A few general suggestions about choice of tests, however,

may be helpful to the recently trained reading expert. When it is determined on the basis of the difference between reading grade and reading expectancy that the degree of retardation is moderate, the *Durrell Analysis of Reading Difficulty* or selected parts of the *Gates-McKillop Reading Diagnostic Tests,* or some comparable program, such as the Spache *Diagnostic Reading Scales,* will be found appropriate. Ordinarily, informal techniques of diagnosis are useful supplements to these tests. In cases of relatively mild retardation, they may furnish all the information needed for the remedial program. But for severe and complicated cases of reading disability, the complete Gates-McKillop program or the Monroe, or some comparable program which will yield a thoroughgoing diagnosis is indicated. The experienced reading expert at times finds it helpful to use parts of more than one diagnostic series for the testing of a particular case.

23 *Appraisal in Specific Areas*

The sequence of steps in diagnosing reading disability ordinarily follows a general pattern.* First of all, the problem cases must be identified. This is done by determining the discrepancy between the reading grade obtained by a survey test and the reading expectancy grade derived by one of the methods described in Chapter 21. If this discrepancy is large enough, one-half to one and one-half grades depending upon the grade at which the child is located, analysis of the difficulty follows. This next step usually consists of administering one or more group diagnostic tests. For certain mild cases, the information thus obtained may be enough to proceed with the remedial instruction. In many cases, however, a further step is indicated. This consists of administering an appropriate, individually given analytical, i.e., diagnostic, test. Such a test is frequently supplemented by parts of other diagnostic tests or informal tests constructed or organized by the teacher.

With the test data in hand, the reading specialist organizes the instructional program to relieve the deficiencies discovered. This program must always be based upon diagnostic findings. But the initial diagnosis and instructional program should always be considered tentative. If the remedial instruction does not bring improvement during a reasonable length of time, there should be a re-evaluation of the diagnosis and perhaps some additional testing. This is especially true for many of the more complicated disability cases. It is gratifying that diagnostic and remedial

* This discussion is based partly upon material written by M. A. Tinker in Chapter 16, *Teaching Elementary Reading*, 2nd ed., by Tinker and McCullough (320).

reading procedures enable a well-trained reading expert or clinician to help all or nearly all disability cases substantially.

Appraisal of word identification and word recognition tends to be a continuing necessity, especially during the primary grades. During these early school years, the day-by-day adjustment of instruction to individual needs must be based upon such appraisal. The alert teacher will frequently check the progress of her pupils in mastering use of the clues and techniques employed for identification and recognition of words: word-form clues, picture clues, verbal-context clues, the basic phonetic skills, structural analysis including syllabification, and consulting the dictionary. At any specific time during day-by-day and week-by-week instruction, the appraisal is ordinarily devoted to the clues and techniques then being taught. For instance, when use of verbal context is being taught, most of the appraisal deals with determining how well the pupils are mastering use of meanings in the verbal context as a way of identifying new words. Other deficiencies uncovered will, of course, also receive the teacher's attention. Periodically, the appraisals will also check on what was taught earlier.

For short-range appraisal of skill in word identification and recognition, informal teacher-made tests are employed in addition to teacher observation. Suggestions and examples for teacher-made tests are found in the teacher manuals and workbooks accompanying basal reader series. At times the material in workbooks can be used without modification. The specially constructed readiness and achievement tests which are devised to be used with each step in the *Ginn Basic Readers* are good sources of testing material.

An excellent method for appraising proficiency in using word identification and recognition clues and techniques is to give an oral reading test. As noted earlier, the teacher must have experience in recording errors and noting a child's behavior during the reading. In such a test, the efficiency with which the pupil uses all the clues and techniques listed above, except referring to the dictionary, is readily determined. In other words, such a test will reveal how well the child comes to grips with new or difficult words. Most satisfactory data are obtained with such standard-ized oral reading tests as the *Gray Oral Reading Test*, the *Gil-more Oral Reading Test*, and the oral reading sections in such a diagnostic test as that of Gates-McKillop, Spache, or Durrell. For a thorough inventory of word recognition strengths and weaknesses, the *Bond-Clymer-Hoyt Silent Reading Diagnostic Tests*, the *McCullough Word Analysis Tests*, or the *Doren Diag-nostic Reading Test of Word Recognition Skills* may be used. All three of these measure the word recognition skills that should have been mastered. Consequently, these tests should be used in the latter part of the third grade or in the intermediate grades. Any one of the three may be administered by the class-room teacher who is well qualified to teach reading if she fol-lows directions *exactly as specified* in the manual of directions. A satisfactory measure of word recognition for the sight vocab-ulary that is supposed to be mastered by the beginning of the third grade is the *Dolch Basic Sight Word Test*. The words in this test make up two-thirds of the words that occur in the read-ing material of the primary grades, and nearly 60 per cent of the words in books written for grades 4 to 6. The frequency with which these "sight" words occur in children's literature indicates how important it is for pupils to master them. For annotated lists of reading tests, see Tinker and McCullough (320), or Harris (114), or Buros (37).

Appraisal of vocabulary knowledge can take place ordinarily along with that of word recognition. Both informal (not stand-ardized) and standardized tests are employed for measurement and evaluation. But teacher observation tends to be less useful for appraisal of vocabulary understanding. It is better, there-fore, for the teacher in her day-by-day evaluations to depend upon either teacher-made tests or other informal tests found in workbooks to guide instruction in vocabulary growth. This in-formation obtained from informal tests should be supplemented periodically by results from appropriate standardized tests. In-formation on several of these for each grade level may be found in almost any list of reading tests. Most tests for use in the pri-mary grades are concerned with general vocabulary meanings.

At higher grade levels a few tests deal with vocabularies relevant to specific subject matter fields.

Appraisal of comprehension is achieved most satisfactorily by use of informal and formal, i.e., standardized, tests. Nearly all standardized reading tests measure some aspect of comprehension. In a number of tests, several aspects are measured, such as sentence or paragraph comprehension, ability to understand directions, larger meanings, comprehension of details, and interpretations. As stated by Tinker and McCullough (320), "As in other areas of reading, the formal standardized tests are most useful for appraisals of growth over an interval such as three months, a semester, or a school year. An accumulation of scores makes it a simple matter to trace growth in each of the comprehension skills measured. Relative proficiency in the different kinds of comprehension is revealed by reference to norms." (Page 317.) To discover readily where instruction is needed to improve some aspect of a child's comprehension, scores for all his reading abilities, including comprehension, are arranged in tabular or profile form. Since these scores will ordinarily be listed by grade level, a child's strengths and weaknesses are easily noted. In addition, by examination of the profiles of all her pupils, the teacher can see what the class as a whole needs. That is, an area in which the whole class tends to be deficient will show up.

In order to adjust instruction to individual needs and to the necessary emphases in her instructional program, the teacher will have to have more frequent evaluation than that usually secured by use of standardized tests. In fact, most teachers carry on a more or less continuous evaluation to discover how well her pupils are acquiring the comprehension skills. Observation of the children's performance alone is of relatively small help. The day-by-day evaluation will be obtained chiefly by the use of informal teacher-made tests and workbook tests and exercises. By this procedure, she will find out how well the students are grasping the comprehension skills being taught in the sequential program. At the same time she will discover pupil difficulties which require supplementary individual guidance for their correction.

283

Some teachers find it helpful to use a check list covering various aspects of the comprehension skills. At any desired time a pupil can be rated on the items in the check list and these ratings then consulted in making appraisals. For instance, the standing of a child in the item "Understands relations between words in sentences" can be rated 1, 2, or 3 to indicate that the child is making less than satisfactory, average, or excellent progress in this aspect of a skill. A variety of comprehension skills that might be rated in this manner can be found in Chapter 8 of Tinker and McCullough (320). The teacher and the reading objectives she is emphasizing will determine what items to rate and how frequently the rating is to be done.

The more complex comprehension skills, such as skimming or generalizing, and the study skills, such as locating information or organizing material, are interrelated. As stated by Tinker and McCullough (320), "In general, the *study skills*, such as locating information, using reference materials, interpreting graphs and tables, organizing material, and adjusting the rate at which unfamiliar material is tackled, play an important role when one or another *comprehension skill* is employed. This relationship is particularly obvious in reading in the social studies, in literature, or in science and mathematics." (Page 186.)

Appraisal of the more complex comprehension skills (skimming, reading for the main idea, following and predicting sequence of events, reading to apprehend details, following directions, generalizing or drawing conclusions, critical evaluation) is accomplished by many kinds of techniques. A variety of standardized tests are available and may be employed for periodic appraisals. In addition, the teacher should frequently use informal testing to ascertain, as her instruction progresses, in which comprehension skills each child needs further training. This information is obtained by use of appropriate workbook exercises, by observation, and by use of tests constructed by the teacher.

Appraisal of the study skills (remembering what is read, locating information, organizing and summarizing material, adjusting speed of reading) employs on occasion all the techniques discussed above. But teacher observation and use of informal tests tend to be most rewarding and most preferred, particularly for the day-to-day evaluation. A few standardized tests are available for periodic testing in intermediate and higher grades.

More specific appraisal of study skills is in order as the pupils advance beyond the primary grades. One approach is to check the speed and accuracy in use of indexes, library card catalogs, and a dictionary or an encyclopedia. Observation may be used to check a pupil's efficiency in locating a specific fact in a textbook or a reference book, or his proficiency in selecting and evaluating pertinent information. Certain workbook exercises are designed to develop specific study skills. When coordinated with the classroom program, they may be employed to furnish some information concerning progress in the use of one or another study skill. But teacher-constructed tests and her observations tend to yield more information, especially when checking skill in reading graphs, tabular material, charts, and maps.

Appraisal of the specialized reading skills required for successful reading of material in the content fields must be made mostly by informal techniques plus teacher observation. Few standardized tests are available for measuring these skills. Those that are available ordinarily measure comprehension, specialized vocabulary knowledge, and interpretation. Nevertheless, use of standardized achievement tests supplemented by observation and teacher-constructed tests on the acquisition of skill and understanding will show whether a pupil is progressing satisfactorily in history, mathematics, or some other content subject. A pupil's difficulty in mastering a content subject may be due to deficiency in the specialized reading skills required. To find the source of the difficulty, the teacher must necessarily investigate the child's performance in reading that particular content material.

Other factors need to be checked. The difficulty may reflect a failure to master the fundamental and/or the more complex reading skills and procedures, such as basic vocabulary knowledge, word recognition techniques, comprehension and study skills. If the pupil is weak here, this deficiency should first be corrected. But, if this is not the problem, the trouble may be due to one or two other factors. First, the pupil may be unable to adjust his reading skills and the procedures previously learned to the unique requirements for effective reading of the specific subject matter. Or, the pupil may lack the necessary specialized vocabulary knowledge and related concepts. No child can do satisfactory work in a particular content subject without adequately mastering the unique vocabulary and concepts involved. "Observation of pupil responses in classwork, in teacher-made tests, in workbook exercises, supplemented if necessary by personal conferences, will reveal the degree of proficiency in technical vocabulary and in the handling of related concepts. If standardized tests of technical vocabulary are available, they may be employed for periodic checking to ascertain grade standing of the pupils." (320, page 300.) Actually the teaching of reading and evaluation of proficiency in the various content areas are at present not very satisfactory. Consequently, for the time being, the teacher must rely largely upon her own ability to devise and use informal methods of appraisal.

Appraisal of speed in reading involves, of course, appraisal of speed of comprehension for whatever is read. Appraising speed of reading has three aspects: ascertaining the best rate for achieving the purpose of the reading and for the kind of material read; determining whether reading of specific materials is so slow that it represents dawdling; and finding out whether a child can adjust his speed to the nature of the material and the purpose of the moment for which it is read. The pupil should be able to read rapidly when that is indicated, and slowly with care, and even to reread when this is appropriate for full understanding. There is no such thing as one speed of reading that is appropriate for various purposes and for all kinds of material. Appraisal of speed of reading must always be in some specific area, such as geography or literature. Speed of reading in one area bears little relation to speed in another if the reader adjusts his rate to the nature of the material as all good readers do. All concerned should realize that the rate of reading easy material such as appears in most standardized speed of reading tests bears little or no relation to rate of reading other kinds of material. Consequently, standardized speed of reading tests are of little use to the teacher.

It is necessary, therefore, for the teacher to organize materials in test form, which is a relatively easy task. She selects representative passages from a certain kind of material. These selections are then to be read for a specific purpose which the pupil clearly understands. Also he will know in advance that comprehension will be checked. A 3 to 5 minute sample of reading is appropriate and the timing should be accurate. With duplicated material, the whole class can be tested in a group.

Results of the testing give guidance in instructional procedures. Too fast or too slow reading for a particular purpose or for specific material, such as science or fiction, calls for corrective procedures. Merely informing a pupil how many words he reads per minute and suggesting that it is slow reading usually motivates him to read somewhat faster. When reading is too fast, it can be slowed down to a rate which is satisfactory for the requirements of the material read (i.e., rather slow for science, very slow for mathematics), or for a specific purpose, by insisting upon a high level of comprehension. This is supplemented by informing the pupil that a high level of comprehension is best achieved by reading slowly and carefully.

Training to increase speed of reading as such is seldom justified in the elementary school, except for dawdlers. Undesirably slow reading by a pupil is usually due to some deficiency in word recognition techniques, vocabulary knowledge, or comprehension skills. The most effective way to get a child to read at an appropriate rate in one or another kind of material is to provide him with a clearly understood purpose and to furnish him with the necessary concepts and techniques so that he can be prepared to comprehend fully what he is to read. When this is done, most pupils will tend to adjust their reading to a rate that is proper for the situation.

Frequent *appraisal of oral reading* is necessary to provide the basis for adjusting instruction where deficiencies are discovered. The use of standardized oral reading tests, as noted above, is not particularly helpful for diagnosing efficiency in reading aloud to an audience. What is needed is a procedure for evaluating skill in oral reading as a form of communication. The day-by-day observation of the teacher yields helpful information which should be recorded in anecdotal notes for each pupil's folder. In addition, the teacher should make systematic observations and ratings of the performance of each pupil while he reads selected passages aloud. The passages chosen should consist of easy material which contains considerable conversation. In general, this evaluation should be made while the pupil reads material he has prepared for oral presentation. Suggestions for items to be rated might well include enunciation, phrasing, word recognition skill, loudness, expression, rate, tension manifestation, confidence, voice quality, and rhythm.

Appraisal of reading interests and tastes is not easy. Nevertheless, if the teacher is to exercise guidance to broaden interests and to develop improved tastes, appraisal is essential. Initial appraisal will serve to determine current breadth and strength of interests and the level of tastes. Later assessment will then show what changes have taken place because of personal experience and teacher guidance. Informal procedures of appraisal are the only ones available. The evaluation is based upon a coordination of information derived from teacher observation, anecdotal records, conferences with pupils, and use of check lists of preferred activities and interests. Check lists made by the teacher tend to be more useful than published inventories. However, suggestions for the construction of such lists may be obtained by inspecting those published by Harris (114, pages 480–481) and by Witty (353, pages 302–307). Considerable information on interests and tastes can be derived from analysis of the data assembled by the procedures described above. These appraisals are, of course, largely subjective but nevertheless useful. Breadth of interests is indicated by the varieties of activities and of reading taking place. And the strength of an interest pattern is indicated by the time and effort devoted to a given activity or type of reading material. Standards of taste in reading are subjective. But, when the level of taste of a child is discovered, it is

288

possible to note whether added experience and teacher guidance lead to the reading of "better" books.

Appraisal of attitudes that promote growth in reading, and teacher guidance to improve them, should be a continuing process, for their growth is gradual. The relevant attitudes include those toward the teacher, books, the school, the reading situation, and class activities, plus the various habits the child has acquired while learning to read. Appraisal of attitudes must depend entirely, or nearly so, on teacher observation aided by analysis of anecdotal records based on observation.

Satisfactory appraisal is possible only when adequate records are kept to facilitate guidance in teaching reading. Furthermore, each pupil's cumulative record folder must be kept up to date if it is to be thoroughly useful for guidance. A valuable aid to evaluation is a record form in which is tabulated such items as mental test results, standardized reading test scores, initial and subsequent evaluations, and the various kinds of informal appraisals made. Tinker and McCullough (320) give a sample "Pupil's Reading Evaluation Form" on page 326. Probably most teachers will want to organize a somewhat different outline form to meet their special needs and then duplicate it so as to have a copy for each pupil. In a similar manner, it is helpful to enter scores of standardized tests on a profile. A sample, which may be adapted by the teacher, is given on page 327 in Tinker and McCullough.

Appraisal is absolutely essential if the teaching of reading is to be effective. It is generally accepted that the instruction must be adjusted to individual differences in the class although too often this is not done. In any case, such an adjustment is impossible to any appreciable extent without appraisal. And the appraisal, to be of maximum use, must be thoroughly carried out by administering both standardized and informal tests in addition to relying upon teacher observation. It is worth repeating that administering tests and making anecdotal records accomplish nothing unless the results are appropriately applied in the instructional program.

Any remedial teaching can succeed only when based upon an

appraisal of a child's strengths and weaknesses. With adequate appraisal, the classroom can and should be able to give remedial instruction to a large majority of children who have difficulty in learning to read. But a reading specialist will have to handle the severe and complicated cases. For these, the reading specialist will necessarily make appraisals by administering the proper analytical diagnostic tests to gain information required for remedial instruction.

Remedial instruction is primarily by individual prescription for individual needs. It should be emphasized that many of the specialized materials and gadgets employed by some reading specialists tend to have less value than the more meaningful, richer, more challenging, and more natural content used by good classroom teachers. As noted by Gates (88), "remedial instruction, with rare exceptions, would be more fruitful if the remedial materials were more like, indeed better than, those used in the best classroom practice in such respects as interest-provoking qualities, educative values, and general utility in content" (page 122). The main difference between remedial instruction and ordinary classroom teaching is that in the remedial instruction there is, for the time being, a greater emphasis upon individual work with the child in difficulty. And all this depends upon satisfactory appraisal as a basis for instruction.

Bibliography

Bibliography

1. Abernethy E. M., Photographic records of eye movements in studying spelling. J. Educ. Psychol., 1929, 20, 695–701.
2. Ahrens, A., *Untersuchungen ueber die Bewegung der Augen beim Schreiben.* Rostok, 1891.
3. *American standard guide for school lighting.* New York (347 East 47th Street): Illuminating Engineering Society, 1962.
4. Anderson, I. H., Studies in the eye movements of good and poor readers. Psychol. Monog., 1937, 48, 1–35.
5. Anderson, I. H., An evaluation of some recent research in the psychology of reading. Harvard Educ. Rev., 1937, 7, 330–339.
6. Anderson, I. H., The opthalm-o-graph and metron-o-scope evaluated in the light of recent research in the psychology of reading. Teach. Coll. J., 1941, 12, 60–63.
7. Anderson, I. H., and C. W. Meredith, The reading of projected books with special reference to rate and visual fatigue. J. Educ. Res., 1948, 41, 453–460.
8. Anderson, I. H., and W. F. Dearborn, *The Psychology of teaching reading.* New York: Ronald Press Company, 1952.
9. Arnold, D. C., and M. A. Tinker, The fixation pause of the eyes. J. Exper. Psychol., 1939, 25, 271–280.
10. Austin, M. C., C. L. Bush, and M. H. Huebner, *Reading evaluation: Appraisal techniques for school and classroom.* New York: Ronald Press Company, 1961.
11. Austin, M. C., and C. Morrison, *The first R: The Harvard report on reading in elementary schools.* New York: Macmillan Company, 1963.
12. Baird, J. W., The legibility of a telephone directory. J. Appl. Psychol., 1917, 1, 30–37.
13. Ballantine, F. A., Age changes in measures of eye movements in silent reading. In *Studies in the psychology of reading.* University of Michigan Monographs in Education, No. 4. Ann Arbor: University of Michigan Press, 1931. Pp. 65–111.
14. Bayle, E., The nature and causes of regressive movements in reading. J. Exper. Educ., 1942, 11, 16–36.
15. Bell, H. M., The comparative legibility of typewriting, manuscript

and cursive script: I. Easy prose, letters and syllables. J. Psychol., 1939, 8, 295–309.

16. Bell, H. M., The comparative legibility of typewriting, manuscript and cursive script: II. Difficult prose and eye-movement photography. J. Psychol., 1939, 8, 311–320.

17. Bell, L., Chromatic aberration and visual acuity. Elec. World, 1911, 57, 1163–1166.

18. *Better reading instruction — A survey of research and successful practice.* Research Bulletin of the National Education Association, Vol. 13, No. 5. Washington, D.C.: Research Division of the National Education Association, 1935, 273–325.

19. Betts, E. A., A study of paper as a factor in type visibility. Optometric Weekly, 1942, 33, 229–232.

20. Betts, E. A., *Foundations of reading instruction.* New York: American Book Company, 1957.

21. Bitterman, M. E., Heart rate and frequency of blinking as indices of visual efficiency. J. Exper. Psychol., 1945, 35, 279–292.

22. Blackhurst, J. H., Investigations in the hygiene of reading. Baltimore: Warwick and York, 1927.

23. Blackwell, H. B., Development and use of a quantitative method for specification of interior illumination levels. Illum. Engng., 1959, 54, 317–334.

24. Blackwell, H. R., Visual basis of desirable standards of quantity and quality of illumination. Amer. J. Optom. and Arch. Amer. Acad. Optom., 1963, 40, 581–613.

25. Boice, M. L., M. A. Tinker, and D. G. Paterson, Color vision and age. Amer. J. Psychol., 1948, 61, 520–526.

26. Bond, G. L., and M. A. Tinker, *Reading difficulties.* New York: Appleton-Century-Crofts, 1957.

27. Bond, G. L., and E. B. Wagner, *Teaching the child to read*, 3rd ed. New York: Macmillan Company, 1960.

28. Bowden, J. H., Learning to read. Elem. Sch. J., 1911, 12, 21–33.

29. Breland, K., and M. K. Breland, Legibility of newspaper headlines printed in capitals and lower case. J. Appl. Psychol., 1944, 28, 117–120.

30. Bremer, N., Do readiness tests predict success in reading? Elem. Sch. J., 1959, 59, 222–224.

31. Broom, M. E., The reliability of the reading graph yielded by the ophthalm-o-graph. Sch. and Soc., 1940, 52, 205–208.

32. Broom, M. E., M. A. A. Duncan, D. Emig, and J. Stueber, *Effective reading instruction*, 2nd ed. New York: McGraw-Hill Book Company, 1951.

33. Brozek, J., Quantitative criteria of oculomotor performance and fatigue. J. Appl. Physiol., 1949, 2, 247–260.

34. Brozek, J., E. Simonson, and A. Keys, Changes in performance and in ocular functions resulting from strenuous visual inspection. Amer. J. Psychol., 1950, 63, 51–66.

35. Bryan, A. I., Legibility of Library of Congress cards and their reproductions. College and Research Libraries, 1945, 6, 447–464.

36. Buckingham, B. R., New data on the typography of textbooks. In *The textbooks in American education*. Thirtieth Yearbook, Part II, of the National Society for the Study of Education. Chicago: University of Chicago Press, 1931. Pp. 93–125.

37. Buros, O. K. (ed.), *The fifth mental measurements yearbook* (plus the four earlier editions). Highland Park, N.J.: The Gryphon Press, 1959.

37a. Burtt, H. E., H. C. Beck, and E. Campbell, Legibility of backbone titles. J. Appl. Psychol., 1928, 12, 217–227.

38. Buswell, G. T., *An experimental study of the eye-voice span in reading.* Suppl. Educ. Monog., No. 17, 1920.

39. Buswell, G. T., *Fundamental reading habits: A study of their development.* Suppl. Educ. Monog., No. 21, 1922.

40. Buswell, G. T., *Diagnostic studies in arithmetic.* Suppl. Educ. Monog., No. 30, 1926.

41. Buswell, G. T., *A laboratory study of the reading of modern languages.* New York: Macmillan Company, 1927.

42. Buswell, G. T., *How adults read.* Suppl. Educ. Monog., No. 45, 1937.

43. Buswell, G. T., *Remedial reading at the college and adult levels.* Suppl. Educ. Monog., No. 50, 1939.

44. Butsch, R. L. C., Eye movements and the eye-hand span in typewriting. J. Educ. Psychol., 1932, 23, 104–121.

45. Carmichael, L., and W. F. Dearborn, *Reading and visual fatigue.* Boston: Houghton Mifflin Company, 1947.

46. Cason, E. B., *Mechanical methods for increasing the speed of reading.* Teach. Coll. Contr. Educ., No. 878, 1943.

47. Cattell, J. M., Ueber die Zeit der Erkennung und Benennung won Schriftzeichen, Bildern und Farben. Phil. Stud., 1885, 2, 634–650.

48. Clark, B., The effect of binocular imbalance in the behavior of the eyes during reading. J. Educ. Psychol., 1935, 26, 530–538.

49. Clark, B., and N. Warren, A photographic study of reading during a 65 hour vigil. J. Educ. Psychol., 1940, 31, 385–390.

50. Cobb, P. W., Some experiments on speed of vision. Trans. Illum. Engng. Soc., 1924, 19, 150–175.

51. Cole, L., *The improvement of reading.* New York: Holt, Rinehart, and Winston, 1938.

52. *Color and the use of color by the illuminating engineer.* New York: Illuminating Engineering Society, 1961.

53. Commery, E. W., and C. E. Stephenson, *How to decorate and light your home.* New York: Coward-McCann, 1955.

54. Cox, W. E., *Lighting and lamp design.* New York: Crown Publishers, 1952.

55. Crosland, H. R., *An investigation of proofreader's illusions.* Uni-

versity of Oregon Publication, Vol. 2, No. 6. Eugene: University of Oregon Press, 1924.

56. Crouch, C. L., The relation between illumination and vision. Illum. Engng., 1945, 40, 747–784.

57. Davidson, H. P., *An experimental study of the bright, average and dull children at the four year mental level.* Genet. Psychol. Monog., 1931, Vol. 9, Nos. 3–4.

58. Dearborn, W. F., *The psychology of reading.* New York: Columbia University Contr. to Phil. and Psychol., Vol. 14, No. 1, 1906.

59. Dearborn, W. F., On the possible relations of visual fatigue to reading disabilities. Sch. and Soc., 1940, 52, 532–536.

60. Dearborn, W. F., and I. H. Anderson, A new method for teaching phrasing and for increasing the size of reading fixations. Psychol. Rec., 1937, 1, 459–475.

61. Delabarre, E. B., A method of recording eye movements. Amer. J. Psychol., 1898, 9, 572–574.

62. Dixon, W. R., Studies of the eye movements in reading of university professors and graduate students. In *Studies in the psychology of reading.* University of Michigan Monog. in Educ., No. 4. Ann Arbor: University of Michigan Press, 1951, 115–178.

63. Dodge, R., Visual perception during eye movement. Psychol. Rev., 1900, 7, 454–465.

64. Dodge, R., Five types of eye movement in the horizontal meridian of the field of regard. Amer. J. Physiol., 1903, 8, 307–329.

65. Dodge, R., The illusion of clear vision during eye movement. Psychol. Bull., 1905, 2, 193–199.

66. Dodge, R., *An experimental study of visual fixation.* Psychol. Rev. Monog. Suppl., 1907, 8, No. 4.

67. Dodge, R., and T. S. Cline, The angle velocity of eye movements. Psychol. Rev., 1901, 8, 145–157.

68. Durrell, D. D., *Improving reading instruction.* New York: Harcourt, Brace, and World, 1956.

69. English, E., A study of the readability of four newspaper headline types. J. Quarterly, 1944, 21, 217–229.

70. Erdmann, B., and R. Dodge, *Psychologische Untersuchungen ueber das Lesen auf experimenteller Grundlage.* Halle: Max Niemeyer, 1898.

71. Ferree, C. E., and G. Rand, The power of the eye to sustain clear seeing under different conditions of lighting. J. Educ. Psychol., 1917, 8, 451–468.

72. Ferree, C. E., and G. Rand, An investigation of the reliability of the "li" test. Trans. Illum. Eng. Soc., 1927, 22, 52–75.

73. Ferree, C. E., and G. Rand, Intensity of light and speed of vision studied with special reference to industrial situations: Part I. Trans. Illum. Engng. Soc., 1927, 22, 79–110.

74. Ferree, C. E., and G. Rand, Visibility of objects as affected by

color and composition of light: Part I. With lights of equal luminosity or brightness. Person. J., 1931, 9, 475–492.

75. Ferree, C. E., and G. Rand, Visibility of objects as affected by color and composition of light: Part II. With lights equalized in both brightness and saturation. Person. J., 1931, 10, 108–124.

76. Ferree, C. E., and G. Rand, The effect of intensity of illumination on the near point of vision and a comparison of the effect for presbyopic and non-presbyopic eyes. Trans. Illum. Engng. Soc., 1933, 28, 590–611.

77. Ferree, C. E., G. Rand, and E. F. Lewis, The effect of increase of intensity of light on the visual acuity of presbyopic and non-presbyopic eyes. Trans. Illum. Engng. Soc., 1934, 29, 293–313.

78. Flesch, R., *Why Johnny can't read.* New York: Harper and Row, 1955.

79. Foster, H., A comparative study of three tests of color vision. J. Appl. Psychol., 1946, 30, 135–143.

80. Frandsen, A., *An eye-movement study of objective examination questions.* Genet. Psychol. Monog., 1934, 16, 79–138.

81. Freeman, F. N., *Experimental education.* Boston: Houghton Mifflin Company, 1916.

82. Freeman, F. N., Clinical study as a method in experimental education. J. Appl. Psychol., 1920, 4, 126–141.

83. Futch, O., A study of eye movements in reading Latin. J. Genet. Psychol., 1935, 13, 434–463.

84. Gans, R., *A study of critical reading comprehension in the intermediate grades.* New York: Bureau of Publications, Teachers College, Columbia University, 1940.

85. Gates, A. I., What do we know about optimum lengths of lines in reading? J. Educ. Res., 1931, 23, 1–7.

86. Gates, A. I., The necessary mental age for beginning reading. Elem. Sch. J., 1937, 37, 497–508.

87. Gates, A. I., A further evaluation of reading readiness tests. Elem. Sch. J., 1940, 40, 577–591.

88. Gates, A. I., *The improvement of reading,* 3rd ed. New York: Macmillan Company, 1947.

89. Gates, A. I., and E. Boeker, A study of initial stages in reading by preschool children. Teachers College Record, 1923, 24, 469–488.

90. Geldard, F. A., *The human senses.* New York: John Wiley and Sons, 1953.

91. Gilbert, A. J., and D. W. Gilbert, Reading before the eye-movement camera versus away from it. Elem. Sch. J., 1942, 42, 443–447.

92. Gilbert, L. C., *An experimental investigation of eye movements in learning to spell words.* Psychol. Monog., 1932, 43, No. 196.

93. Gilbert, L. C., A genetic study of growth in perceptual habits in spelling. Elem. Sch. J., 1940, 40, 346–357.

94. Gilbert, L. C., *Functional motor efficiency of the eyes and its rela-*

tion to reading. Univ. Calif. Publ. Vol. 11, No. 3. Berkeley: University of California Press, 1953.

95. Gilbert, L. C., and D. W. Gilbert, *Training for speed and accuracy of visual perception in learning to spell: A study of eye movements.* Univ. Calif. Publ. Educ. No. 7. Berkeley: University of California Press, 1942.

96. Gilbert, L. C., and D. W. Gilbert, The improvement of spelling through reading. J. Educ. Res., 1944, 37, 458–463.

97. Gilliland, A. R., The effect on reading of changes in the size of type. Elem. Sch. J., 1923, 24, 138–146.

98. Glanville, A. D., G. L. Kreezer, and K. M. Dallenbach, The effect of type size on accuracy of apprehension and speed of localizing words. Amer. J. Psychol., 1946, 59, 220–235.

99. Glock, M. D., Effect upon eye movements and reading rate at the college level of three methods of training. J. Educ. Psychol., 1949, 40, 93–106.

100. Goldscheider, A., and R. F. Müller, Zur Physiologie und Pathologie des Lesens. Zsch. f. Klin. Med., 1893, 23, 131–167.

100a. Gould, P. N., L. C. Raines, and C. A. Ruckmick, The printing of backbone titles on thin books and magazines. Psychol. Monog., 1921, 30, 62–76.

101. Gray, C. T., *Types of reading ability as exhibited through tests and laboratory experiments.* Suppl. Educ. Monog., No. 5, 1917.

102. Gray, L., *Teaching children to read,* 3rd ed. New York: Ronald Press Company, 1963.

103. Gray, W. S., Diagnostic and remedial steps in reading. J. Educ. Res., 1921, 4, 1–15.

104. Gray, W. S., *Remedial cases in reading: Their diagnosis and treatment.* Suppl. Educ. Monog., No. 22, 1922.

105. Gray, W. S., A study of reading in fourteen languages. In *The teaching of reading and writing: An international study.* Chicago: Scott, Foresman, 1956.

106. Gray, W. S., and B. Rogers, *Maturity in reading: Its nature and appraisal.* Chicago: University of Chicago Press, 1956.

107. Grayum, H. S., An analytic description of skimming: Its purpose and place as an ability in reading. *Studies in Education* (Theses Abstract Series). Bloomington: School of Education, Indiana University, 1952. Pp. 137–143.

108. Greene, E. B., The legibility of typewritten material. J. Appl. Psychol., 1933, 17, 713–728.

109. Griffing, H., and S. I. Franz, On the condition of fatigue in reading. Psychol. Rev., 1896, 3, 513–530.

110. Hackman, R. B., *An analysis of certain factors operating in the reaction of the eye to suddenly appearing peripheral stimuli.* Ph.D. Thesis, University of Minnesota, 1938.

111. Hackman, R. B., and M. A. Tinker, Effect of variation in color

of print and background upon eye movements in reading. Amer. J. Optom. and Arch. Amer. Acad. Optom., 1957, 34, 354–359.

112. Hamilton, F. M., *The perceptual factors in reading.* Archives of Psychology, Vol. 1, No. 9, 1907.

113. Hamilton, J. A., *Toward proficient reading.* Claremont, Calif.: Saunders Press, 1939.

114. Harris, A. J., *How to increase reading ability,* 4th ed. New York: Longmans, Green, and Company, 1961.

115. Harrison, M. L., *Reading Readiness,* rev. ed. Boston: Houghton Mifflin Company, 1939.

116. Hecht, S., and J. Mandelbaum, Dark adaptation and experimental human vitamin A deficiency. Amer. J. Physiol., 1940, 130, 651–664.

117. Henig, M. S., Predictive value of a reading readiness test and of teacher's forecasts. Elem. Sch. J., 1949, 50, 41–46.

118. Hildreth, G., *Teaching reading.* New York: Holt, Rinehart, and Winston, 1958.

119. Hill, M. B., A study of the process of word discrimination in individuals beginning to read. J. Educ. Res., 1936, 29, 487–500.

120. Hincks, E. M., *Disability in reading and its relation to personality.* Harvard Monog. in Educ., No. 7, 1926.

121. Hoffman, A. C., Eye movements during prolonged reading. J. Exper. Psychol., 1946, 36, 95–118.

122. Hoffman, A. C., B. Wellman, and L. Carmichael, A quantitative comparison of the electrical and photographical techniques of eye-movement recording. J. Exper. Psychol., 1939, 24, 40–53.

123. Hoffmann, J., Experimentelle psychologische Untersuchungen ueber Leseleistungen von Schulkindern. Arch. f. d. ges. Psychol., 1927, 58, 325–388.

124. Holmes, G., The relative legibility of black print and white print. J. Appl. Psychol., 1931, 15, 248–251.

125. Holt, E. B., Eye movement and central anaesthesia. Psychol. Monog., 1903, 4, No. 17.

126. Holway, A. H., and D. Jameson, *Good lighting for people at work in reading rooms and offices.* Boston (Soldiers Field): Harvard Business School, Division of Research, 1947.

127. Hovde, H. T., The relative effect of size of type, leading and context. Part I. J. Appl. Psychol., 1929, 13, 600–629.

128. Hovde, H. T., The relative effect of size of type, leading and context. Part II. J. Appl. Psychol., 1930, 14, 63–73.

129. Huey, E. B., Preliminary experiments in the physiology and psychology of reading. Amer. J. Psychol., 1898, 9, 575–586.

130. Huey, E. B., On the psychology and physiology of reading. Amer. J. Psychol., 1900, 11, 283–302; 1901, 12, 292–313.

131. Huey, E. B., *The psychology and pedagogy of reading.* New York: Macmillan Company, 1908.

132. *IES lighting handbook*, 3rd ed. New York: Illuminating Engineering Society (145 East 47th Street), 1962.

133. Imus, H. A., J. W. M. Rothney, and R. M. Bear, *An evaluation of visual factors in reading*. Hanover, N.H.: Dartmouth College Publication, 1938.

134. Imus, M. A., J. W. M. Rothney, and R. M. Bear, Photography of eye movements. Amer. J. Optom. and Arch. Amer. Acad. Optom., 1943, 20, 231–247.

135. Javal, E., Essai sur la physiologie de la lecture. Annales D'Oculistique, 1879, 82, 242–253.

136. Javal, E., *Physiologie de la lecture et de l'ecriture*, 2nd ed. Paris: Librairie Felix Alcan, 1906.

137. Johnson, P. O., and R. W. B. Jackson, *Introduction to statistical methods*. Englewood Cliffs, N.J.: Prentice-Hall, 1953.

138. Jones, H. E. and D. M. Morgan, Twin similarities in eye-movement patterns. J. Hered., 1942, 33, 167–172.

139. Judd, C. H., C. N. McAllister, and W. M. Steele, Introduction to series of studies of eye movements by means of kinetoscope photographs. Psychol. Rev., 1905, 6, 1–16.

140. Judd, C. H., and G. T. Buswell, *Silent reading: A study of the various types*. Suppl. Educ. Monog., No. 23, 1922.

141. Karlin, R., The prediction of reading success and reading readiness tests. Elementary English, 1957, 34, 320–322.

142. Kirschmann, A., Uber die Erkennbarkeit geometrischer Figuren und Schriftzeichen in indirekten Sehen. Arch. f. d. Gesamte Psychol., 1908, 13, 352–388.

143. Komzweig, A. L., *Physiological effects of age on the visual process*. Special Publication No. 195 of the National Society for the Prevention of Blindness, New York, 1954. Reprinted from the Sight-Saving Review, Vol. 24, No. 3.

144. Kunz, J. E., and R. B. Sleight, Effect of target brightness on "normal" and "subnormal" visual acuity. J. Appl. Psychol., 1949, 33, 83–91.

145. Landolt, S., Nouvelles researches sur la physiologie des mouvements des yeux. Archives D'Ophthal., 1891, 11, 385–395.

146. Larson, L., *Lighting and its design*. New York (18 East 55th St.): Whitney Library of Design, 1964.

146a. Laycock, F., Significant characteristics of college students with varying flexibility in reading rate: 1. Eye movements in reading prose; 2. Motor and perceptual skill in "reading" material whose meaning is unimportant. J. Exper. Educ., 1955, 23, 311–330.

147. Ledbetter, F. G., Reading reactions for varied types of subject matter: An analytical study of eye movements of 11th grade pupils. J. Educ. Res., 1947, 41, 102–115.

148. *Lighting keyed to today's homes*. New York: Illuminating Engineering Society, 1961.

149. Lofquist, L., *Eye movements in a special reading situation.* M.A. Thesis, University of Minnesota, 1941.
150. Luckiesh, M., Monochromatic light and visual acuity. Elec. World, 1911, 58, 450–452.
151. Luckiesh, M., The influence of spectral character of light on effectiveness of illumination. Trans. Illum. Engng. Soc., 1912, 7, 135–152.
152. Luckiesh, M., Visual acuity in white light. Elec. World, 1913, 62 1160.
153. Luckiesh, M., *Light, vision and seeing.* New York: D. Van Nostrand Company, 1944.
154. Luckiesh, M., Reading and the rate of blinking. J. Exper. Psychol., 1947, 37, 266–268.
155. Luckiesh, M., and F. K. Moss, Seeing in sodium-vapor light. J. Opt. Soc. Amer., 1934, 24, 5–13.
156. Luckiesh, M., and F. K. Moss, *The new science of seeing.* Cleveland: General Electric Company, 1934.
157. Luckiesh, M., and F. K. Moss, Visibility: Its measurement and significance in reading. J. Franklin Inst., 1935, 220, 431–466.
158. Luckiesh, M., and F. K. Moss, Seeing in tungsten, mercury and sodium lights. Trans. Illum. Engng. Soc., 1936, 31, 655–674.
159. Luckiesh, M., and F. K. Moss, *The science of seeing.* New York: D. Van Nostrand Company, 1937.
160. Luckiesh, M., and F. K. Moss, The visibility of various type faces. J. Franklin Inst., 1937, 223, 72–82.
161. Luckiesh, M., and F. K. Moss, Visibility and readability of print on white and tinted papers. Sight-Saving Rev., 1938, 8, 123–134.
162. Luckiesh, M., and F. K. Moss, Frequency of blinking as a clinical criterion of ease of seeing. Amer. J. Ophthal., 1939, 22, 616–621.
163. Luckiesh, M., and F. K. Moss, The readability of stencil duplicated materials. Sight-Saving Rev., 1939, 9, December 3–12.
164. Luckiesh, M., and F. K. Moss, Criterion of readability. J. Exper. Psychol., 1940, 27, 256–270.
165. Luckiesh, M., and F. K. Moss, Boldness as a factor in type-design and typography. J. Appl. Psychol., 1940, 24, 170–183.
166. Luckiesh, M., and F. K. Moss, Vision and seeing under light from fluorescent lamps. Illum. Engng., 1942, 37, 81–88.
167. Luckiesh, M., and F. K. Moss, *Reading as a visual task.* New York: D. Van Nostrand Company, 1942.
168. Luckiesh, M. and F. K. Moss, Visual tasks in comic books. Sight-Saving Rev., 1942, 12, March, 19–24.
169. Luckiesh, M., S. K. Guth, and A. A. Eastman, The blink rate and ease of seeing. Illum. Engng., 1947, 42, 584–588.
170. Luckiesh, M., and A. H. Taylor, Radiant energy from fluorescent lamps. Illum. Engng., 1945, 40, 77–88.
171. Lyon, O. C., The telephone directory. Bell Telephone Quarterly, 1924, 3, 175–185.

172. Lythgoe, R. J., *The measurement of visual acuity*. London: His Majesty's Stationery Office, 1932.

172a. Martin, L. C., and R. W. B. Pearse, The comparative visual acuity and ease of reading in white and coloured light. Brit. J. Ophthal., 1947, 31, 129–144.

173. May, C. H., and C. A. Perera, *Manual of the diseases of the eye*, 18th ed. New York: William Wood and Company, 1943.

174. McCullough, C. M., About practices in teaching reading. English Journal, 1957, 46, 475–490.

175. McCullough, C. M., Context aids in reading. The Reading Teacher, 1958, 11, 225–229.

176. McCullough, C. M., Conditions favorable to comprehension. Education, 1959, 79, 533–536.

177. McFarland, R. A., A. H. Holway, and L. M. Hurvich, *Studies in visual fatigue*. Boston (Soldiers Field): Graduate School of Business Administration, Harvard University, 1942.

178. McNamara, W. G., D. G. Paterson, and M. A. Tinker, The influence of size of type on speed of reading in the primary grades. The Sight-Saving Rev., 1953, 23, 28–33.

179. Meek, L. H., *A study of learning and retention in young children*. Teachers College Contr. to Educ., No. 164. New York: Bureau of Publications, Teachers College, Columbia University, 1925.

180. Messmer, O., Zur Psychologie des Lesen bei Kindern und Erwachsennen. Arch. f. d. ges. Psychol., 1903, 2, 190–298.

181. Miles, W. R., The peep-hole method for observing eye movements in reading. J. Genet. Psychol., 1928, 1, 373–374.

182. Miles, W. R., Horizontal eye movements at the onset of sleep. Psychol. Rev., 1929, 36, 122–141.

183. Miles, W. R., and D. Segal, Clinical observation of eye movements in the rating of reading ability. J. Educ. Psychol., 1929, 20, 520–529.

184. Miles, W. R., and E. Shen, Photographic recording of eye movements in the reading of Chinese in vertical and horizontal axes: Method and preliminary results. J. Exper. Psychol., 1925, 8, 344–362.

185. Milne, J. R., The arrangement of mathematical tables. In *Napier Tercentenary Memorial Volume*. London: Longmans, Green and Company, 1915. Pp. 293–316.

186. Miyake, R., J. W. Dunlap, and E. E. Cureton, The comparative legibility of black and colored numbers on colored and black backgrounds. J. Gen. Psychol., 1930, 3, 340–343.

187. Morgan, D. H., Twin similarities in photographic measures of eye movements while reading prose. J. Educ. Psychol., 1939, 30, 572–586.

188. Morse, W. C., A comparison of the eye movements of average fifth and seventh grade pupils reading materials of corresponding difficulty. In *Studies in the psychology of reading*. University of Michi-

gan Monog. in Educ., No. 4. Ann Arbor: University of Michigan Press, 1951. Pp. 1–64.

189. Munoz, J. M., J. B. Odoriz, and J. Tavazza, Registro de los movemientos occulares durante lectura. Rev. Sociedad Argentina Biologia, 1944, 20, 280–286.

190. Nelson, L. P., *Employee handbook printing practices*. Minneapolis: Industrial Relations Center, University of Minnesota, 1949.

191. North, A. J., and L. B. Jenkins, Reading speed and comprehension as a function of typography. J. Appl. Psychol., 1951, 35, 225–228.

191a. Ogg, O., *The 26 Letters*. New York: Thomas Y. Crowell Company, 1961.

192. Ovink, G. W., *Legibility, atmosphere-value and forms of printing types*. Leiden: A. W. Sitjthoff's Uitgeversmaatschappij N. V., 1938.

193. Paterson, D. G., and M. A. Tinker, Time-limit vs. work-limit methods. Amer. J. Psychol., 1930, 42, 101–104.

194. Paterson, D. G., and M. A. Tinker, Studies of typographical factors influencing speed of reading: VI. Black type versus white type. J. Appl. Psychol., 1931, 15, 241–247.

195. Paterson, D. G., and M. A. Tinker, Studies of typographical factors influencing speed of reading: X. Styles of type face. J. Appl. Psychol., 1932, 16, 605–613.

196. Paterson, D. G., and M. A. Tinker, The part-whole illusion in printing. J. Appl. Psychol., 1938, 22, 421–425.

197. Paterson, D. G., and M. A. Tinker, *How to make type readable*. New York: Harper and Row, 1940.

198. Paterson, D. G., and M. A. Tinker, Influence of line width on eye movements. J. Exper. Psychol., 1940, 27, 572–577.

199. Paterson, D. G., and M. A. Tinker, Influence of line width on eye movements for six point type. J. Educ. Psychol., 1942, 33, 552–555.

200. Paterson, D. G., and M. A. Tinker, Influence of size of type on eye movements. J. Appl. Psychol., 1942, 26, 227–230.

201. Paterson, D. G., and M. A. Tinker, Eye movements in reading type sizes in optimal line widths. J. Educ. Psychol., 1943, 54, 547–551.

202. Paterson, D. G., and M. A. Tinker, Eye movements in reading optimal and non-optimal typography. J. Exper. Psychol., 1944, 34, 80–85.

203. Paterson, D. G., and M. A. Tinker, Readability of newspaper headlines printed in capitals and lower case. J. Appl. Psychol., 1946, 30, 161–168.

204. Paterson, D. G., and M. A. Tinker, The relative readability of newspaper and book print. J. Appl. Psychol., 1946, 30, 454–459.

205. Paterson, D. G., and M. A. Tinker, Influence of leading upon the

readability of newspaper type. J. Appl. Psychol., 1947, 31, 160–163.

206. Perry, D. K., Speed and accuracy of reading Arabic and Roman numerals. J. Appl. Psychol., 1952, 36, 346–347.

207. Pillsbury, W. B., A study in apperception. Amer. J. Psychol., 1897, 8, 315–393.

208. Pollock, M. C., and L. C. Pressey, An investigation of the mechanical habits in reading of good and poor readers. Educ. Res. Bull., 1925, 4, 273–275.

209. Pratt, C. C., A note on the legibility of items in a bibliography. J. Appl. Psychol., 1924, 8, 562–564.

210. Pressey, L. C., *A manual of reading exercises for freshmen.* Columbus: Ohio State University Press, 1928.

211. Pressey, L. C., *Pressey's diagnostic tests in the fundamental reading habits.* Bloomington: Public School Publishing Company, 1928.

212. Preston, K., H. P. Schwankl, and M. A. Tinker, The effect of variations in color of print and background on legibility. J. Gen. Psychol., 1932, 6, 459–461.

213. Pyke, R. L., *Report on the legibility of print.* London: His Majesty's Stationery Office, 1926.

214. Quantz, J. O., *Problems in the psychology of reading.* Psychol. Rev. Monog. Suppl., 1897, Vol. 2, No. 1.

215. Rebert, G. N., A laboratory study of the reading of familiar numerals. J. Educ. Psychol., 1932, 23, 35–45.

216. Rebert, G. N., A laboratory study in the reading of familiar formulas. J. Educ. Psychol., 1932, 23, 192–203.

217. *Recommended practice of library lighting.* New York: Illuminating Engineering Society, 1950.

218. *Recommended practice for supplementary lighting.* New York: Illuminating Engineering Society, 1953.

219. *Recommended practice for residence lighting.* New York: Illuminating Engineering Society, 1953.

220. *Recommended practice for office lighting.* New York: Illuminating Engineering Society, 1960.

221. *Report of the Committee appointed to select the best faces of type and modes of display for government printing.* London: His Majesty's Stationery Office, 1922.

222. Robinson, F. P., and P. G. Murphy, The validity of measuring eye movements by direct observation. Science, 1932, 76, 171–172.

223. Robinson, F. P., and W. E. Hall, *Concerning reading readiness tests.* Bulletin of the Ohio Conference on Reading, No. 3. Columbus, Ohio: Ohio State University Press, 1942.

223a. Robinson, H. M. (ed.), *Evaluation of reading.* Suppl. Educ. Monog. No. 88, 1958.

224. Roethlein, B. E., The relative legibility of different faces of printing types. Amer. J. Psychol., 1912, 23, 1–56.

Bibliography

225. Ruediger, W. C., *The field of distance vision.* Archives of Psychology, 1907, 1, No. 5.
226. Russell, D. H., Opinions of experts about primary-grade basic reading programs. Elem. Sch. J., 1944, 44, 602–609.
227. Russell, D. H., Reading and child development. In *Reading in the elementary school.* Forty-eighth Yearbook, Part II, National Society for the Study of Education. Chicago: University of Chicago Press, 1949, 10–32.
228. Russell, D. H., *Children learn to read,* 2nd ed. Boston: Ginn and Company, 1961.
229. Russell, D. H., and O. Ousley, *Manual for teaching the reading readiness program.* Boston: Ginn and Company, 1957.
230. Sanford, E. C., The relative legibility of the small letters. Amer. J. Psychol., 1888, 1, 402–435.
231. Schackwitz, A., Apparat zur Aufzeichnung der Augenbewegungen beim zuzammenhängenden Lesen. Zsch. f. Psychol., 1913, 63, 442–453.
232. Schmidt, W. A., *An experimental study of the psychology of reading.* Suppl. Educ. Monog, 1917, 1, No. 2.
233. *School lighting application data.* New York: Illuminating Engineering Society, 1962.
234. Schubert, D. G., Visual immaturity and reading difficulty. Elementary English, 1957, 34, 323–325.
235. Scott, W. D., *The theory of advertising.* Boston: Small, Maynard, and Company, 1903.
236. Seibert, E. W., Reading reactions for varied types of subject matter: An analytical study of eye movements of eighth grade pupils. J. Exper. Educ., 1943, 12, 37–44.
237. Shen, E., An analysis of eye movements in the reading of Chinese. J. Exper. Psychol., 1927, 10, 158–183.
238. Sievers, C. H., and B. D. Brown, *Manual for improving your eye movements in reading.* Wichita: McGuin Publishing Company, 1946.
239. Sisson, E. D., *The role of habit in eye movements of reading.* Ph.D. Thesis, University of Minnesota, Minneapolis, Minnesota, 1936.
240. Sisson, E. D., Habits of eye movements in reading. J. Educ. Psychol., 1937, 28, 437–450.
241. Sisson, E. D., Eye-movement training as a means of improving reading ability. J. Educ. Res., 1938, 32, 35–41.
242. Sister Mary Caroline, *Breaking the sound barrier.* New York: Macmillan Company, 1960.
243. Skordahl, D. M., Effect of sloping text upon speed of reading and upon visibility. Unpublished paper, University of Minnesota, 1958.
244. Smith, H. P., and E. V. Dechant, *Psychology in teaching reading.* Englewood Cliffs, N.J.: Prentice-Hall, 1961.

245. Soar, R. S., Readability of typography in psychological journals. J. Appl. Psychol., 1951, 35, 64–67.

246. Soar, R. S., Height-width proportion and stroke width in numerical visibility. J. Appl. Psychol., 1955, 39, 43–46.

247. Spache, G. D., A rationale for mechanical methods of improving reading. In *Significant elements in college and adult reading improvement.* The Seventh Yearbook of the National Reading Conference for Colleges and Adults. Fort Worth: Texas Christian University Press, 1958. Pp. 115–132.

248. Spache, G. D., *Toward better reading.* Champaign, Ill.: Garrard Publishing Company, 1963.

248a. Stanley, J. C., *Ross's measurement in today's schools*, 3rd ed. New York: Prentice-Hall, 1954.

249. Stanton, F. M., and H. E. Burtt, The influence of surface and tint of paper on speed of reading. J. Appl. Psychol., 1935, 19, 685–693.

249a. Starch, D., *Advertising.* Chicago: Scott, Foresman, 1914.

250. Starch, D., *Principles of advertising.* Chicago: A. W. Shaw Company, 1923.

251. Stone, L. C., Reading reactions for varied types of subject matter: An analytical study of eye movements of college freshmen. J. Exper. Educ., 1941, 10, 64–77.

252. Stromberg, E. L., The relation of lateral muscle balance to the convergence and divergence movements of the eyes during reading. J. Gen. Psychol., 1938, 29, 437–439.

253. Stromberg, E. L., Binocular movement of the eyes in reading. J. Gen. Psychol., 1938, 18, 349–355.

254. Stromberg, E. L., The reliability of monocular photography in the investigation of reading. J. Educ. Psychol., 1942, 33, 118–127.

255. Summer, F. C., Influence of color on legibility of copy. J. Appl. Psychol., 1932, 16, 201–204.

256. Taylor, C. D., The relative legibility of black and white print. J. Educ. Psychol., 1934, 25, 561–578.

257. Taylor, E. A., *Controlled reading.* Chicago: University of Chicago Press, 1937.

258. Taylor, N. W., New light on visual contrast. Illum. Engng., 1962, 57, 177–186.

259. Taylor, S. E., *Eye-movement photography with the reading eye.* Huntington, N.Y.: Educational Developmental Laboratories, 1959.

260. *Technical recommendations for psychological tests and diagnostic techniques.* Supplement to Psychological Bulletin, Vol. 51, No. 2, Part 2, March 1954. Published by American Psychological Association, Washington, D.C.

261. Terman, S., and C. C. Walcutt, *Reading: Chaos and cure.* New York: McGraw-Hill Book Company, 1958.

262. Terry, P. W., The reading problem in arithmetic. J. Educ. Psychol., 1921, 12, 365–377.
263. Terry, P. W., *How numerals are read.* Suppl. Educ. Monog., 1922, No. 18.
264. Tiffin, J., Simultaneous records of eye movements and voice in oral reading. Science, 1934, 80, 430–431.
265. Tiffin, J., *Industrial Psychology*, 2nd ed. Englewood Cliffs, N.J.: Prentice-Hall, 1947.
266. Tinker, M. A., Reading reactions for mathematical formulae. J. Exper. Psychol., 1926, 9, 444–467.
267. Tinker, M. A., Numerals versus words for efficiency in reading. J. Appl. Psychol., 1928, 12, 190–199.
268. Tinker, M. A., How formulae are read. Amer. J. Psychol., 1928, 40, 476–483.
269. Tinker, M. A., Eye-movement duration, pause duration, and reading time. Psychol. Rev., 1928, 35, 385–397.
270. Tinker, M. A., The relative legibility of the letters, the digits, and of certain mathematical signs. J. Gen. Psychol., 1928, 1, 472–496.
271. Tinker, M. A., *A photographic study of eye movements in reading formulae.* Genet, Psychol. Monog., 1928, 3, No. 2.
272. Tinker, M. A., Photographic measures of reading ability. J. Educ. Psychol., 1929, 20, 184–191.
273. Tinker, M. A., The relative legibility of modern and old style numerals. J. Exper. Psychol., 1930, 13, 453–461.
274. Tinker, M. A., Physiological psychology of reading. Psychol. Bull., 1931, 28, 81–98.
275. Tinker, M. A., Apparatus for recording eye movements. Amer. J. Psychol., 1931, 43, 115–127.
276. Tinker, M. A., The influence of form of type on the perception of words. J. Appl. Psychol., 1931, 16, 167–174.
277. Tinker, M. A., The relation of speed to comprehension in reading. Sch. and Soc., 1932, 36, 158–160.
278. Tinker, M. A., Cautions concerning illumination intensities used for reading. Amer. J. Optom. and Arch. Amer. Acad. Optom., 1935, 12, 43–51.
279. Tinker, M. A., Time taken by eye movements in reading. J. Genet. Psychol., 1936, 48, 468–471.
280. Tinker, M. A., Eye movements in reading. J. Educ. Res., 1936, 30, 241–277.
281. Tinker, M. A., Motor efficiency of the eye as a factor in reading. J. Educ. Psychol., 1938, 29, 167–174.
282. Tinker, M. A., Reliability and validity of eye-movement measures of reading. J. Exper. Psychol., 1939, 19, 732–746.
283. Tinker, M. A., The effect of illumination intensities upon speed of perception and upon fatigue in reading. J. Educ. Psychol., 1939, 30, 561–571.

284. Tinker, M. A., Illumination standards for effective and comfortable vision. J. Consult. Psychol., 1939, 3, 11–20.
285. Tinker, M. A., Effect of visual adaptation upon intensity of light preferred for reading. Amer. J. Psychol., 1941, 54, 559–563.
286. Tinker, M. A., Experimental study of reading. Psychol. Bull., 1934, 31, 98–110.
287. Tinker, M. A., Individual and sex differences in speed of saccadic eye movements. In *Studies in Personality*. New York: McGraw-Hill Book Company, 1942, 271–280.
288. Tinker, M. A., Readability of comic books. Amer. J. Optom. and Arch. Amer. Acad. Optom., 1943, 20, 89–93.
289. Tinker, M. A., Illumination intensities for reading newspaper type. J. Educ. Psychol., 1943, 34, 247–250.
290. Tinker, M. A., Criteria for determining the readability of type faces. J. Educ. Psychol., 1944, 35, 385–396.
291. Tinker, M. A., Illumination intensities preferred for reading with direct lighting. Amer. J. Optom. and Arch. Amer. Acad. Optom., 1944, 21, 213–219.
292. Tinker, M. A., The effect of visual adaptation upon intensity of illumination preferred for reading with direct lighting. J. Appl. Psychol., 1945, 29, 471–476.
293. Tinker, M. A., The study of eye movements in reading. Psychol. Bull., 1946, 43, 93–120.
294. Tinker, M. A., Illumination standards for effective and easy seeing. Psychol. Bull., 1947, 44, 435–450.
295. Tinker, M. A., Readability of book print and newsprint in terms of blink rate. J. Educ. Psychol., 1948, 39, 35–39.
296. Tinker, M. A., Effect of vibration upon reading. Amer. J. Psychol., 1948, 61, 386–390.
297. Tinker, M. A., Cumulative effect of marginal conditions upon rate of perception in reading. J. Appl. Psychol., 1948, 32, 537–540.
298. Tinker, M. A., Involuntary blink rate and illumination intensity in visual work. J. Exper. Psychol., 1949, 39, 558–560.
299. Tinker, M. A., Fixation pause duration in reading. J. Educ. Res., 1951, 44, 471–479.
300. Tinker, M. A., Derived illumination specifications. J. Appl. Psychol., 1951, 35, 377–380.
301. Tinker, M. A., The effect of intensity of illumination upon speed of reading six-point italic print. Amer. J. Psychol., 1952, 65, 600–602.
302. Tinker, M. A., Effect of vibration upon speed of perception while reading six point print. J. Educ. Res., 1953, 46, 459–464.
303. Tinker, M. A., Readability of mathematical tables. J. Appl. Psychol., 1954, 38, 436–442.
304. Tinker, M. A., Light intensities preferred for reading. Amer. J. Optom. and Arch. Amer. Acad. Optom., 1954, 31, 55–66.

305. Tinker, M. A., The effect of slanted text upon the readability of print. J. Educ. Psychol., 1954, 45, 287–291.
306. Tinker, M. A., Prolonged reading tasks in visual research. J. Appl. Psychol., 1955, 39, 444–446.
307. Tinker, M. A., *Tinker speed of reading test*. Minneapolis: University of Minnesota Press, 1955.
308. Tinker, M. A., Perceptual and oculomotor efficiency in reading materials in vertical and horizontal arrangements. Amer. J. Psychol., 1955, 68, 444–449.
309. Tinker, M. A., Effect of sloped text upon the readability of print. Amer. J. Optom. and Arch. Amer. Acad. Optom., 1956, 33, 189–195.
310. Tinker, M. A., Effect of angular alignment upon readability of print. J. Educ. Psychol., 1956, 47, 358–363.
311. Tinker, M. A., Effect of curved text upon readability of print. J. Appl. Psychol., 1957, 41, 218–221.
312. Tinker, M. A., Recent studies of eye movements in reading, Psychol. Bull., 1958, 54, 215–231.
313. Tinker, M. A., Length of work periods in visual research. J. Appl. Psychol., 1958, 42, 343–345.
314. Tinker, M. A., Print for children's textbooks. Education, 1959, 80, No. 1, 37–40.
315. Tinker, M. A., Brightness contrast, illumination intensity and visual efficiency. Amer. J. Optom. and Arch. Amer. Acad. Optom., 1959, 36, 221–236.
316. Tinker, M. A., Legibility of mathematical tables. J. Appl. Psychol., 1960, 44, 83–87.
316a. Tinker, M. A., Legibility of print for children in the upper grades. Amer. J. Optom. and Arch. Amer. Acad. Optom., 1963, 40, 614–621.
317. Tinker, M. A., *Legibility of print*. Ames, Iowa: Iowa State University Press, 1963.
318. Tinker, M. A., Influence of simultaneous variation in size of type, width of line and leading for newspaper type. J. Appl. Psychol., 1963, 47, 380–382.
319. Tinker, M. A., and A. Frandsen, Evaluation of photographic measures of reading. J. Educ. Psychol., 1934, 25, 96–100.
320. Tinker, M. A., and C. M. McCullough, *Teaching elementary reading*, 2nd ed. New York: Appleton-Century-Crofts, 1962.
321. Tinker, M. A., and D. G. Paterson, Influence of type form on speed of reading. J. Appl. Psychol., 1928, 12, 359–368.
322. Tinker, M. A., and D. G. Paterson, Studies of typographical factors influencing speed of reading: III. Length of line. J. Appl. Psychol., 1929, 13, 205–219.
323. Tinker, M. A., and D. G. Paterson, Studies of typographical factors influencing speed of reading: VII. Variation in color of print and background. J. Appl. Psychol., 1931, 15, 471–479.

324. Tinker, M. A., and D. G. Paterson, Studies of typographical factors influencing speed of reading: IX. Reduction in size of newspaper print. J. Appl. Psychol., 1932, 16, 525–531.

325. Tinker, M. A., and D. G. Paterson, Studies of typographical factors influencing speed of reading: XI. Role of set in typographical studies. J. Appl. Psychol., 1935, 19, 647–651.

326. Tinker, M. A., and D. G. Paterson, Studies of typographical factors influencing speed of reading: XIII. Methodological considerations. J. Appl. Psychol., 1936, 20, 132–145.

327. Tinker, M. A., and D. G. Paterson, Influence of type form on eye movements. J. Exper. Psychol., 1939, 25, 528–531.

328. Tinker, M. A., and D. G. Paterson, Eye movements in reading a modern type face and old English. Amer. J. Psychol., 1941, 54, 113–114.

329. Tinker, M. A., and D. G. Paterson, Reader preferences and typography. J. Appl. Psychol., 1942, 26, 38–40.

330. Tinker, M. A., and D. G. Paterson, Differences among newspaper body types in readability. J. Quarterly, 1943, 20, 152–155.

331. Tinker, M. A., and D. G. Paterson, Eye movements in reading black print on white background and red print on dark green background. Amer. J. Psychol., 1944, 57, 93–94.

332. Tinker, M. A., and D. G. Paterson, Wartime changes in newspaper body type. J. Quarterly, 1944, 21, 7–11.

333. Tinker, M. A., and D. G. Paterson, Effect of line width and leading on readability of newspaper type. J. Quarterly, 1946, 23, 307–309.

334. Tinker, M. A., and D. G. Paterson, Readability of mixed type forms. J. Appl. Psychol., 1946, 30, 631–637.

335. Traxler, A. E., Value of controlled reading: summary of opinions and research. J. Exper. Educ., 1943, 11, 280–292.

336. Vernon, M. D., The errors made in reading. In *Studies in the psychology of reading*. Medical Research Council, Special Report Series, No. 130. London: His Majesty's Stationery Office, 1929. Pp. 5–40.

337. Vernon, M. D., Characteristics of proof-reading. Brit. J. Psychol., 1931, 21, 368–381.

338. Vernon, M. D., *The experimental study of reading*. Cambridge: Cambridge University Press, 1931.

339. Vernon, M. D., *Visual perception*. Cambridge: Cambridge University Press, 1937.

340. Vernon, M. D., *The movements of the eyes in reading*. Special Series, No. 148, Medical Research Council. London: His Majesty's Stationery Office, 1930.

341. Walker, R. Y., The eye movements of good readers. Psychol. Monog., 1933, 44, 95–117.

342. Walker, R. Y., A qualitative study of eye movements of good readers. Amer. J. Psychol., 1938, 51, 472–481.

343. Waterman, J. T., Reading patterns in German and English. The German Quart., 1954, 26, 225–227.
344. Webster, H. A., and M. A. Tinker, The influence of paper surface on the perceptibility of print. J. Appl. Psychol., 1935, 19, 145–147.
345. Webster, H. A., and M. A. Tinker, The influence of type face on the legibility of print. J. Appl. Psychol., 1935, 19, 43–52.
346. Weston, H. C., Effects of age and illumination upon visual performance with close sights. Brit. J. Ophthal., 1948, 32, 645–653.
347. Weston, H. C., Proposals for a new lighting code. Trans. Illum. Engng. Soc. (London), 1943, 8, 17–32.
348. Weston, H. C., *Sight, light and efficiency.* London: H. K. Lewis and Company, 1949.
349. Weston, H. C., *The relation between illumination and visual efficiency. I. The effect of size of work.* Medical Research Report. London: His Majesty's Stationery Office, 1935.
350. Weston, H. C., *The relation between illumination and visual efficiency — The effect of brightness contrast.* Industrial Health Research Board Report, No. 87. London: His Majesty's Stationery Office, 1945.
351. Westover, F. L., *Controlled eye movements versus exercises in reading: A comparison of methods of improving reading speed and comprehension.* Teach. Coll. Contr. Educ., 1946, No. 917.
352. Wiggins, R. H., *The effects of lower-case alphabet length, length of line and spacing on speed of reading 8 point Regal type.* Ph.D. thesis, School of Journalism, the State University of Iowa, 1964.
353. Witty, P., *Reading in modern education.* Boston: D. C. Heath and Company, 1949.
354. Woodworth, R. S., Vision and localization during eye movements. Psychol. Bull., 1906, 3, 68–70.
355. Woodworth, R. S., and H. Schlosberg, *Experimental psychology,* rev. ed. New York: Holt, Rinehart, and Winston, 1954.
356. Zeitler, J., Tachistoskopische Versuche ueber das Lesen. Phil. Stud., 1900, 16, 380–463.

Index

Index

Abernethy, E. M., 99
Ahrens, A., 55
All-capital printing: early experiment, 136; interpretations, 136–37; and word form, 137; use of, 137–38
Anderson, I. H., 26, 28, 59, 60, 197
Anglo-Saxon words, 20
Arabic numerals, 193
Arnold, D. C., 68
Artisan enamel paper, 166
Audiometer test, 260, 268
Austin, M. C., 255, 257, 258, 259, 260, 261, 263, 264, 265

Babbage, C., 192
Backbone titles of books, legibility of, 200
Baird, J. W., 118, 198
Ballantine, F. A., 82, 149
Bayle, E., 75
Bear, R. M., 60
Beck, H. C., 200
Bell, H. M., 196
Bell, L., 222
Betts, E. A., 40, 161, 273
Bibliographies, legibility of identifying key in, 198
Bifocal age, 210
Binet test, 257
Bitterman, M. E., 118, 219
Black print vs. white print: eye movements in reading, 158; perceptibility of, 158–60; influence of meaning in perceiving, 159–60; with sans-serif type, 159; interpretations, 160. *See also* Colored print on colored paper
Blackhurst, J. H., 151, 152
Blackwell, H. B., 231, 232
Blink rate: involuntary, 118; and illumination for reading, 218–19

Boeker, E., 28, 29
Boice, M. L., 209
Boldface type: experiment with, 135; preferences for, 136
Bond, G. L., 34, 35, 42, 207, 255, 256, 258, 259, 260, 261, 263, 265, 273, 276
Bond-Clymer formula for reading expectancy, 259, 271
Bond-Clymer-Hoyt Silent Reading Diagnostic Tests, 282
Bowden, J. H., 28
Breland, K., 177, 178
Breland, M. K., 177, 178
Bremer, N., 265, 266
Brightness ratio, 236, 237
Broom, M. E., 59, 106
Brown, B. D., 106, 107
Brozek, J., 94
Bryan, A. I., 199
Buckingham, B. R., 151
Buros, O. K., 263, 265, 282
Burtt, H. E., 161, 167, 200
Bush, C. L., 255, 257, 258, 259, 260, 261, 263, 264, 265
Buswell, G. T., 76, 81, 82, 84, 85, 86, 87, 90, 95, 96, 98, 108, 109, 110, 111, 149
Butsch, R. L. C., 101

California Test of Mental Maturity, Non-Language Section, 257
Campbell, E., 200
Capital letters, *see* All-capital printing
Carmichael, L., 58, 59, 93, 94, 118, 197
Carse, R., 165
Cason, E. B., 108
Catalog cards, legibility of reproductions of, 199
Cataract, 207–8

315

Index

McAllister, C. N., 55
McCullough, C. M., 5, 10, 23, 24, 30, 31, 32, 35, 40, 41, 42, 43, 253, 254, 255, 256, 263, 264, 265, 266, 267, 271, 282, 283, 284, 286, 289
McCullough Word Analysis Tests, 276, 282
McFarland, R. A., 91, 118
Machines, use of to control reading, 110
McNamara, W. G., 150
Mandelbaum, J., 209
Mary Caroline, Sister, 35
Mat-surface paper, 166
Mathematical tables, legibility of, 194–95
May, C. H., 206
Meek, L. H., 28
Mental set in testing, 123
Meredith, C. W., 197
Messmer, O., 16, 17, 18
Metron-o-scope, 108, 109
Microfilm, legibility of projected, 197
Miles, W. R., 54, 55, 65, 67, 106
Milne, J. R., 192
Mixed type forms, unfortunate use of, 138, 180
Miyake, R., 162
Modern numerals, 192–93
Monochromatic light, effects on vision, 222–23
Monroe Diagnostic Reading Examination, 275, 277, 279
Morgan, D. H., 104
Morse, W. C., 89
Moss, F. K., 117, 118, 161, 167, 196, 216, 217, 218, 223, 224, 226
Motor habits, short-lived, 73, 74
Müller, R. F., 16, 22
Munoz, J. M., 103
Murphy, P. G., 55
Myopia: incidence of, 206; progressive, 206

National Society for the Study of Education, 4
Nelson, L. P., 128
Nelson Silent Reading Test, 269
Nervous muscular tension, and ease of seeing, 219
Newspaper headlines: all capitals vs. lower case, 177; single column, 177–78, 179; banner, 178–79; evaluation, 179–80
Newspaper print: importance of legibility, 169; survey of practice, 170; effect of narrowing letters, 171; legibility of typefaces, 171–72; leading in, 172–73, 176; effect of type size, 173, 176; versus book print, 174; reduction in reproduction, 174–76; effect of context on legibility, 176; simultaneous variation of typographical factors, 176–77; headlines, 177–80
Norms, 264, 269, 270
North, A. J., 188
Numerals: eye movements in reading, 97–98; opinions on legibility, 192; Modern vs. Old Style, 192–93; Roman vs. Arabic, 193; versus words, 194

Objective questions, eye movements in reading, 101–2
Oculomotor efficiency: assumptions about, 77; experiments on, 77–80; evaluation of, 79–80
Odoriz, J. B., 103
Ogg, O., 122
Old Style numerals, 192–93
Ousley, O., 267
Ovink, G. W., 118, 126

Pacing eye movements, 107, 108
Page, *see* Position of reading page, Spatial arrangement of printed page
Paper: in children's books, 154; opinions on color, 157; legibility of black print on tinted, 161; legibility of colored print on colored, 162–66; surfaces of, 166–68
Paterson, D. G., 118, 120, 123, 128–50 *passim,* 155, 158, 163–86 *passim,* 209
Perception: general process, 9; of words, 10; and meaning, 11; dependence on in reading, 11; by word wholes, 15; of unfamiliar words, 21, 22; by children, 25–32; studies of practices, 30; clues and techniques in developing, 31–38
Perceptual span: number of items in, 13–14; subjective grouping in, 14
Perera, C. A., 206

319